Grace, Beauty & Banjos

Michael Kilgarriff has been wielding the gavel as 'Mr Chairman' for over 30 years at the legendary Players' Theatre, London. An accomplished actor, he lays his claim to being the tallest March Hare in show business (6ft 6ins standing at ease) in a tour of *Alice in Wonderland*. An acknowledged authority on British Music Hall, his many books include *It Gives Me Great Pleasure*, *It Gives Me Further Pleasure*, *Music Hall Miscellany* (Samuel French), and *Sing Us One of the Old Songs* (Oxford University Press). He also wrote the music for *Mad Dan*, the BBC Radio play on the life of Dan Leno. Aspiring Music Hall aficionados may care to note that Mr Kilgarriff's illustrated lecture on the history of the Halls continues to be seen everywhere from Bolton Public Library to the QE2. His many TV appearances include John Brown to Miriam Margolyes' Queen Victoria, the social reformer to Charles Booth, and the evil Cybercontroller (and sundry other monsters) in Dr Who. Married with one daughter, he lives in Ealing, an area of West London which for over a century has basked in the soubriquet *The Queen of the Suburbs*.

THE SISTERS CHESTER
Originally Florrie, Grace and Laura.

GRACE, BEAUTY & BANJOS

Michael Kilgarriff

Tall and in the Dark Handsome

In which attention is focussed upon a little-regarded aspect
of the Performing Arts, providing an unique repository
of information never before assembled in one volume.

OBERON BOOKS
LONDON

First published in 1998 by Oberon Books Ltd
(incorporating Absolute Classics)
521 Caledonian Road, London N7 9RH
Tel: 0171 607 3637 / Fax: 0171 607 3629
e-mail: oberon.books@btinternet.com

First published in paperback 1999

A CIP catalogue record for this book is available from the British Library.

ISBN: 1 84002 116 0

Cover photograph: Kaufmann's Trick Cyclists (The Theatre Museum)

Cover design and typography: Richard Doust

Printed in Great Britain by MPG Books Ltd, Bodmin.

'Mrs Crummles was the original Blood Drinker.'

'Was she indeed?'

'Yes. She was obliged to give it up, though.'

'Did it disagree with her?' asked Nicholas.

'Not so much with her, as with her audiences,' replied Mr Crummles. 'Nobody could stand it. It was too tremendous. You don't quite know what Mrs Crummles is, yet.'

Nicholas ventured to insinuate that he thought he did.

'No, no, you don't,' said Mr Crummles. 'You don't, indeed. *I* don't and that's a fact. I don't think her country will, till she is dead. Some new proof of talent bursts from that astonishing woman every year of her life. Look at her, mother of six children, three of 'em alive, and all upon the stage!'

'Extraordinary!' cried Nicholas.

'Ah! extraordinary indeed,' rejoined Mr Crummles, taking a complacent pinch of snuff, and shaking his head gravely. 'I pledge you my professional word I didn't even know she could dance, till her last benefit, and then she played Juliet, and Helen Macgregor, and did the skipping-rope hornpipe between the pieces. The very first time I saw that admirable woman, Johnson,' said Mr Crummles, drawing a little nearer, and speaking in the tone of confidential friendship, 'she stood upon her head on the butt-end of a spear, surrounded with blazing fireworks.'

'You astonish me!' said Nicholas.

'*She* astonished *me!*' returned Mr Crummles, with a very serious countenance. 'Such grace, coupled with dignity! I adored her from that moment!'

Nicholas Nickleby, Charles Dickens

Acknowledgements

Grateful thanks are extended to the following for their help and advice: Eve Aldridge, Nigel M Anderson, Larry Barnes (*Inner Magic Circle*), Robert Bain (*Scottish Music Hall Society*), Chris Beeching, Timothy Bentinck, Bobby Bernard (*Inner Magic Circle*), the late J O Blake, British Actors' Equity Association, The British Library Music Department, The British Library Newspaper Library, Peter Brough, Cliff Castle, Peter Charlton, Graeme Cruickshank (*Palace Theatre*), Barry Cryer, Alan Curtis, Pamela Cundell, Fred Dell, Jean Fergusson, Will Fyffe jnr, Catherine Haill (*The Theatre Museum*), John M Hall, Michael D Hine, Peter Honri, Len Howe, Roy Hudd, Jan Hunt, P W Hurst, Peter John, Bob Johnson, Dominic Le Foe, Ian Liston, Jimmy Logan OBE DLitt FRSAMD, Henry McGee, Jeanne Mackinnon, Larry Macari, Raymond Mander & Joe Mitchenson Theatre Collection, Gerald Moon, Patrick Newley, Larry Parker, Bill Pertwee & Marion, Gordon Peters, John Roscoe, Victor Seaforth, Jack Seaton, Harry Seltzer, Barrie Stacey, Renée Stepham, Allan Stirland, Roza Thompson, Frank Thornton, Veronica Twidle, Dennis Warrilow, Pamela Watford, Westminster Reference Library, Mrs D Wiseman, Christopher Woodward (*The London Palladium Theatre Collection*).

My gratitude is also extended to Audrey Lane and those residents of Brinsworth House and Denville Hall who were so generous with their precious memories; finally I must thank that most distinguished of Variety artistes, *The Golden Voiced Goon* himself, Sir Harry Secombe, who so kindly and so aptly supplied the Foreword.

MK

Contents

Illustrations

Copyright holders are given in brackets.

Back flap: Michael Kilgarriff
(John Fletcher)
Frontispiece: Sisters Chester
(Tony Barker)
Facing Foreword: Sir Harry Secombe
(British Music Hall Society)

Between pp. 80-81
1. The Three Aberdonians
   (Michael Kilgarriff)
2. Julie Andrews
   (Mander & Mitchenson)
3. Max Bacon (BMHS)
4. Joséphine Baker
   (Mander & Mitchenson)
5. Barbette (Mander & Mitchenson)
6. Billy Bennett
   (Mander & Mitchenson)
7. Bessie Bonehill
   (Mander & Mitchenson)
8. Walford Bodie
   (Mander & Mitchenson)
9. Caicedo (Mander & Mitchenson)
10. Harry Claff (BMHS)
11. Bonar Colleano (BMHS)
12. Peg-Leg Bates
    (Mander & Mitchenson)
13. Billy Cotton
    (Mander & Mitchenson)
14. Dehl Trio (BMHS)
15. Delfont & Toko (BMHS)
16. Phyllis Dixey
    (Mander & Mitchenson)
17. Phyllis Dixey
    (Mander & Mitchenson)
18. Drum & Major
    (Mander & Mitchenson)
19. Norman Evans
    (Mander & Mitchenson)

Between pp. 160-161
20. Sid Field (Mander & Mitchenson)
21. Gracie Fields (Theatre Museum)
22. Flanagan & Allen
    (Mander & Mitchenson)
23. George & Beryl Formby and Max
    Miller (Mander & Mitchenson)
24. Harry Fragson & Father
    (Mander & Mitchenson)

25. Gaston & Andrée
    (Mander & Mitchenson)
26. Tommy Handley
    (Mander & Mitchenson)
27. Jenny Hill (Mander & Mitchenson)
28. Herschel Henlere (BMHS)
29. Nat Jackley (Michael Kilgarriff)
30. Betty Jumel (Michael Kilgarriff)
31. Jumpin' Jax (BMHS)
32. Kaufmann's Lady Cyclists
    (Theatre Museum)
33. Koringa (Mander & Mitchenson)
34. Lucan & McShane (BMHS)
35. Dan Leno (Terry Lomas)
36. Dan Leno (Terry Lomas)
37. Marie Lloyd (Terry Lomas)
38. Marie Lloyd (Terry Lomas)

Between pp. 224-225
39. La Milo (Mander & Mitchenson)
40. Evelyn Nesbit
    (Mander & Mitchenson)
41. La Belle Otero
    (Mander & Mitchenson)
42. Eugene Sandow
    (Mander & Mitchenson)
43. Joseph Pujol
    (Mander & Mitchenson)
44. George Robey (Michael Kilgarriff)
45. Daisy Squelch (Michael Kilgarriff)
46. Wilson Keppel & Betty
    (Mander & Mitchenson)
47. Elsie & Doris Waters
    (Mander & Mitchenson)
48. Poster, New Theatre, Oxford
    (Mander & Mitchenson)
49. Bransby Williams
    (Michael Kilgarriff)
50. George Williams (BMHS)
51. Zazel (Mander & Mitchenson)
52. Poster, Hippodrome, Brighton,
    1955 (BMHS)
53. Poster, Hippodrome, Brighton,
    1955 (BMHS)
54. Poster, Hippodrome, Brighton,
    1958 (BMHS)
55. Poster, Grand, Derby, 1938
    (BMHS)

HARRY SECOMBE c1950

Foreword

Sir Harry Secombe CBE

Bill-matter has always fascinated me. As a lad going to school I had to pass Weaver's Flour Mills on Swansea's East Side, and on one of its walls was the poster site for the Swansea Empire. It was always a thrill to see who was coming to grace our fair town the following week. The names leapt out at me: Roy Fox and his Band, Arthur Tracy *The Street Singer*, Revnell & West *The Long and the Short of It*. I was hooked from those days on.

When the time came for my own name to go on Variety theatre bills it was decided by my agent Jimmy Grafton that *The Golden Voiced Goon* would be most appropriate. It made me cringe at the time, especially when it came out as *The Golden Voiced Coon*. Spike Milligan decided to take the mickey out of the process by billing himself as *The Performing Man* or *Late of the Human Race*. He would, wouldn't he?

I've forgotten most of the act descriptions now except for Mushie *The Forest Bred Lion* or the famous Kardoma *He Fills the Stage with Flags*. I do recall, however, inventing fantasy turns such as Moira Pules *The Underwater Soprano* and Jim Crint *The Whistling Goldfish*; how marvellous to find within these pages details of real-live performers just as unlikely and even more bizarre.

Variety has gone now, more's the pity, and I am so glad that Michael has chronicled bill-matter for posterity. I shall treasure this book because it's part of *my* history.

Harry Secombe

INTRODUCTION

O n the first day of pantomime rehearsals at the London Palladium the yet-to-be-knighted Harry Secombe, bemused by our inordinate height of six and a half feet, cried out 'Michael Kilgarriff! He fills the stage with him!'

An amusing quip to be sure, but there is more to this joke than may appear, for at that time as Sir Harry notes in his Foreword there still flourished on the Halls one Kardoma, a conjuror famed for his promise to *Fill the Stage with Flags*. Of similar vintage was Gaston Palmer (*All the Spoons in All the Glasses*), an act of almost unbearable tension and it must be admitted not a little tedium. Ted Ray's *Fiddling and Fooling* told you exactly what he offered, just as *Cleopatra's Nightmare* gave us the precise flavour of Wilson, Keppel & Betty.

Such encapsulations of an act's essence were known as billing- or bill-matter, their creation a discipline which expired with Variety, its principal sponsor. The heydays for these showbiz strap-lines were the inter-war years, for prior to 1914 performers saw little need for a personalised slogan, contenting themselves with such bald descriptions as *Singer*, *Comedian*, or *Dancer*. Only speciality acts showed a degree of imaginativeness, perhaps too much so in the case of Madame Gascoyne who in the 1890s declared herself to be *The Only Clock-Eyed Lady in the World*.

Quite what this estimable lady did to enchant the Great British Public took some ferreting out (*see page 114*), but we cannot begin to guess at the exhibition displayed by Rusty Warren, tantalisingly touted in the 1920s and 1930s as *The Knockers Up Girl*. We can reveal, however, that Mr and Miss Nemo's *Impalement Act*, seen at all the best Metropolitan Halls in the 1870s, exhibited nothing more outré than knife-throwing. Only in his last few tragic years was the great Dan Leno billed as anything other than *Comedian*, wary perhaps after a visit to New York where he was puffed as *The Funniest Man on Earth*, a claim resented by New Yorkers who decided to discourage such Limey braggadocio by declining to be amused.

At Sadler's Wells Theatre in 1895 the manager, George E Belmont, not a man to hide his stars' lights under any bushels, advertised a certain sparky young performer's charms as *Tasty, Trippy, Twiggy, Timely, Telling, Tender, Tempting, Toothsome, Transcendent, Trim, Tactical, Twinkling, Tricksy,*

Triumphal, Tantalizing. This was none other than the 25-year-old Miss Marie Lloyd, who was surely all of those things.

Required viewing for the Music Hall enthusiast in the 1890s must have included Miss Nellie Gertine, *Lady Character Baritone Vocalist,* and the one and only Miss Marie Gilchrist whose turn was described as *Congress of Nations.* Of the thousands of billings listed in this volume our favourite, positively reeking with fin-de-siècle charm and giving us our title, is that borne by The Sisters Chester: *Grace, Beauty and Banjos.*

Just a few years later, also at the Old Mo', you could admire Miss Daisy Squelch *with her Big Brass Six.* Squelch might not seem the most glamorous name to emblazon across a billboard, but what imp of mischief persuaded Miss Lydia Rudge to become Lydia Flopp? Or Miss Clarice Etrulia de Bucharde to become Truly Shattuck, *The California Nightingale?* In our sniggering teens how delicious was the awareness that Britain's home-grown siren of the silver screen Miss Diana Dors (*Swingin' Dors in Person*) had been born Diana Fluck, a name impossible for a public figure. And not too easy in private, we would suggest.

One of the few major Music Hall stars to recognise the value of a pithy individualised caption was Miss Vesta Tilley who from the 1880s invariably described herself as *The London Idol.* And if, around the turn of the century, you didn't know who *The Prime Minister of Mirth* was you must have spent a very long time in a very far-flung corner of Empire indeed. This eminent personage was of course the darling of the Halls: Sir George Robey. Despite this trail-blazing it was not until the 1920s that catchy bill-matter became as much part of a pro's equipment as clean shoes and readable band-parts, with Joe Musaire (*The Harry Lauder of the Canadian Tanks*) reminding us of his time in uniform, Billy Bennett defiantly declaring himself to be *Almost a Gentleman* and Billy Russell assuring us that he would be speaking *On Behalf of the Working Classes.*

In the 1930s Dave & Joe O'Gorman were promising *Laughter in the Roar* and a little-known Sid Field was billed as *The Destroyer of Gloom,* though comedienne Dorrie Dene's *The Indescribable* can have had significance only for her admirers. Also in this decade Joan Elliott & Billie Roche are awarded a commendation for their teeth-grindingly cute *2 Girls 2 Good 2 Miss.*

Animal acts in particular tended to encourage the extravagant and the bizarre such as Fink's Mules (*Vaudeville's Equine Joy Fest*), Vogelbein's

Bears (*Bruins at their Best*), Bob Bemand's Comedy Pigeons (*Flying Funsters*), Van der Koors (*Quack Illusionists with Felix, the Mind-Reading Duck*), and finally – and barely comprehensibly – Laurie and her Dogs (*Enjoyment does their Gladness Injustice*).

Demobilisation at the end of Hitler's war prompted an influx of eager talent from the Armed Forces. These fresh faces – Harry Secombe (*The Golden Voiced Goon*), Frankie Howerd (*The Borderline Case*), Norman Vaughan (*Aspirin to Fame*), Michael Bentine (*The Happy Imbecile*) – were still in the late 1940s setting out their wares in customary fashion, and it was at this time that a Sussex schoolboy, intoxicated with the peacetime novelties of lights in the streets and bananas in the shops, was taken regularly in the holidays to his local Hippodrome. There he would lean on the plush-covered rail at the back of the huge amphitheatre and gaze at the performers, demi-gods from beyond the rainbow.

A Variety programme was inevitable and immutable: after the overture, greeted with politely perfunctory applause, came the opening duo – it was always a duo, and it was always a mute dance routine ('while they're getting their coats off'). Variety boasted no compère, no concerteds, no finale; each act was self-contained, identified by illuminated numbers on either side of the proscenium which corresponded with the printed programme. The dancers, the comics, the singers, the jugglers, the magicians, the sea-lions, the instrumentalists, the acrobats, the impressionists, the ventriloquists, the wire-walkers, all succeeded one another in a well-defined and comforting sequence. Variety was predictable undemanding fare, and for half a century, after the demise of Music Hall, it served the British public well.

By the late 1950s bill-matter had all but disappeared from flyers and posters; the practice was perceived as dated, Archie Rice-ish, and even, like yesterday's catch-phrase, an embarrassment. 'When I'm gone the game's over,' Max Miller would say, and indeed within a year or two of *The Cheeky Chappie's* death in 1963 twice-nightly weekly Variety had also expired, helped on its way by bingo and television. The oriflamme passed to a collateral branch of the entertainment industry All-In Wrestling, but the appeal of the grunt-'n'-groan boys such as Cyanide Sid Cooper (*Rotten to the Core*) was short-lived, and the singers and stand-up comics who fill today's theatres, halls, pubs, and cabaret rooms are disinclined to revive a custom discarded over a generation ago.

Perhaps they are wise; older artistes don't want to remind us they go back that far and the younger ones don't want to be associated with a restricting and outmoded practice. Today only such slogans – usually on pantomime bills – as *Gazza's Sister** and *The Cat from Coronation Street** are left to remind us of a poignantly evocative half-forgotten corner of literary endeavour.

Michael Kilgarriff
Ealing, January 1998

The generosity of our estimable publisher, Mr James Hogan (b1943), in bringing out this paperback edition has provided a welcome opportunity for some additions and, it must be confessed, the occasional correction.

Michael Kilgarriff
Ealing, June 1999

*Gazza: Paul Gascoigne, a talented but wayward player of soccer
*Coronation Street: a popular television serial

A

ABBOTT, ANNIE MAY (1866-1943)
The Georgia Magnet

Volunteers from the audience were unable to lift or even move the artiste unless she so willed, yet Miss Abbott 'only had to lift a little finger to heave bulky men off their feet'. We are informed by a member of the Inner Magic Circle that this ability is based not so much upon supranormal powers as upon well-established mechanical principles and muscular co-ordination.

In *The Era* of November 14th 1917 a similar exhibition was given by a lady calling herself Mona Magnet, and at the Victoria Palace in 1922 there appeared one Resista who was also seemingly able to alter her weight at will. This lady's assistant, Miss Ward Smith, was described, uniquely in our experience, as 'Oratress'.

See MAGICIANS, JOAN RHODES

ABERDONIANS, THE THREE (fl1929-48)
Too Mean to Tell You What They Do
(a.k.a. Barr Brothers & Roza)

This team – brothers Charles and Thomas Barr with Roza Louise Thompson (b1916) – were comedy acrobatic dancers whose bill-matter is fondly iterated by Variety memorialists. Their performance at the London Coliseum in the mid-1930s was reviewed as 'in a class by itself. Working with ease and precision, the boys did some exceptionally clever feats of balance and acrobaticism while the lissome girl...turned one hand somersaults, high kicked and tumbled with gracefulness. A running exchange of comedy patter throughout added to the attractiveness of the act'.

ADAMS, ANNIE (1843-1905)
Queen of Serio-Comic Vocalists

A serio-comic was one who performed songs both dramatic and sentimental or lightly humorous. Originally a description of either a lady or a gentleman vocalist, by the end of the 19th century the term was applied exclusively to females. Miss Adams was a heavily built, homely looking *chanteuse* who was not so much a subtle as a likeable performer, for it is indisputable that she was mightily popular.

The artiste's husband was Harry Wall (b1838) who would stand uxoriously in the wings to pin up his wife's skirts as she left the stage to keep them clean. In the profession Mr Wall was known unaffectionately as *The Copyright Demon* from his habit of buying up song copyrights and demanding vast usage fees from unsuspecting singers. In 1888 this gentleman overstepped the mark by passing himself off as a solicitor and was sent to prison for three months.

For other serios see BEATRICE LILLIE and MARIE LLOYD. Also see ELLA RETFORD.

ADLER, LARRY (b1914)
The Virtuoso of the Mouth Organ

Also a virtuoso of the mouth, from which orifice well-honed anecdotes of the good, the bad, and the ill-favoured emerge seamlessly whenever a microphone is in the offing. Mr Adler's celebrated rendition upon the mouth organ (we understand he eschews the word harmonica) of the solo part in Mr George Gershwin's orchestral piece *Rhapsody in Blue* represents an unique musical marriage of the bathetic and the meretricious.

Mr Adler does however deserve respect for intestinal fortitude in the face of the American anti-Communist hearings conducted c1950 by the egregious Senator McCarthy; his other much-rehearsed distinction is 'almost' to have been engaged to the lustrous Swedish depictress Miss Ingrid Bergman.

In the same line of business should be mentioned Max Geldray (b1916) *with his Harmonica*, Ronald Chesney *Virtuoso of the Harmonica*, and Morton Fraser (c1910-82) who ran his eponymous Harmonica Rascals from 1949 until the 1960s. Further raucous rascality was provided by Borrah Minevitch (c1904-55), whose troupe wheezed their way round the Halls from 1926 until the 1950s, though from 1939 their leader was Johnny Puleo (1907-83).

Other puffers of fond memory were The Three Monarchs (fl c1946-81) billed as *Comedy Harmonica Virtuosos* or, a touch strainedly, *Harmonicomedians,* and whose original personnel were John Crowe, Les (Cedric) Henry and Eric Yorke (d February 8th 1998). Space must also be found for Arthur Tolcher (1912-87), famous for appearances on television with MORECAMBE & WISE in which his attempts to play *The Flight of the Bumblebee* were invariably frustrated by Eric Morecambe's quiet but firm 'Not now, Arthur'.

AFRIQUE (1907-61)
Impersonator of Celebrities

Alexander Witkins was born in Johannesburg, South Africa, hence his stage cognomen. A head-liner in his day this entry was intended initially for the law but then trained for the operatic stage. In London the young colonial first appeared with the Old Vic-Wells Opera Company for the redoubtable Miss Lilian Baylis (1874-1937). By 1934 opera had been abandoned and the 6ft 4ins artiste was making his West End début as an impressionist at the WINDMILL THEATRE. Was the notoriously out-spoken Miss Baylis behind this curious career switch, we wonder? Whatever the truth of the matter, Mr Afrique's impression of the then Prince of Wales was particularly admired.

ALBA, THEA (b c1904)
The Woman with Ten Brains

This extraordinary Berliner so impressed President Woodrow Wilson that he was moved to devise for her the slogan: *Whatever Else You Miss, Don't Miss This Miss This Week!*. Other eminent admirers include Maxim Gorky ('Genius or phenomenon? I believe she is both') and ex-Kaiser Wilhelm II ('Miss Alba, you are a whole secretariat in yourself'). But what did this entry do to earn such golden opinions?

With chalks attached to her fingers Miss Alba could write ten different words simultaneously; she could write backwards, forwards and upside down with both hands, with both feet and with her mouth in several of the twenty-five languages at her disposal; she could draw two different pictures in colour at the same time; she could – but enough is enough. It is a relief to learn that the lady married a German actor and lived in retirement 'in a small but tastefully furnished flat in the heart of Wiesbaden'.

Two names in the rarefied field of instant mental arithmetic are Professor William S Hutchings (fl1850s-60s) *The Mathematical Phenomenon and Lightning Calculator* and Jacques Inaudi (fl1880s-1910s)

The Man with Two Brains and *The Marvellous Lightning Calculator*. But how, we wonder, were answers in pre-computer days verified?

See DATAS, MAY ERNE, GEORGE JESSEL

ALBERT, BEN (1876-1925)
The Dry Old Stick

This Ulsterman was a popular Music Hall grotesque whose repertoire included *On The Day King Edward Gets His Crown On*, the first verse of which runs as follows:

> *The lodger's going to get blind drunk as soon as day begins,*
> *Sister's wearing bloomers fixed up with safety-pins,*
> *To celebrate the great event mother will have twins,*
> *On the day King Edward gets his crown on.*

None of Mr Albert's other songs is half so memorable.

ALBERT, FRED (1845-86)
The Inventive Gentleman

This Mr Albert (no relation to the preceding) was another warbler of topical songs though not always as comical as that just quoted. *Brave Captain Webb, A Cheer For Plimsoll, The Prince Of Wales In India* and *We Will Beat Back The Russians* were typical of his earnest offerings, all of which were his own work, though *The Mad Butcher* would suggest a modicum of hilarity.

ALDRIDGE, IRA (1805-67)
The African Roscius

This bill-matter is inspired by the legendary Roman actor Quintus Roscius Gallus (120-c62BC). Mr Aldridge was a black American tragedian whose interpretations of the great Shakespearean rôles of Othello, King Lear and Macbeth earned him an international reputation. Accounts of his early life are sketchy and conflicting; that he was a protégé of the great actor-carouser Edmund Kean (1787/90-1833) is undeniable, as were his triumphs in Britain and on the Continent where, after 1853, he played for most of his career. In 1863 during the American Civil War he became a British citizen, an action from which we are tempted to draw conclusions.

Also named for Roscius were Master WILLIAM BETTY and SAM COWELL.

ALI, SHEK BEN (1912-78)

The Comedy Prince of Magic; Mysteries of the Orient; Nobody Inside – Nobody Outside

Mohari Alli was born in Calcutta, India, under the Raj. The magician came to the Mother Country first in 1929, and after establishing a sound reputation on the Halls took the plunge into management, running his own all-Indian show at the Indian Theatre, Skegness. We regret to report that he lost every rupee. *Nobody Inside etc.* was spoken while presenting the now achingly familiar lady-vanishing-from-cabinet effect. As may readily be imagined this artiste was much in demand at pantomime time as the wicked wizard Abanazar in *Aladdin*, a telling rôle in which we venture to suggest we ourself have made no little mark.

ALLAN, MAUD (1873-1956)

The Symphonic Dancer; The Vision of Salome

The most significant event in Miss Allan's early life was the regrettable hanging of her brother Theo in San Quentin prison for double murder. Despite this handicap to public acceptability, and having being born in Toronto, the future world-celebrity studied piano in San Francisco and Berlin under the great Busoni (1866-1924); what passed between them we can but speculate, but we do know that in Vienna in 1903 Miss Allan made her début as a dancer. Free expression, exoticism, and bare feet were the lady's hallmarks; her Salome dance in which she kissed the severed head of the Baptist on its platter in particular caused scandal, uproar and derision in equal measure. This artiste enjoyed an immense vogue for a brief period during which she was thoroughly burlesqued on four continents. Miss Allan retired in 1928, and not before time.

See MY FANCY

ALLEN, DAVE (b1936)
God's Own Comedian

This critically respected comedian's upbringing, as might be expected of his birthplace of Templegate near Dublin, was fervently Roman Catholic, though he was later to describe the nuns of his tender years as being like the Gestapo in drag. In his chosen mode of occupation Mr Allen began humbly enough as a Butlin's redcoat. By 1967 the artiste was well enough regarded to secure the top position for a light entertainer in those days, and that was to compère ATV's *Sunday Night at the London Palladium*, since when Mr Allen has had many television shows of his own. He is an elegant, urbane comedian specialising in a wry look at life interspersed with regrettable obscenities. It is this latter aspect of his art which causes such dismay to his many admirers, as well as his habit of leaning an elbow on the microphone stand, acceptable from a third-rate club MC but not, we suggest, an artiste of Mr Allen's genuine wit and accomplishments.

ALLEN, FRED (1894-1956)
Vaudeville's Voltaire

We do not know to what extent the philosophies of the great French visionary impinged upon this comedian's work though his stage name was taken from the American Revolutionary hero Ethan Allen.

Fred Allen was born John F Sullivan in Cambridge, Massachusetts, and was an established vaudevillian by the time he started broadcasting in 1932. For the next twenty years and more this entry wrote almost all of the 273 radio shows in which he was to star with his wife, Portland Hoffa.

In feature films Mr Allen was celebrated as much for the prominent bags under the eyes as for his laconic delivery. His original avocation as a juggler was pursued under the name of Freddie St James, *The World's Worst Juggler*.

See MOREY AMSTERDAM, BIG BILL CAMPBELL, JUGGLERS

ALMA, Mlle (1868-1908)
The Human Fly

Ceiling walking, achieved either by suction or, less vulnerably, the use of loops into which the shoes are hooked, has ever been a popular circus and fair-ground attraction. Who can forget the scene in *At The Circus* in which Eve Arden persuades Groucho Marx to walk upside down with her, only to find his stolen wallet slipping from her bosom? Mlle Alma had more than one string to her bow for we find her billed at the Palace, London, in October 1898 as *The Electric Flying Wonder of the Pneumatic Globe.*

Others to assume the appellation *Human Fly* have been Charles Bliss (1826-1906), Olav Czarnowski (d1914), ALOIS PETERS, and William P Smith (d1919). George Morisco (c1842-1919) had a slight variant in that he called himself *Man Fly*, just as Berenetta Miller was *The Fly Girl*, and Hervio Nano (1804-47) (who was in all probability a midget) was billed variously as *The Gnome Fly*, *Man Monkey*, and *What is It?* (see M. GOUFFÉ). Finally let us record Professor Eugene Hermann *American Wizard & Ceiling Walker* who flourished in the 1850s-60s.

See MAGICIANS

AMES, CARLOS (1902-67)

A Harp – a Piano – a Voice; The Wizard of the Harp

Born in Mill Hill, North London, this musician boasted a diploma from the Royal College of Music, but it should be noted that his bill-batter *The Wizard of the Harp* was being used by another Music Hall artiste, Mr Roxy La Rocca by name, when the young Carlos was still in short trousers. And in 1922 when he would have graduated into long trousers but not yet from the Royal College we find one Marie Lawton *(The Harp – the Piano – the Voice)* had also pre-empted his alternative slogan. Mr Ames later stated that he had devised a harp act suitable for the Halls 'due to lack of orchestral opportunities'. We should not presume of course that this was due to any lack of mastery of his instrument.

In the 1930s there flourished one Gilbert Gerard *The Human Harp*. We have no documentary evidence on the musician so we suppose that he plucked himself.

AMSTERDAM, MOREY (1909-96)

The Human Joke Machine

At one time this Chicagoan comedian was on American radio so frequently that FRED ALLEN observed 'the only thing I can turn on without getting Morey Amsterdam is the faucet!' On this side of the Atlantic the artiste is remembered principally for his role as Buddy the wise-cracking script writer in *The Dick Van Dyke Show* (1961-66) which was so very popular here. But although Mr Amsterdam's smart-alec quickfire delivery was effective within the confines of a television situation comedy his style as a solo comedian was not appreciated within these shores. We once saw an audience totally freeze up on him, a memory which still makes our toes curl. This artiste was also responsible for the American lyrics of that most lachrymose of burlesque ballads *Your Baby Has Gone Down The Plug-Hole.*

ANDERSON, JOHN HENRY (1814-74)
The Wizard of the North

Mr Anderson claimed to have been given his title by none other than Sir Walter Scott, though what authority the literary giant possessed to confer such honorifics remains lost in the Gaelic mists. As part of his show Wizard Anderson performed a mentalism act, one of the first of its kind, with his daughter Louise, giving rise to her billing as *Second-Sighted Sybil,* and, less restrainedly but even more learnedly, *Retro-Reminiscent Mnemosyne.* For those without the benefit of a classical education Sybil (more properly Sibyl) was a prophetess famed for her notoriously ambiguous prognostications; Mnemosyne was the goddess of memory.

See GEORGE BARNARDO EAGLE, J W LISKARD, MAGICIANS, THE ZANCIGS

ANDREWS, JULIE (b1935)
The Amazing Child Singer

For once the bill-matter does not exaggerate for Miss Andrews, a schoolgirl from Walton-on-Thames in Surrey, did possess a phenomenal soprano from a remarkably early age, stopping the 1946 Hippodrome show *Starlight Roof* in its tracks. That she was accompanied by VIC OLIVER makes her triumph all the more remarkable. (Also making his West End début in this show was MICHAEL BENTINE.) A later highlight of this artiste's early career was to provide the musical interludes in the bafflingly popular BBC radio series *Educating Archie* (see PETER BROUGH & ARCHIE ANDREWS).

Miss Andrews' finest stage hour was as Eliza Doolittle in *My Fair Lady*; infamously denied the film rôle this entry found consolation in *Mary Poppins*, a picture which brought her lasting popularity. Certain uncouth journalists are wont to imply that Miss Andrews is lacking in animality. What we say to these gentlemen is we would rather have Miss Andrews with nothing on than them in their best suits.

See TED ANDREWS, BEATRICE LILLIE

ANDREWS, TED (1907-66)
The Canadian Troubadour: Songs and a Guitar

Mr Andrews (1907-66) arrived in Britain from the Dominion in 1937 intending to find work as a music arranger. In 1939 after establishing himself as a performer on the Variety circuits he teamed up with Barbara Ward Morris (b c1910) as *The Canadian Troubadour, with Barbara at the Piano*. Miss Morris had a promisingly talented daughter, Julie, from whose father she was separated. There was a divorce and a swift re-marriage, so that by 1946 the act had become Ted & Barbara Andrews (*and their daughter Julie*). Little Julie's rise to world celebrity (as outlined in the previous entry) is surely one of the most heartening show business stories of the century.

See MARGARET COOPER

ANIMAL & BIRD ACTS

Sonya Allen
See ELLEN BRIGHT

Millie Betra (fl1890s)
Serpent Queen
See Mlle Paula *infra*

Fred Bithell's (b1881)
...Performing Crows

Leoni Clarke (1852-1927)
The Bird King, Champion Pigeon
Charmer of the World; The Cat King

Pauline De Vere
See ELLEN BRIGHT, 'Lord' GEORGE SANGER

Claire Heliot
See ELLEN BRIGHT

ANIMAL & BIRD ACTS (continued):

Polly Hilton
See ELLEN BRIGHT

Charles Kellogg (1869-1949)
The Bird Man; California's Nature Singer

Laurie & Her Dogs (fl c1950s)
Enjoyment does their Gladness Injustice

Ellen Marvelle (fl c1900)
...with her Performing Cockatoos

Mme Marie Marzella (fl1890s-1900)
Queen of the Feathered World/Tribe;
The Wonder of the Age
Married Max Rose, an acrobat.

Mlle Paula (fl1890s)
Crocodile Conjurer & Serpent Subjugator;
Water Queen & Snake Charmer
Another ophidian dominatrice was Millie Betra (see *supra*).
Also see KORINGA.

Charles Prelle (fl1910s)
...with his Ventriloquial Dogs
See VENTRILOQUISTS

Rafayette's Dogs (fl1920s-30s)
Elopement by Motorcycle

Maud Rochez (1886-1930)
Monkey Music Hall

Jimmy Rogers (fl1930s-60s)
...with his Elusive Doves

Edna Squire-Brown (c1920-?)
Dance of the Doves

See also entries for: BETTY AUKLAND, HARRY BALL, BOB BEMAND'S COMEDY PIGEONS, ELLEN BRIGHT, THE GREAT (JAMES) CARTER, CARL HERTZ, KORINGA, MUSHIE, NAPOLEON, Colonel PARKER, THE THREE LOOSE SCREWS, ISAAC VAN AMBURGH, MIKE & BERNIE WINTERS

ARROL, DON (1928-67)
Dial M for Madness; A Nut in a Hut

Mr Arrol was too much a perfectionist and worrier for his own good, and it must be considered that his over-sensitivity and anxiousness to be thought well of contributed to his untimely demise. Despite the lowliest of theatrical beginnings – as a scene-shifter at the Glasgow Empire – he made his initial mark with the famous *Fol de Rols* concert-party. Wider success eluded him and twice he left the profession, lack of confidence smothering his ambition. But perseverance was rewarded in 1960 when the comedian landed the plum engagement of compère of *Sunday Night at the London Palladium*, then Britain's foremost television light entertainment programme. His predecessor was BRUCE FORSYTH, and although Mr Arrol's diffident manner could scarcely have been more different from Mr Forsyth's brashly confident persona, his initial three week trial was extended by Val Parnell (see FRED RUSSELL) to a year. At the time of his fatal syncope Mr Arrol was resident comedian with BBC tv's *Black & White Minstrel Show*, a hugely popular programme which ran for many years in various media and under various titles.

ARTEMUS (1890-1986)
...and his Incompetent Assistants

Arthur Hull Hayes was born in Dublin, Ireland, but after serving an apprenticeship as a compositor in London this entry emigrated to America where he developed the act which he himself described as 'comedy, hokum and slapstick conjuring'. He also avowed that he had been inspired as a boy by the antics of Walton & Lester *The World's Worst Wizards* and *The World's Worst Hypnotists*, and that he 'always tried to master the comedy side of conjuring without vulgarity'. Very edifying, though we feel that slapstick without vulgarity must surely also be deeply dull. Mr Artemus' membership number of the International Typographical Union of North America was 30180.

See PETER CASSON, MAGICIANS

ASKEY, ARTHUR (1900-82)
Big-Hearted Arthur

This much-loved comedian first saw the light of day in Liverpool, a city which has nurtured so many in his line of business. Mr Askey did not turn professional until 1924, commencing a long novitiate in summer seasons, Variety, pantomimes (notably as Dame), and above all in concert-party (billed at one time as *The Ultra-Violet Ray of Sunshine*), eventually graduating to the *Fol de Rols*.

The entertainer was also hugely in demand for Masonic evenings, flitting between as many as six lodges a night though it is not thought that he ever turned up a ceremonial trouser leg himself. A bespectacled little man with a wide personality and an engaging chuckle, Mr Askey came to national prominence in 1938 with Richard Murdoch in the iconoclastic BBC radio series *Band Waggon*. His records sold in their millions and he also appeared in several films, notably a version of that perennial thriller *The Ghost Train*. We once saw this artiste struggling for laughs in a pantomime routine early in the run. 'This'll be funny when we've worked it up,' he said cheerily.

See WILKIE BARD, PETER CAVANAGH

ATLAS, CHARLES (1893-1972)
The World's Most Perfectly Developed Man

At the age of ten the future male paradigm emigrated from Calabria with his family to the USA. The legendary humiliation when sand was kicked in his face by a lifeguard who then walked off with his inamorata occurred at Coney Island beach. By 1922 Mr Atlas' body-building triumphs prompted the magazine publisher Bernard Macfadden to confer on him the famous soubriquet quoted *supra*. Such was the enduring power of the sand-in-the-face story that advertisements featuring Mr Atlas' barrel-chest and big smile were still shifting his exercise and diet regimes nearly half a century later.

An earlier hunk was Henry E Dixey (1859-1943) *The Perfect Adonis*.

See EUGENE SANDOW

ATLAS & VULCANA (fl1890-c1920)
King and Queen of Athletes; Society Athlete

Vulcana (1872-1946) also billed herself improbably as *The Champion Lady Athlete of the World*. We would assume that these two fine physical specimens were husband and wife, though we have no direct evidence. Atlas was born William Hedley Roberts in 1864; his description of himself as *Society Athlete* puzzles us; did the artiste demonstrate his lissom prowess in evening dress and sporting a monocle?

See THE GREAT ATROY

ATROY, THE GREAT (1873-1952)
Society Juggler

In justification of his bill-matter did Mr Atroy abandon balls and clubs like the general run of his ilk and juggle with coats of arms and the family silver?

See ATLAS & VULCANA, JUGGLERS

ATWELL, WINIFRED (1913/9-83)
...and her Other Piano; Dusky Queen of the Keys; Queen of the Keyboard

This Trinidadian artiste arrived in London in 1946 as a concert pianist, turning to light music in 1948 in a strip show named, after the fashion of the time, *Peek-a-Boo*. The performer's 'Other Piano' was of the honky-tonk variety, specially tuned to enable Miss Atwell to delight her admirers by playing *Twelfth Street Rag*, her best-selling record.

The musician was a lady of ample girth, a big smile, great charm and not inconsiderable technique who removed to Australia, where her act had always aroused inordinate enthusiasm.

Other disturbers of the dominoes were Peggy 'Piano' Desmond (b1913) *Queen of the Ivories*, HERSCHEL HENLERE, and Charlie Kunz (1896-1958) *Clap Hands – Here Comes Charlie* and *Radio's Wizard of the Piano*.

Will H Fox (1858-1929) was *The First of the Trick Piano Playing Acts* and *Paddywhiski*. Two others who coasted along on the réclame of the renowned Polish pianist Ignacy Jan Paderewski (1860-1941) were Mendel (b1875) *The Marvellous Blind Pianist* and *The Paderewski of the Halls*, and Al Trahan (1897-1966) *The American 'Paderoughski'* and *Reunion in Moscow*.

For piano-entertainers see MARGARET COOPER.

AUGER, Captain GEORGE (1883-1922)
The Cardiff Giant

This gentleman wrote Music Hall sketches in which he worked with midgets thus accentuating to an unseemly degree his height of, allegedly, 8ft 4ins. We have always sympathised with persons of exceptional height, being ourself just a shade under 6ft 6ins, or two metres. We are thus the tallest actor to play virtually every rôle we have ever essayed.

Other exceptionally tall persons, all of whom exaggerated their heights by anything up to eighteen inches, were Martin Van Buren Bates (1845-1919) *The Kentucky Giant* who married Anna Swan (1846-88) *The Nova Scotian Giantess*, Chang Woo Gow (1847-93) *The Chinese Giant*, Robert Hales (1820-62) *The Norfolk Giant*, and Fyodor Machnow (1881-1905) *The Russian Giant* who claimed a height of 9ft 8ins but was in fact a mere 7ft 3¼ins. Patrick Cotter O'Brien (1760-1806) was *The Irish Giant*, as was Brian O'Brien (b1853) whose wife Christianna D Dunz (b1863) was advertised as reaching 7ft 4ins and thus twelve inches shorter than her husband.

Mention might be made here of Hugo (1868-1916) *The Tallest Man in the World*, who took over the name and billing from his brother. But which, we wonder existentially, was the brother?

Also see JAN VAN ALBERT, KATYA VAN DYK.

AUKLAND, BETTY (d c1988)
Queen of the English Concertina

This lady began her career in 1919 with her concertina-playing father Sam as The Auklands. From 1924 their act included Little Tweet, *The Canary Caruso*, after Enrico Caruso (1873-1921) the greatest tenor of the era. Despite this preposterous bill-matter the bird was – at least originally – a budgerigar. Listeners to 2LO radio station in 1926 were captivated by the avian artiste which for a while was a major draw round the best West End cabaret rooms and the nation's Number One Halls.

For other Carusos see TOM BURKE, JIMMY DURANTE, HARRY FRAGSON, and Count JOHN McCORMACK. Other concertinists listed are PERCY HONRI and Professor MacCann (KING OF...). Also see ANIMAL & BIRD ACTS.

AUSTIN, CHARLES (1877-1942)
Parker, PC

This extremely resourceful performer went on to score a huge success with his own sketch company, especially in burlesque playlets built around that ever-popular figure of fun, the comic policeman.

Mr Austin's inspiration for *Parker, PC* was the curious sight of a To Let sign seen outside an empty police station.

It is not sufficiently appreciated by observers of British Music Hall that comedy sketches were an immense draw. Dramatic sketches were also on offer from the likes of GEORGE GRAY and JOHN LAWSON and, after the introduction of double-licensing in 1911, from leading lights of the legitimate theatre such as Sir George Alexander and Sir Herbert Beerbohm Tree.

The only dumb sketch in the old Victorian tradition that we ourself ever saw in Variety took the form of a dozen or so men engaged in a brawl in a Wild West saloon. We cannot now recall the name of the troupe, but we do remember the participants falling downstairs and off balconies and smashing through windows. It was not until years later that we appreciated the strain and the tedium of performing so exhausting and dangerous a sketch *fourteen times a week!*

See FRED KARNO, LYTTON & AUSTIN, SKETCH ARTISTES

B

BAARTMAN, SAARTJE (1790-1815)
The Hottentot Venus

Fashionable London and Paris were fascinated by this entry who was brought to Europe in 1810 by a venal Boer to be exhibited as a human curiosity. Miss Baartman's pronounced steatopygia excited much unwholesome interest, the naturalist Baron Cuvier observing that 'the protuberance of her buttocks was not muscular but of an elastic trembling consistency – whenever the woman moved, she vibrated!'

The young Hottentot became an unwitting symbol of black female eroticism, a combination which had even the august Academie Française in a muck sweat, for after her early death the Immortals subjected Miss Baartman's remains to a lengthy series of prurient quasi-scientific autopsies. The most disgraceful part of this unsavoury story is that until as recently as the mid-1970s could be seen on public display at the Musée de l'Homme in Paris the poor young woman's excised pudenda.

BACON, MAX (1904-69)
Heavyweight Champion of Humour

Max Bacon was a small, rotund drummer who carved himself a niche in comedy cameo roles in stage shows, films and television. We are personally acquainted with an actress of considerable repute who in her youth found Mr Bacon extremely attractive, and indeed admitted to me that she slaked her desires on his person. Not long after this the actress decided that her proclivities tended more to the Sapphic and from thenceforth confined her venereous conjunctions almost exclusively to her own gender, enabling the present writer on one occasion to her delight to observe that we had known her 'before she was gay'.

BAILEY, HARRY (1910-89)
The King of Blarney

Harry Daniels was born in Limerick, Ireland, into a circus family. As a stripling this performer was trained in many of the disciplines traditionally associated with the sawdust ring; as an adult he utilised these arts as tightrope walker, as strong-man, and, with Fossett's Circus, as ring-master.

We had the pleasure of working with the artiste in pantomime at the Pavilion, Liverpool, for the 1958/9 season in which he comicked and tumbled and played a one-string fiddle. Mr Bailey was so lovable as Idle Jack – what Idle Jack was doing in *Robin Hood* need not detain us here – that after one matinée the children in the audience refused to leave. 'We want Jack! We want Jack!' they chanted, long after the walk-down, the final curtain and the National Anthem. Eventually Mr Bailey appeared to tell them the show was over and that they must all go home.

A few years later we were again in pantomime in Liverpool, this time at the Empire. Accompanying the popular vocalist Tommy Steele to a night club we were delighted to discover that the cabaret artiste was none other than Harry Bailey, who bravely and most skilfully won over an uninterested and talkative audience to receive an ovation at the end of his forty-five-minute appearance.

BAKER, HYLDA (1908-86)

Britain's Greatest Comic-ess; Britain's Queen of Comedy; I Wonder How They Know; 101% Pure; She Knows Y'Know

'I think I can say without fear of contraception...' was but one of the comical Malapropisms which spiced this entry's utterances, though the comedienne's principal source of humour was derived from one-sided conversations with her toweringly tall and apparently simple-minded friend Cynthia, a non-speaking rôle customarily essayed by a young man in drag.

Miss Baker was just under five feet in height, her figure was dumpy and her features homely. Bitterness, frustration, and loneliness contributed to a notorious abrasiveness of manner off-stage, though we cannot but sympathise with one whose memory lapses while still at the height of her powers first warned her of the dread onset of 'Alka Seltzer's'.

Other ladies assuming the purple as *Queen of Comedy* were BESSIE BELLWOOD, MARIE LLOYD, GLADYS MORGAN, SUZETTE TARRI, VESTA VICTORIA, and NELLIE WALLACE. In the 1920s slight variations were offered by Lily Morris (1884-1952) *Queen of Comediennes* and May Sherrard *Queen of Mirth.*

See QUEEN OF..., Mrs SHUFFLEWICK

BAKER, JOSÉPHINE (1906-74)

The Black Venus

Miss Baker was a ravishingly beautiful and lithe American singer, dancer, mime, and comedienne who went to Paris in 1925 with *La Revue Nègre* and, finding French society congenial for a person of colour, stayed. Her wartime work as an entertainer and with the Red Cross and the Free French Air Force earned this mesmeric and pantherine performer the Légion d'Honneur, the Croix de Guerre and the Rosette de la Résistance.

From 1950 the artiste devoted her energies to the orphanage which she established on her estate in the Dordogne, regularly coming out of retirement to raise funds for its maintenance. Despite becoming a French citizen in 1937 Miss Baker was not indifferent to events in the country of her birth, in the 1960s travelling to the United States to take part in civil rights activities.

It is heartening to record that the year before she died Joséphine Baker made a trimphant return to New York, where her five valedictory performances at the Carnegie Hall were received with acclamation.

BALL, HARRY (1841-88)

The Great and Original Temperance Band Comedian and Vocalist; The Tramp Musician with his Wonderful Performing Dog Fathead

Recent research shows that Ball was this artiste's family name, though he more usually, in private life, was *k.a.* William Henry Powles. Mr Ball was the father of one of the greatest of all British Music Hall artistes VESTA TILLEY and could perhaps be accused of exploiting his daughter for she was the sole supporter of herself, her parents, and twelve siblings before reaching her teens. But Miss Tilley herself speaks of him most affectionately in her recollections so we must assume that this entry was as kind and loving as could be wished.

See ANIMAL & BIRD ACTS, NAPOLEON

BAMBERG, THEO (1875-1963)
Europe's Greatest Shadowist

A shadowist, or shadowgraphist, is one who produces shadows on a screen by dextrous use of the hands and fingers, a rarely seen art nowadays. Mynheer Bamberg was one of a remarkable family of Dutch entertainers; his great-great-grandfather, Eliaser Bamberg (1760-1833), was known as *The Crippled Devil*, owing to a wooden leg cunningly fitted with secret compartments the better to bamboozle 18th-century Nederlands burghers.

As well as his shadowgraphy Theo Bamberg, who was rendered almost totally deaf after a childhood swimming accident, worked an Oriental illusion act under the name of Okito. Other notables in this line were Bradley & Partner, Clivette, and Cazman the Great (fl c1890) who described himself as *The Leading Escamoteur and Shadowist*. Our French dictionary informs us that 'escamoteur' translates as juggler, conjurer, and/or pickpocket. And finally, a gentleman named Chassino (fl c1900) was advertised as *Bird Imitator & Shadowgraphist* from which we may infer that his performance featured avian representations.

See CHARLES JOANNYS, JUGGLERS, FELICIEN TREWEY

BAMBERGER, FREDDIE (& PAM) (fl1930s-60s)
Jest Artiste

Mr Bamberger (1909-75) described himself as a pianist-raconteur; originally he had been one of The Two Hoffmans, a double-piano act, and he had also played for Jack Hylton (1893-1965). The 'Jesting' came about when Mr Bamberger was scheduled to perform the customary straight double act with his wife. Mrs Bamberger was suddenly taken ill and at very short notice her husband improvised a comedy act; so successful was it that humour remained the core of the act ever after. How common such serendipity seems to be in the happy-go-lucky world of show business! We once waited outside a stage-door for Mr & Mrs Bamberger to sign our autograph book which, we are sorry to say, was later stolen.

See MARGARET COOPER

BARBETTE (1904-73)

The Enigma

Van der Clyde Broodway was a male trapezist and tightrope walker who worked as a beautiful blonde. A Texan who had worked for the Ringling Brothers circus Mr Broodway reached Paris in 1923 where he was a sensation at the Casino de Paris. At the conclusion of the act 'her' wig would be whipped off, to gasps of amazement. No less an intellectual than Jean Cocteau declared Barbette to be 'an angel, a flower, a bird'.

For sixteen years *The Enigma* remained a headline attraction not only in the French capital but in London, Berlin, and New York, and we wonder why, since Barbette's true gender was so well known, audiences continued to be surprised at the revelatory discarding of his *postiche*. Perhaps the contrast of blonde curls with the balding pate underneath gave a *frisson* even to those familiar with the act.

Male performers who dress as women are *k.a.* female impersonators or drag artistes, from the costume which is one's 'drag'. This is a subject too complex to be analysed here – even supposing we understood it – but the following artistes in this field demand mention by right of eminence: DOUGLAS BYNG, Herbert Clifton (1884-1947) *The Vocalist with the £1,000 Voice*, BERT ERROL, ?Lind? *The Male Melba* and *Who Is It?*, Karyl Norman (1896-1947) and Francis Renault (1893-1955) who were both *The Creole Fashion Plate* (the latter was also sometimes *The Last of the Red-Hot Papas* – see SOPHIE TUCKER), MALCOLM SCOTT, Mrs SHUFFLEWICK, JAMES UNSWORTH and Billy Wells (c1909-89) *Second Hand Rose of Washington Square*.

Representing the many drag double-acts are Ford & Sheen *Those Fascinating Frauds* (fl1936-c80) and Hayes & Gardner *Two Misleading Ladies*.

Two ventriloquial female impersonators were BOBBIE KIMBER and LYDIA DREAMS; two aerial drag artistes were Mlle Lu-Lu (see EL NINO FARINI) and Jack 'Dental' Riskit (b1879) *The Girl on the Slack Wire* (see Mme SENYAH). We do not include low comics like NORMAN EVANS, DAN LENO, LITTLE TICH or GEORGE ROBEY whose pantomime Dame-like females were parodic rather than mimical.

For male impersonators see ST GEORGE HUSSEY.

BARCLAY & PERKINS (fl1890?-95)
Brewers of Mirth

After George Barclay (1868-1944) retired from performing the ex-comedian became an extremely successful agent, so much so that from 1927 he was known as *King of the Agents*. Mrs Barclay was on the Halls as KATE CARNEY.

The first Music Hall agency was founded in 1856 by the singer Ambrose Maynard (1819-89). He became famously wealthy on his commissions, leading us to compare his nickname of *Mr Five Per Cent* with the customary present-day commission level of ten per cent, twenty per cent and even more.

A singular *Brewer of Mirth* was George Braley (fl1930s-50s) while The Dewars (fl1920s-30s) had a similar but higher-proof slogan with their *Distillers of Mirth*.

BARD, WILKIE (1874-1944)
The Funniest Man Alive

This entry was born in Manchester as William Augustus Smith, a cotton spinner's clerk who chose to go on the Halls after amateur triumphs. Often such encouragement can be illusory, but Mr Bard was a genuinely talented comedian particularly effective in broad characterisations and as pantomime Dame. Alas, his bizarre appearance and make-up rendered him old hat after the First World War and the artiste became notoriously sullen and unreliable.

The bill-matter quoted above was used in New York, and indeed for his first visit the comic was rapturously received. (See TOM BURKE, DAN LENO and ROBB WILTON for similarly provocative billing.) But Mr Bard's second visit was more of a struggle, for even in vaudeville the days of weirdly accoutred grotesques were beginning to fade.

It is interesting to note that long after comedians had taken to wearing smart lounge suits or evening dress they still tended to wear funny hats – *cf* ARTHUR ASKEY, REG DIXON, ARTHUR ENGLISH, FRED FORDHAM, JEWEL & WARRISS, MAX MILLER, TED RAY, TOMMY TRINDER, MAX WALL, JIMMY WHEELER. JACK SEATON has reminded us that until, say, the 1940s men were customarily covered when out of doors. As the standard backing for a comic was a street-cloth – often decorated with advertisements for local enterprises – a hat would have been *de rigueur*.

BARNES, FRED (1884-1938)
The Prince of Light Comics

This most elegant of Music Hall singers once quoted with pride a press comment describing him as 'the male VESTA TILLEY', after the celebrated male impersonator. It was just this kind of foolish bravado which brought about his eclipse, for Mr Barnes brandished his homosexuality in defiance of convention and of the law as it then stood. 'Freda', said MARIE LLOYD to him on one well-remarked occasion, 'what have you done to your lashes? They look like bloody park railings!' Miss Lloyd, it should be pointed out, was referring to Mr Barnes' *off*-stage maquillage. His vocal talents, immaculate attire, and wondrous good looks made him one of the brightest stars in the Music Hall firmament, but rampant indiscretion and the demon drink tried the patience of managers just too often. His fall from grace was swift and pitiful and he was discovered dead in a gas-filled bed-sitter in Margate.

BARNES, LARRY (b1926)
The Viceroy of Versatility

This subscript is the only one between these covers devised by the present chronicler, for Mr Barnes is a personal friend and colleague of many years' standing. The artiste, who, by the by, is Pearly King of Thornton Heath, lays good claim to being a guitarist, a magician, a paper tearer, a balloon modeller, a lightning sketch artist, an escapologist, and a Music Hall singer whose repertoire extends to nigh on a hundred titles! Mr Barnes is also no mean actor, having, during his lengthy and varied career, graced many a legitimate enterprise. We are proud to have supplied this remarkable performer with an appellation which is as just as it is appropriate.

The doyenne of British paper tearers is the legendary Miss Terri Carol *The Tearaway*, with whom we had the honour of appearing at the Weymouth Pavilion on Sunday, August 3rd, 1969.

See MAGICIANS

BARNES, PAUL J (1919-83)
The Man of a Thousand Voices

This unimaginative bill-matter has been used by any number of mimics and what are now termed 'voice-artistes' including HAROLD

BERENS, MEL BLANC, and JOAN TURNER.

Another *Man of a Thousand Voices* was Victor Seaforth (b1917) who told us that the actual number of voices specified depended on the whim of his agent or the local manager, varying between ninety-nine, a hundred, or – subtle touch – a hundred and one. Mr Seaforth married Suma of Johnny Lamonte & Suma (see JUGGLERS).

See list of MIMICS in glossary.

BARNES, SIDNEY (1876-1927)

The Human Ostrich

Identical bill-matter was displayed by one Vitreo but we have no details of these omnivores' feats. On December 27th 1996 the *Daily Mail* reported that 46-year-old Frenchman Michel Lotito, *a.k.a.* M. Mangetout, had in the course of his career consumed computers, bicycles, television sets, beds, chandeliers, and a Cessna light aircraft. 'What I'd really like to do,' stated the intestinal *non pareil*, 'is to retire to a log cabin in the mountains with my dog'. And then, presumably, eat the lot.

See HARRY NORTON, THE MYSTERIOUS WERTH

BARNUM, P(HINEAS) T(AYLOR) (1810-91)

Prince of Humbugs;The Prometheus of the Pleasure Principle

Prometheus was one of the Greek Titans, noted as a benefactor to mortal man. Mr Barnum's beneficence was based entirely on self-interest, so much so that the very name of this American promoter has become synonymous with opportunism, unwholesome sensation, and outright fraud. Naïvely the showman revealed in his 1855 autobiography many of the deceits on which his fortune had been founded, only to be surprised and aggrieved at the harshness of the criticism inspired by these revelations.

The English showman Edward H Bostock (1858-1940) billed himself as *The Barnum of Britain* though he was far from being a charlatan, for Mr Bostock was a member of Glasgow City Council, a JP and a Fellow of the Zoological Society.

See HENRY COLLARD, JENNY LIND, TONY PASTOR, VALENTINE

BARR, IDA (1884-1968)

Britain's Premier Singer of Rag-Time Melodies; The Ragtime Girl; Red-Headed and Proud of It; Red-Headed but Clever; A Star with the Personality of a Star

The strapping daughter of an Army sergeant-major Maud Barlow saved her father's blushes by adopting the name Maud Laverne on making her Music Hall début in 1897. Eleven years later she became Ida Barr, her six feet of solid femininity prompting the comment 'Ida Barr? She could 'ide a bloomin' pub!'

The artiste married comic singer GUS HARRIS but his jealousy of her superior drawing-power destroyed their union, and, unencumbered by children, she fled to conquer the New World.

Despite years of intercontinental stardom and a repertoire of such standard favourites as *Oh, You Beautiful Doll* and *Everybody's Doin' It Now* Miss Barr died in a public ward leaving only £637.

See DOLLY HARMER

BARRETT, T W (1851-1935)

A Nobleman's Son

This entry's bill-matter derives not from his lineage – his father was a Birmingham shoemaker – but from the title of his first song success. Other ditties in Mr Barrett's repertoire such as *Peg Leg Polly*, *Blow Me Up An Apple Tree*, and *I'm Not Its Father* show that coarseness was by no means absent from his material. Mr Barrett was said to have originated the 'dead-pan' style of humorous delivery, a claim, in our opinion, of dubious veracity.

BARRYMORE, ETHEL (1879-1959)

The First Lady of American Theatre

This magnificent actress was the daughter of actors Maurice Barrymore (1847-1905) and his wife Georgiana Drew (1856-93). Her brothers, also distinguished players, were Lionel (1878-1954) and JOHN BARRYMORE. Esteemed in her youth as much for her beauty as her abilties Miss Barrymore was the first to be described as *Glamour Girl*, but her unparalleled series of histrionic triumphs commanded universal respect. That those two other ornaments of the American stage Katherine Cornell (1893-74) and Helen Hayes (1900-93) were also referred to as *The First Lady* could have led to a degree of animus between the three artistes, especially as their careers overlapped by some thirty years. We are sure that all three were above such pettiness and that they invariably greeted each other as devoted sisters in art.

BARRYMORE, JOHN (1882-1942)
The Great Profile

Brother of Lionel and ETHEL BARRYMORE this prodigiously attractive and talented actor was the Hamlet of his generation – his six months in the rôle in London is still a West End record. A beautiful speaking voice and princely appearance proved as effective on screen as on stage, but the vastly greater financial rewards of the newer medium proved this entry's ruination. Mr Barrymore's last years were pitiful; alcoholism and libidinous excess had wrecked him both physically and spiritually and he was but a caricature of his early splendour.

BASSELIN, OLIVIER (1400-50)
The Father of Vaudeville

'Vaudeville' is probably a corruption of the 15th-century French term vaux-de-vire, which were satirical parodies of popular airs sung in the Val or Vau de Vire region of Normandy. Basselin was a noted writer of these scurrilous ballads, hence his title. French vaudeville developed into what we might today call musical comedy, while in the USA vaudeville evolved into a species of disreputable Variety entertainment.

See FATHER OF...

BATES, PEG-LEG (1907-98)
Monoped Dancer

The one-legged dancer was by no means an unusual sight on the Halls, and although we do not recall having seen one ourself we remember our paternal progenitor assuring us that Mr Clayton Bates' exhibition was 'the most beautiful thing you ever saw'. Despite the danger of straying into Peter Cook/Dudley Moore 'unidexter Tarzan' territory we feel that out of respect to those artistes who had the grit to turn what might have seemed a severe handicap into a positive advantage we should list M. Zampi (fl1870s-80s) *The One-Legged Gymnast* who was decidedly out-billed by Eli Bowen (b1844) *Legless Aerial Gymnast*, Charles Raymond (1860-1903) and Donato (d June 10th 1865) who both described themselves simply but aptly as *One-Legged Dancer*, and M. Pierro (fl1880s-90s) who was *The Unipedean Performer* though what he performed we do not know. Bob Evans (1868-1903) was more forthcoming as *One-Legged Song & Dance Artiste* and La Piere (fl1860s), the only female in this category, was *One-Legged Gymnast/Acrobat.*

For armless artistes see UNTHAN.

BAYES, NORA (c1880-1928)
The Greatest Single Woman Singing Comedienne in the World Assisted and Admired by Jack Norworth

Jack Norworth (1879-1959) was Miss Bayes' husband, though as he was only the second of five he didn't get the chance to assist or admire her for very long. While still paired this American couple co-wrote *Shine On Harvest Moon*, a very pleasant song which was premiered by them in *The Ziegfeld Follies of 1908*. Miss Bayes possessed plenty of what used to be called 'pep', and despite her marital misadventures enjoyed great personal success in London during the 1920s.

BEAUCHAMP, GEORGE (1863-1901)
The Quaintest Comedian Living; The Rage of the Colonies; Worth a Guinea a Box

Mr Beauchamp's claim to be *The Rage of the Colonies* should be understood as a whimsicality; *Worth a Guinea a Box* was for half a century and more the slogan employed on advertisements for Beecham's Pills, a medicament whose laxative properties were legendarily efficacious.

'Quaint' occurs in many artistes' bill-matter, including that of HARRY CHAMPION, for a century ago the word meant unusual or odd as well as whimsical. Others were Laurie Howe *The Quaint Comedian* (see DICK EMERY), G W HUNTER, Sydney Edwards (1917?-78) *That Quaint Chap*, NELLIE WALLACE, David Warfield (1866-1951) *High-Class Mimic and Quaint Story Teller*, and GEORGE WILLIAMS.

BELLWOOD, BESSIE (1857-96)
The Comedy Queen; Queen of the Halls

Music Hall audiences' first experience of the Bermondsey rabbit-skinner was as Signorina Ballantino *World-Famous Zither Player.* Recovering from this false start the artiste made her name with *Wotcher, Ria!,* a noisy knees-up kind of song which mirrored its creator's life-style, for Miss Bellwood was a rumbustious, volatile performer with enormous attack but little finesse. This entry was renowned for her strong language both on and off stage, for her charity work and devout Roman Catholicism, and for her earthy discountenancing of hecklers. Miss Bellwood was for many years under the protection of His Grace the Duke of Manchester.

For other Queens of Comedy see HYLDA BAKER. Also see MARIE LLOYD.

BEMAND'S COMEDY PIGEONS, BOB (fl1917-50s)
Flying Funsters

In 1917 Oswald Bemand (b1891) appealed against a rejection of his request for a three-month deferment of his conscription into the Army on the grounds that the time was needed to teach his brother Bob the act, otherwise £2,000 of pigeons and £500 of scenery would go to waste. To the great credit of Field Marshal Haig the appeal was granted.

We were speaking of the *Flying Funsters* to a group of pros a while back and to our surprise one of them remembered seeing the act at the Dudley Hippodrome. 'It was very funny,' averred my informant, 'the pigeons were all painted different colours and they fell off swings and tightropes and things.'

What must have been a similar act was Ancell's Painted Pigeons *The Most Artistic Act in Vaudeville.*

See p.15

BENEDETTI BROTHERS
Musicians in Twenty Positions

These melodious contortionists were Guglielmo (d January 1935) and Eduardo (d June 17th 1940) Benedetti; we have no knowledge of their art and so will refrain from lascivious speculation.

See VALENTINE

BENNETT, BILLY (1887-1942)
Almost a Gentleman

This poetic genius was the son of John R Bennett (c1863-1936) of Bennett & Martell *Those Murderous Knockabouts*, the other half of the act being Robert Martell (c1868-1925) who at one time had been teamed with T E DUNVILLE as The Two Martells.

After the Great War – in which Mr Bennett served most gallantly – the artiste, before fully evolving his seedy poetaster clad in over-sized dress-suit, under-sized waistcoat, brown Army boots, heavy moustache, and hair plastered down in a cow-lick, returned to the Halls briefly as *The Trench Comedian*. The accent in which this entry declaimed his odes was juicy genteel, or Penge posh, and his surreal effusions such as *Christmas Day in the Cookhouse* and *The Green Tie on the Little Yellow Dog* were joyously received by all parts of the house.

The artiste also worked up a black-faced cross-talk double-act, originally for radio, *k.a.* Alexander & Mose. Mr Bennett was Moses Washington Lincoln and the first Alexander was James Carew (1872-1938), the actor and widower of Dame Ellen Terry (1847-1928); the second was ALBERT WHELAN.

For other black-face acts see G H ELLIOTT; for other poets see CYRIL FLETCHER, CHARLES SLOMAN. Also see J MILTON HAYES.

BENNY, JACK (1894-1974)
Aristocrat of Humour; Waukegan's First Citizen

Having been conservatoire-trained as a fiddler Benjamin Kubelsky gravely disappointed his family by becoming a vaudevillian, first of all in a high-toned musical act called Salisbury and Kubelsky. The renowned concert violinist Jan Kubelik considered that the similarity of name might syphon off some of his less observant admirers and threatened to sue; young Kubelsky, now a comedy single, thus became Ben (K) Benny, *The Fiddlin' Kid* or *Fiddle Funology*. This entry then came to the attention of Ben Bernie, an established performer who also purveyed humour and violin playing, forcing a further change in 1918 to the name by which we all remember the comedian whose magisterially slow burns were a source of merriment to his admirers and of wonderment to his peers. Mr Benny's partner both professionally and personally was Sadye Marks (1906-83) *k.a.* Mary Livingstone. His remains are interred at Hillside Memorial Park, Hollywood, in the Hall of Graciousness.

BENTINE, MICHAEL (1922-96)
The Happy Imbecile

A Peruvian Old Etonian, Mr Bentine made his Variety début in 1947 with his phrenetic broken chairback routine at the Nuffield Centre, a booking which brought the ex-RAF Intelligence officer an agent, a West End show (*Starlight Roof*) and the basis of a fine career. One of the original four Goons the comedian was too individualistic to be one of a team; his television shows were noted for their ingenuity and originality. Mr Bentine undoubtedly possessed an exceptionally powerful – even fearsome – intellect which was never perhaps fully focussed. A man of his gifts could and should have made a greater mark in the world than being a comic, not that we denigrate the need for laughter. Many of our best friends are comics.

See p.15, CLAPHAM & DWYER, RONALD FRANKAU, STAN STENNETT

BERENS, HAROLD (1903-95)
Wot a Geezer!

Before establishing his Cockney barrow-boy persona Mr Berens had worked as a 'dialectician' whose billing was the unimaginative *Man of a Thousand Voices*. We were touched to see this entry smiling seraphically through his rôle as JOSEF LOCKE's conductor in the film *Hear My Song* which was such a great critical and popular success, and made such a happy conclusion to the veteran comedian's long career.

See PAUL J BARNES, JOSEF LOCKE

BERLE, MILTON (b1908)
Mr Television

This New Yorker was an advocate of the sock-it-to-'em school of comedy. Such was his popularity that his television series in 1948 is considered responsible for the explosive sale of sets in the US that year. As a boy his bill-matter was *The Wayward Youth*; another much-quoted label, one perhaps not over-relished by the artiste, is *The Thief of Bad Gags* c1960 Alex Donn and Nick Nicols were billing themselves ungrammatically as *The Thiefs of Badgags*.

BERLIN, IRVING (1888-1989)
King of Ragtime

We would not insult the genius of this entry by trying to encapsulate his career in the space available, but we will point out Israel Baline's longevity which was so protracted that he out-lived the copyright on many of his own songs.

The songsmith's lack of musical training, for he could neither read nor write music and could only play by ear in one key, was no bar to an extraordinary capacity for dreaming up both deceptively simple tunes and memorably appropriate lyrics. This son of a desperately poor Jewish family who had fled from the Russian pogroms caught the mood of his era and helped to shape his adopted country's view of itself; after *Alexander's Ragtime Band* (1910) popular song was never the same again.

See EMMA CARUS

BERNARD, CHARLES S (1816-74)
The American Fire King

Despite its fearsome dangers to the performer fire-eating is still a popular novelty in street-carnivals and corporate theme events. Fire-eating is also seen in theatres and clubs though the smell of paraffin makes the act better suited to the open air. Indeed many theatres, mindful of safety precautions, will not permit any naked flame on stage. We once had to inform a juggler who arrived very late for a performance that he could not use his climactic trick of juggling with blazing brands. He was not best pleased.

Other asbestic artistes were Cristoforo Buonocore (fl1850s) *The Italian Fire King* and *The Italian Salamander*, The Fire-Eating Dubarrys (Stanley and Jean {d January 24th 1975}), The Ngfys *Remarkable Human Salamandas*, Mlle Le Never (fl1870s-80s) *The Royal Salamander & Fire Queen*, and Eugene Rivalli (d February 2nd 1900) who billed himself as *The Fire Prince* with his wife Mme Rivalli as *The Fire Princess*. William E Smith (1879-1934) *The Human Torch* was *a.k.a.* Smithy *The High Diver*.

See IVAN IVANITZ CHABERT, THE SALAMBOS

BERNARD, GEORGE & BERT (fl1932-67)
Off the Record

American dancers George Bernard (1912-68) and Bert Maxwell (b1918) originally teamed up in 1932, but it was not until 1946 that they developed the miming-to-records act which was to prove so outstandingly popular. The unseen third member of the act was George

Pierce, for it was he who controlled and manipulated the records off-stage. These artistes did more than just mime, they spoofed the recordings to hilarious effect and we retain the most vivid recollections of their chokingly funny Andrews Sisters. George Bernard's real name was Bernard George; after his death he was succeeded by Les Bernard (no relation).

BETTY, Master WILLIAM HENRY WEST (1791-1874)
The Young Roscius

Master Betty's vogue was brief but all-conquering. For four months in 1804 he held London in thrall, and such was his drawing-power that Parliament adjourned to enable Honourable Members to see this extraordinary child for themselves. The 13-year-old played many of the great dramatic roles, though the freakshow nature of the performances must have been emphasised by the use of adult support casts. But by the end of the season Master Betty couldn't, as the Americans say, get arrested, and his career was over. Any regrets were assuaged by his swiftly acquired fortune which was sufficient to last his days.

Even younger was William Robert Grossmith (1818-99) *The Infant Roscius*, though Master Betty remains the most celebrated of all histrionically precocious children. Across the Atlantic Joseph Santley (1886/9-1971) was allegedly *America's Greatest Boy Actor*.

For other Rosciuses (Roscii?) see IRA ALDRIDGE; for other juvenile performing prodigies see NORMAN CARROL, SAM COWELL, EL NINO FARINI, and DAN LENO.

BEVERLEY SISTERS, THE
Three in Harmony

Daughters of the Variety duo Coram & Mills *Songs and Laughter,* Joy (b1929) and her twin sisters Teddie and Babs (b1932) are East Enders who made very good indeed from the late 1940s until their retirement in 1967 with a string of close-harmony records both sentimental *(I Saw Mommy Kissing Santa Claus)* and novel *(How Much is That Doggy in the Window? –Woof! Woof!).* Blonde, pretty, slim and dizzily loquacious, the Bevs came out of retirement in 1985 at the behest of the egregious hedonist and flash-trash night club entrepreneur Peter Stringfellow and have swept all before them ever since.

BIBB, JOSEPH (1845-95)
The Prince's Grotesque

Mr Bibb awarded himself this title after appearing before the Prince of Wales; we cannot think HRH was overly thrilled – try saying it for yourself...

BI-BO-BI (d April 24th 1928)
The Sousa of the Bells

We may reasonably infer that Émile Deschee Maecker played on tuned bells those rousing marches of the kind composed by John Philip Sousa (1854-1932), the renowned American US Marine Corps bandmaster. But we may be quite wrong.

BICYCLE ACTS

The Abbins
See AL CARTHY

Sam Barton (fl1900s-?)
Stealing a Bicycle; Trying to Ride a Bicycle

Clark & Ritchie (fl1910)
The Messengers of Mirth

P L Clark (b c1887) and W E Ritchie (see *infra*). Clark also ran an act called Clark's Crazy Comedy Cyclists as well as working solo under the name of Auntie *A Gate, A Bike and A Gamp*.

The Elliotts (c1880-c1914)
The World's Cycling Wonders

With another family *k.a.* The Elliotts and Savonas or The Musical Elliott Savonas *The Only Saxophone Band in the World* and *The Palace of Orpheus*.

Henri French (b1916)
Laughter on Wheels

Boy Foy (b1918)
England's Youngest Juggler; The Wonder on One Wheel
See (Boy Foy) JUGGLERS

BICYCLE ACTS (continued):

Eddie Gordon (1889-1956) & Nancy
The American Tramp Cyclist; The Silent Humorist
In 1938 received permission to copy machine invented by W E
Ritchie *infra.* Nancy's sister married LEW GRADE.

Joe Jackson (1878-1942)
Trying to Steal a Bicycle
From 1930 worked with son Joe Jackson jnr (b1912) who went
solo after his father's death.
See Sam Barton *ultra*
See Clarke & Ritchie, Eddie Gordon *supra*

Lotto, Lilo & Otto (fl1880s-1900s)
Trick cyclists
Alfred Lotto (1878-1912), Toby Lilo (Walter Eggington
1880-1902) and Otto. Alfred and Otto may have been
brothers; John (Jack) Lotto (1858-1944) may have
been their father.

Ravic & Renée (fl1948-1960s?)
Thrills on Wheels
Husband & wife team: John (b1925) and Eileen (b1926)
Lilley. Without Eileen the act was *k.a.* Ravic & Partner or
Ravic & Babs *Thrills Awheel.* In *The Stage* for April 16th
1959 billed as Ravic & Babs (2).

W E Ritchie (1872-1943)
The (Original) Tramp Cyclist
Also ran a troupe called Ritchie's Reckless Rough Riders.

Ad Robbins (fl c1900-39)
Canadian Cycle Tamer

Lalla Selbini (1878-1942)
*The Bathing Belle on the Bicycle; The Girl with the
Perfect Form; A Wow on Wheels*
Daughter of Lily (1858-1930) and Jack (1854-1932) Selbini.
Inherited THE GREAT LAFAYETTE's show.

Verno & Voyce (fl1890s-1900s)
The Fin-de-Cycle Bicyclists; The Singing Cyclists
Sydney Verno and brother Albert Voyce (b1870).

Sydney died 1897; replaced by Barney Stuart. Also presented sketches, e.g. *The German Jockey* and *John Bull's Cash-Box*.

See JOE COLVERD, VICTORIA MONKS, SKETCH ARTISTES, TOM TINSLEY

See also entries for: KAUFMANN'S TRICK CYCLISTS, SLIM RHYDER

BLACK, JOE
Crazy but Harmless

This entry began his professional life as a singer and dancer; in the late 1930s Laurie Howe, father of DICK EMERY, perspicaciously suggested that Mr Black switch to comedy. Since then the artiste, a small man of simple charm, has enlivened many a Variety bill, revue and pantomime – his Dame is especially admired.

The performer has not been so successful at picking winners, for he confided to us that unreliable horses had cost him not one house but two.

BLANC, MEL (1908-89)
The Man of a Thousand Voices

Mr Blanc's entrée into the esoteric world of cartoon voicing was only achieved by persistence. For eighteen months the artiste auditioned once a fortnight without a whiff of an engagement. Then the person conducting the auditions suddenly died and this entry secured his first booking, as a drunken bull.

This was the start of a glorious list of characterisations to include Daffy Duck, Woody Woodpecker, Porky Pig, Tweety Pie, Sylvester, Pepe le Pew, Speedy Gonzales, and Barney Rubble. Nor can we omit the immortal Bugs Bunny, despite the irony of his vocal creator's allergy to carrots.

See PAUL J BARNES. Also see list of MIMICS in glossary.

BLONDIN (1824-97)
The Hero of Niagara; The Little Wonder

Émile Gravelet's feat of crossing Niagara Falls on a tightrope in 1859 made him a personage of world renown. The following year he offered to take the Prince of Wales across on his back, and it is said that HRH had to be restrained by an equerry from accepting.

Having retired from the rope M. Blondin founded a wine-importing business in London, but the Frenchman's balancing skills did not extend to book-keeping and he lost his fortune. At an advanced age the *Wonder*, no longer so *Little*, had perforce to go back aloft, carrying his doubtless dismayed consort. We are pleased to report that he died peacefully in his bed at Ealing, West London, where Blondin Avenue and Niagara Avenue memorialise their illustrious resident.

Such was this artiste's fame that his name was regularly, one might say almost routinely, invoked by his fellow funambulists. *Female Blondin* was the billing displayed by, amongst many others, Mrs Ben Biddle (d January 1907), Mlle Carlotte (1848-1928), PAULINE VIOLANTE, and SELINA YOUNG.

Master Alfred Corello (fl1860s) was, almost inevitably, *The Juvenile Blondin* and *The Juvenile Léotard*, while Carlos Trower (1848-89) was *The African Blondin*. Forepaugh's Circus in New York even included a 'tightrope-walking Blondin horse'.

See CAICEDO, JULES LÉOTARD, GRIFFITHS BROTHERS; note also the grim entry for Mme GENEIVE.

BLOW, WINDY (1910-86)
The Balloonatic; The Balloonologist

This entry had a performing *alter ego* as Charles Cole *The World's Fastest Lightning Cartoonist*. The artiste was not only devoted to his audiences but also his Unions, for he worked indefatigably for many years for the Variety Artistes' Federation and then, after amalgamation, for the British Actors' Equity Association. Another union which occupied his attention is found under YVONNE PRESTIGE.

BODIE, Dr WALFORD (& CO) (1870-1939)
Electric Wizardry; The Talkies' Only Rival

An Aberdonian, Samuel Bodie (Walford was his brother-in-law's surname) was one of the most flamboyantly dubious characters ever seen on the Halls. Unlike your average conjurer who baffles us through honest trickery this entry purported that his supernormal powers were real and his electrical apparatus genuinely therapeutic. Hypnotism, psychic surgery, and a phoney doctorate added to his extravagantly

extravagantly puffed reputation as a healer, and many sufferers were given false hopes by his bogus claims.

At one time the Bodie company included his sister Mystic Marie (1885-1906), his wife Princess RUBIE, her 'galvanic' sister *k.a.* La Belle Electra, and Florrie Robertshaw (b1908) who in 1932 became his second wife. Mr Bodie's degree came from an American postal academy; numerous other claimed qualifications were equally worthless. Perhaps the most outrageous catchline in this charlatan's long litany of self-aggrandisement was *The Protector of Suffering Humanity*. The only genuine mystery in his career is how he kept out of jail.

See THE GREAT CARLTON, CASEY'S COURT, PETER CASSON, MAGICIANS

BOLTON, GEORGE (1897-1981)
The Funniest of Funny Men; The New Gagster

This artiste's career displays an interesting example of the stratification of popular entertainment during the first half of the 20th century, for although Mr Bolton was a principal comedian in revue both in Britain and Australia from his teens he did not make his solo début in Variety until the age of 37. Above revue in the scale of social acceptability was musical comedy with the dramatic stage capping them all. Pantomime, due to the 'vulgarising incursion of Music Hall artistes', had lost caste but Mr Bolton went on to become one of the country's most popular and sought-after Dames.

BONEHILL, BESSIE (1855-1902)
England's Gem

Born in West Bromwich, Miss Bonehill solicited public approbation as a male impersonator specialising in patriotic songs. Many artistes presented one or the other but it was this performer's popular wheeze to offer the two together – *Here Stands a Post*, *Waiting for the Signal*, and *The British Tar* were typical of her repertoire.

The lady's strapping figure and forthright manner were especially admired in New York, where she received an average of a dozen proposals of marriage a week. Miss Bonehill was however married to Lew Abrahams, manager of the Queen's Poplar, one of the better suburban halls, and she died, alas, in the proud plenitude of her powers.

See ST GEORGE HUSSEY

BONN, ISSY (1903-77)
Radio's Hebrew Comedian; The Star of Stars; Wisecracking Songster

After some ten years as one of The Three Rascals Ben Levin went solo as Benny Leven *A Voice and a Smile*. In 1936 came his first broadcast as Issy Bonn, and his mixture of sentimental songs and humorous sketches with The Finkelfeffer Kids immediately caught the public affections. This entry was a large man and not perhaps the ideal Buttons, but when delineating the rôle at the Brixton Empress he ensured that Cinderella's response to her Fairy Godmother's request for three wishes would be (1) to go to the ball, (2) to have a lovely gown, and (3) to hear Issy Bonn sing *My Yiddishe Momme*.

Others working Jewish *shtik* were Ike Freedman (1899-1960) *The Jocular Hebrew*, Abraham Goldfaden (1840-1908) *The Yiddish Shakespeare*, GUS HARRIS, HAYMAN & FRANKLIN, DAVY KAYE, JOHN LAWSON, MARIE LOFTUS, Ikey Moe (see JIMMY CLITHEROE), Peel & Curtis *Kosher Komics* and *The Only Two Scotch Jews In Captivity*, Julian Rose (1879-1935) *Our Hebrew Friend*, and Yorke & Adams (fl1910s) *The Hebrew MPs*.

BORGE, VICTOR (b1909)
The Unmelancholy Dane

The gloomy Dane was Shakespeare's Hamlet, in this bill-matter contrasted with the revered musical raconteur who has delighted the civilised world for more than three generations. At the 1996 *Royal Variety Performance* Mr Borge showed he had lost none of his consummate skill, timing, and relaxed charm. Trained as a concert pianist the artiste still displays, amid the hilariously inconsequential remarks, tantalising flashes of a brilliant technique. As an entertainer this entry remains *sui generis* but see MARGARET COOPER also fellow countryman and knight CARL BRISSON.

BOW, CLARA (1905/6-65)
The Hottest Jazz Baby in Films; The 'It' Girl

It was this entry's starring role in the 1927 silent-film version of Elinor Glyn's novel *It* which bestowed her cognomen upon her, the title implying allure of a kind then not generally discussed in polite society. Those in the know were also aware of the grossly improper etymology of the word 'Jazz'. Miss Bow's strong Brooklyn accent, instability of temperament, and persistent indulgence in what was then contractually described as moral turpitude ensured that by 1933 her film career was over.

As a matter of historical record we should state that Miss Glyn herself always denied that *It* bore any carnal implications; 'I mean by *It,*' said the authoress, 'a magnetic quality of the spirit'.

BOWER, ELSIE (fl1930s-40s)
The Joy Bomb

We know nothing of this lady; her delicious billing makes us wish that we did.

See DAVE WILLIS for similar bill-matter.

BOWLLY, AL (1899-1941)
Britain's Ambassador of Song

This still-popular crooner arrived in London in the late 1920s to flit promiscuously from one fashionable dance-band to another, including those of Maestri Roy Fox (1901-82), Geraldo (1904-74), Ray Noble (1903-78), Oscar Rabin (1899-1958), and Lew Stone (1898-1969). It was with these last two especially that Mr Bowlly made the dozens of recordings which earned him such vast popularity, especially amongst the ladies.

A land-mine dropped by the Germans on April 17th 1941 near his Jermyn Street flat stilled his voice forever, though we have to say that his singing, while pleasant enough, gives us no especial *frisson*, and his screen presence is, in our opinion, decidedly wooden.

BREWSTER & LOTINGA (fl1930s-50s)
Ignorance Blistered; Nutical Naughties

This team were Max Brewster (b1889) – formerly *k.a.* Max Avieson – and his wife Betty Lotinga (b1915). This was not an act distinguished in the annals of British comedy but we include it to show the kind of desperate punning which was a feature of bill-matter from the 1930s. Mrs Brewster's father was Henry Lotinga of the Six Brothers Luck (SKETCH ARTISTES), making her the niece of Ernie Lotinga (SKETCH ARTISTES). We mention this to avoid confusion.

BRIGHT, ELLEN (1832-50)
Lion Queen

Female big cat-tamers were routinely dubbed *Lion Queen*, the first allegedly being Polly Hilton who died at a reputed age of 104. Ellen Bright (not Blight as is sometimes incorrectly stated), niece of the circus and menagerie proprietor George Wombwell (1777-1850), came to a grisly end when at a private performance in Chatham a tiger ripped her leg open, caught her by the throat and killed her. The 17th-year-old's ghastly death turned the public against *Lion Queens*, but not for long.

Pauline de Vere (see GEORGE SANGER) was *The Lady of the Lions*, as were Claire Heliot (fl c1900s) and Sonya Allen (fl1940s-50s).

See ANIMAL & BIRD ACTS, THE GREAT CARTER

BRIGHTLING, BIRDIE (fl1880s-90s)
Banjo Queen

Of Miss Brightling we know little so we shall expatiate instead upon her instrument. The banjo was introduced into Britain by T D RICE from America and popularised by J Arnold Cave (1823-1912) who clandestinely made a copy of Rice's instrument. Some say these gentlemen deserve in consequence to be consigned to the lowest circle of Hades, but where would the New Orleans Trad Band be without the banjo's plangent plunking?

Other plucky professors were Reuben R Brooks (1861-1906) *The King of Banjoists*, SISTERS CHESTER, Sonny Farrar (1905-79) *Five Foot of Fun and a Banjo*, Winifred E Johnson (see R G KNOWLES), Franco Piper (see JUGGLERS), Troise (b1893) *and his Banjoliers* who were sometimes billed as Troise *and his Mandoliers*, and W H Vane (1858-91) *The Banjo King*.

BRISSON, CARL (1895-1958)
The Smiling Star of Songs

This artiste must be forgiven so unimaginative a strap-line on account of having the misfortune to be a foreigner. Mr Brisson, whose height of 6ft 1in may not have made him a Great Dane but certainly made him a larger one than usual, first achieved celebrity as a champion welter-weight boxer; at the age of 21 he made his début as a dancer with his sister Tilly and five years later had reached the Finsbury Park Empire. Before the decade was out he was a film star and a staggeringly successful recording artiste, though we would say he appealed principally to the more impressionable shop-assistant class of female. From this caveat we must exclude HM King Frederick IX of Denmark, who in 1949 conferred upon Mr Brisson the honour of knighthood. VICTOR BORGE has also received this distinction but is a lot funnier.

BROUGH, PETER & ANDREWS, ARCHIE
Everybody's Radio Favourites

Peter Brough (b1916) was born in Ealing and became, like his father before him, a ventriloquist. (It was Arthur Brough who so memorably voiced Hugo, the sinister dummy which possessed Michael Redgrave in the film *Dead of Night*.) Archie Andrews was a cheeky schoolboy whose tutelary progress in *Educating Archie* was required British listening on Sunday afternoons from 1950 until 1958. The pair became so celebrated that their likenesses were exhibited in Mme Tussaud's and people queued for hours to see a dummy of a dummy. Spooky.

It is alleged that on one occasion just before transmission a studio-manager was heard to say 'Mr Brough, your voice-level is fine but could you hold Archie a little closer to the mic..?'

See JULIE ANDREWS, TONY HANCOCK, ROBERT MORETON, BERYL REID, VENTRILOQUISTS

BROWN, NEWLAND & LE CLERQ (fl c1886-1911)
Black Justice

Black-face comics Ben Brown (1848-1926), James Newland (1843-1931) and George Le Clerq (1848-1910) worked other sketches such as *Go as You Please* and *The House of Commons* but *Black Justice* was the most celebrated of their 'screaming farces', remaining in their repertoire for over twenty years. We ourself have seen 'Here Come de Judge' sketches in the US and suggest that since Mr Le Clerq spent some time in America *Black Justice* would have been of this type. *Black Justice* was also the bill-matter of Charles Clark (1866-1943).

See G H ELLIOTT, SKETCH ARTISTES

BROWN, TEDDY (1900-1946)
The 'Great' Xylophonist

Abraham Himmebrand's bill-matter paid tribute not only to his artistry but to his girth, for he was a phenomenally fat man. A popular cabaret act in the night clubs of 1920s London, this saxophonist-percussionist developed a Variety act, some of which is fortunately preserved on film. As befits one who spent four years with the New York Philharmonic Orchestra Mr Brown plays with professional dexterity, at one point pirouetting elephantinely and not missing a clunk.

BRUCE, LENNY (1927-66)
America's Number One Vomic

The godfather of confrontational alternative comedy relied more on shock value than on actually being funny. This performer was proud of having been arrested for obscenity in San Francisco, Chicago, and New York; he was proud of being refused entry into Britain, and was probably proud of having died, with sub-cultural appositeness, of a drug overdose. Mr Bruce's bill-matter indicates the reaction he liked to provoke, which cannot have been pleasant for the cleaners.

BURKE, TOM (1890-1969)
The Lancashire Caruso

To invite comparisons with Enrico Caruso (1873-1921), incontestably the world's greatest tenor of his time, might invite odorousness as when in 1920 Mr Burke's US agent puffed him as *The World's Greatest Living Irish Tenor*, thus gravely antagonising the legions of American JOHN McCORMACK worshippers. For other instances of over-enthusiastic bill-matter see WILKIE BARD, DAN LENO, and ROBB WILTON.

For other Carusos see BETTY AUKLAND.

BURNAND, 'Lovely Lively' LILY (b1865)
The Beauty Queen

Lovely and lively this Music Hall singer certainly was, being received with affection and hearty plaudits on both sides of the Atlantic. Miss Burnand was fortunate enough to introduce in 1892 that first-rate song *Two Little Girls in Blue*, a number which ever after stood her in good stead. The artiste's full life history is even as we speak being painstakingly traced by Mr J Garrod, who has not as yet discovered when and where his enchanting great-aunt died. What he has discovered is that Miss Burnand married twice and had an aunt in the New York Salvation Army.

BUX, KUDA (c1905-81)
The Man with the X-Ray Eyes

Mr Bux, we are told, presented an act in which his eyes were covered and yet he was able to divine the nature of objects proffered by members of the audience. An uncomfortable gift, we would have thought.

See MAGICIANS

BYGRAVES, MAX (b1922)
A Good Idea, Son!; I've Arrived and to Prove It I'm Here; Silly but Happy; Still Cleaning Up

Mr Bygraves is one of those artistes who doesn't seem to do very much but, my golly, how we want him to go on doing it. Walter William Smith from Rotherhithe, London, discovered his vocation while in the RAF from 1940-6. In the half century since then this gentleman has proven himself to be one of our most durable performers with a casual almost lazy style which belies a steely technique and a massive but lightly-borne presence. How effortlessly the artiste dominated those huge Moss houses, not to mention the, Palace New York, where he co-starred with Judy Garland, and how audiences exulted in his company! We feel that Mr Bygraves has maintained his stature by shrewd rationing of his television appearances; no game shows, no chat shows, just the occasional 'special' which, because it is so occasional, makes it an event.

BYNG, DOUGLAS (1893-1987)
Bawdy but British

Mr Byng's reputation has grown since his demise and he is now regarded as one of the great pantomime Dames as well as a seminal figure of the sophisticated inter-war London cabaret scene. We confess never to have warmed to this artiste; we never saw him live, but we remember him on the wireless and even in our innocent youth found his archness and coy innuendo quite embarrassing. It always seems to us that Mr Byng's material, for which he was himself usually responsible, exuded a dismal whiff of 1920s concert-party.

See BARBETTE

C

CAICEDO (d May 16th 1920)
King of the Wire

Don Juan Antonio Caicedo was what used to be called an equilibrist, or, even more imposingly, an equipoise artiste. In 1885 the Mexican became the first to turn a full somersault on the wire; he invariably performed without the use of a balancing pole, which of course as everyone knows makes it *much* more difficult.

Wire-walkers' bill-matter suggests only two avenues of inspiration: those who claim to be a Blondin of some kind or another or those who, like this entry, claim Royalty of the Rope. See BLONDIN for the former; the latter include Harold Alanza *King of the High Wire*, Alvantee (fl1860s-1910s) *King of the Slanting Wire* and *The Monarch of the Air*, The Beautiful Jessica (see QUEEN OF...), Rex Fox (1871-1954) *Wire King*, Princess Tetu (fl early 1800s) *Queen of the Wire*, W F Wainratta (fl1860s-80s) *King of the Wire*, and H R Ponchery (fl1920s-30s) *Monarch of the High Rope*. Paul Gordon (fl1920s) declared himself to be *The Wire Wonder*, closely shadowed by Babu Rao (1913-91) *Wonder on the Wire* and *Thrills and Fun on the Slack Wire*.

See M. CANDLER

CAIROLI, CHARLIE (& CO) (1909-80)
Clown Prince of Laughter

This bill-matter's flatness may be due to Mr Cairoli being a Milanese trumpet-playing clown, though on the only occasion we met him his English seemed to be perfect. From 1949 the artiste enjoyed nearly three decades of residency at the Tower Circus, Blackpool; the contact this famed venue gave him with holiday-makers, his pantomime seasons and television exposure all combined to raise him to stellar status, the only clown so regarded in Britain since Grock. While a troupe of clowns was not accommodated within the traditional storylines of English pantomime without occasional incongruity it was a treat to see the well-honed routines in which 'Little' Jimmy Buchanan (1918-95) was on the receiving end of the slapstick and the slosh for thirty-three years.

CALEY, NORMAN (b1920)
The Mad Earl (& Maisie)

Mr Caley averred that he started his career as an entertainer at the age of eight with a Punch & Judy show on the beach of his home town, Bridlington. With the best will in the world we cannot marry up an eight-year-old boy and a Punch & Judy show, unless the lad did the bottling*. It was during World War II in the Middle East that this entry developed his insane toff act, an advertisement for which in our possession shows him wearing a golfing cap, a striped blazer, and a caddish-looking spotted bow tie. He is also sporting a white bristling moustache and a manic expression with *The Acme of Idiotic Entertainment* across the top and *Still Fighting Against Fate* across the bottom. Mr Caley's style of comedy is one which would perhaps today be described as 'wacky' and to which we have the deepest resistance.

See CLAPHAM & DWYER

* Bottling: collecting money from the assemblage.

CALVERT, EDDIE (1922-78)
The Man with the Golden Trumpet

Mr Calvert enjoyed excessive popularity on the strength of his recording of a melody entitled *Cherry Pink*. We always felt that the gold coating on his trumpet muffled its characteristic brassy edge, so when we saw this artiste in the flesh we hoped that personality and presentation would make up for the blandness of his playing, but we were disappointed.

Some years later we took a telephone call at the stage door for a Certain Star. The caller was Eddie Calvert, wanting to know whether the Star was coming to his wedding the following Saturday. When this query was passed on the Star made a bad smell face and said something very, *very* rude. Naturally our relay of this response to Mr Calvert was heavily bowdlerised, but he knew he was being snubbed and responded curtly to our honeyed words. And so ended our only encounter with *The Man with the Golden Trumpet*.

Identical bill-matter was displayed by Murray Campbell; Kenny Baker was billed in 1951 as *Europe's Greatest Trumpeter and Recording Star*.

CALVIN, WYN (b1927)
Clown Prince of Wales

It was in pantomime at the New Theatre Cardiff that we first encountered this most genial and cultured of comics. That Mr Calvin enjoys life so much is because of his determination that everyone around him shall enjoy life; in performance his good-nature sweeps over the footlights (which we still had in those days, children) like a tidal wave. This entry is quite simply a very funny man, a very genuine man, and an incomparable raconteur.

See BILLY CARYLL & HILDA MUNDY

CAMPBELL, BIG BILL (1893-1952)
...and his Hilly-Billy Band; ...and his Rocky Mountain Rhythm; ...and his Rocky Mountaineers; As Big as the West Itself;The Happy Philosopher (as Old Zeke Winters)

Mr Campbell's home town was Medicine Hat in Alberta; his radio show, if memory serves, was built around a group of tired but contented cowboys sitting round the bunkhouse stove after a hard day's cow-poking and enjoying a wholesome singalong. It was all very gentle and innocuous, like the Cliff Adams Singers without the raunch, and regularly featured Old Zeke's crumbs of cracker-barrel philosophy which ended with him saying 'Mighty fine...' in tones of deepest smugness.

The word *Philosopher* makes strangely frequent appearances in bill-matter, the earliest noted being that of M. Testot (fl1824-45) *Professor of Recreative Philosophy*. More recent instances are J MILTON HAYES, Eddie Lawrence (b1921) *The Old Philosopher*, Charles Pastor (d November 6th 1926) *The Laughing Philosopher*, SAM REDFERN, SCOTT SANDERS, and Burt Shepard *a.k.a.* Charles Foster (1882-1929) *The Singing Philosopher*. Also see FRED ALLEN in this regard.

An artiste named Bob Dyer (d1965) used to bill himself as *The Last of the Hill-Billies*; we prefer to award that distinction to Harry Lester *and his Hayseeds* for Mr Lester died in 1993 at the age of 98 and so could claim to be the Last of pretty well anything he chose.

CAMPBELL, HERBERT (1846-1904)
England's Own Comedian

And so he was, this mountain of Lambeth jollity who is chiefly remembered for his fifteen-year pantomime partnership at Drury Lane with the diminutive DAN LENO, whom he preceded to the grave by only three months. Mr Campbell sang comic songs, as his bill-matter might lead one to suppose, but he also specialised in parodies and topical songs, the most celebrated of which was a version by Henry Pettitt of the sabre-rattling *We Don't Want To Fight* – indeed it was the unprecedented popularity of this song which gave rise to the word 'jingoism', meaning bull-necked and insensate patriotism. Mr Campbell's refreshingly down-to-earth version of the chorus ran:

> *I don't want to fight,*
> *I'll be slaughtered if I do;*
> *I'll change my togs,*
> *I'll pop my kit,*
> *And sell my rifle, too.*
> *I don't like the war,*
> *I'm not a Briton true;*
> *And I'd let the Russians have Constantinople!*

CAMPBELL, IRENE (d August 12th 1991)
Scotland's Betty Hutton

Betty Hutton (b1921) was an American musical comedy film star noted for her super-charged energy. Whether Miss Campbell was justified in commandeering a sister-artiste's reputation we cannot say.

CANDLER, M. (fl mid-19th cent.)
The Great Bottle Equilibrist

We can only posit that this artiste performed feats of balance and perhaps contortion whilst poised on up-turned bottles. This does not sound a very exciting spectacle, but it is surprising what a little ingenuity can achieve. We shouldn't be surprised to learn that M. Candler simultaneously juggled and whistled *La Marseillaise* while filling the stage with flags blindfold.

Fellow equilibrists were CAICEDO, BILLY MERSON, and The Pantzer Brothers (fl1900s-1920s) *Society Acrobats and Equilibrists.*

CANTOR & LEE (fl1914)
The Master and the Man

These American vaudeville comedians were Eddie Cantor (1892-1964) and Al Lee (c1892-1945). Prior to their partnership Mr Cantor had appeared for two years in *The Kid Kabaret*, his small stature and preternaturally high voice justifying his inclusion. Despite the lack of inches this artiste became huge on Broadway; his energy, original dancing style, and huge round eyes – *Banjo Eyes* was the title of one of his shows – made him one of the biggest draws on the Great White Way. Mr Cantor's boisterous talents transferred well to the big screen and to radio, with such songs as *Makin' Whoopee, Yes Sir That's My Baby* and *If You Knew Susie* helping to consolidate his popularity.

CARLTON, THE GREAT (1880-1942)
Champion Card Manipulator; The Hanki-Homey Showman; The Human Hairpin

This performer was a bizarre and not entirely wholesome sight on stage. He was 6ft ½in high but weighed only nine stone, with his thinness accentuated by a tight-fitting costume and high heels. He also wore a high-domed bald wig and eccentric make-up. The result was a figure from Hiëronymous Bosch, but Mr Carlton's presentations were not for the squeamish for he also toured with Bobby Dunlop (d1912), an unfortunate American gentleman who weighed forty stone, and assorted freaks. Mr Carlton included hypnotism as part of his entertainment, but we are not persuaded that the artiste added much to the gaiety of nations.

See Dr WALFORD BODIE, PETER CASSON, MAGICIANS, WILL OLIVER

CARNEY, KATE (1868-1950)
The Coster Queen; The People's Favourite

This popular singer of Cockney songs was originally *k.a.* Kate Paterson *The Hibernian Star.* In 1889, doubtless at the instigation of her agent and husband George Barclay, Miss Carney changed her name and line of business; in her new incarnation she was an immediate and lasting success, with such fine songs as *Are We To Part Like This, Bill?* and *Three Pots A Shilling* to her credit.

Mr Barclay assiduously nursed his wife's career, and Miss Carney used to joke a trifle indelicately that she was the only Music Hall artiste to sleep with her agent and 'still hold her head up in public'. Her grandson informs us that the artiste had a sister, Rose, who had two natural sets of teeth.

See BARCLAY & PERKINS, PAT FEENEY

CARROL, NORMAN (1890-1954)

Never 'Eard of Him

a.k.a. Sydney Brandon *The Boy Barry Sullivan of the Music Halls*, after the provincially popular Irish barn-storming tragedian who died in 1891 at the age of 70. In 1919 Master Brandon became Mr Carrol, by which time *The Boy Barry Sullivan* must have seemed suspiciously mature. The now-adult performer spent his first year as a comedian burlesqueing the material he had previously played seriously. Did the man have no integrity?

See Master WILLIAM BETTY

CARTER, THE GREAT (1813-47)

Lion King

A gentleman who trained lions for public display was customarily given the title of *Lion King* (see ELLEN BRIGHT for the distaff equivalent). James Carter was brought over from America to Astley's in 1839 where he thrilled London by driving a team of lions in a chariot. That is, he was in the chariot, not the lions. An unrelated Great Carter may be found under MAGICIANS.

See ANIMAL & BIRD ACTS

CARTHY, AL (fl1943-80s?)

...and his Mechanical Man

The is-it-real-or-not? appeal of the humanoid is presented at its most fascinating by this brilliantly worked act whose shock ending never fails to provoke gasps of bewilderment. We will not divulge any further details so that, dear reader, should you have the rare treat of witnessing this entry you shall not have cause to complain that we spoilt it for you.

Others worthy of mention in this sphere are The Amazing Robots, confusingly billed as *Too Real to be True*, Cire (MAGICIANS), Phroso (fl c1900) *The Mysterious Mechanical Doll*, and René Mazie *The Mechanical Man*, billing also assumed by Mr Robot, who in private life was Harry Rose (1909-71).

CARUS, EMMA (1879-1927)
The Human Dialect Cocktail

'I'm not pretty,' was this American artiste's customary opening line, 'but I'm good to my family.' And in truth Miss Carus had a piggy face and matching circumference. But she also had a useful singing voice and a talent for comedy which more than made up for any lack of conventional charms, for this entry graced many musical comedies and was in the very first Ziegfeld Follies (1907).

Miss Carus' greatest claim to our attention today is to have given as a 'female baritone' in 1911 the first public performance of the song which created a seismic sensation in Tin Pan Alley, IRVING BERLIN's *Alexander's Ragtime Band.*

CARYLL, BILLY & MUNDY, HILDA (fl1925-39)
The Great Lovers; The Home-Coming of George; Those Friendly Enemies

This husband and wife team's on-stage comic rows were inspired by an off-stage tiff. The pair were in George Black's *Crazy Week* productions at the London Palladium in 1931 and 1932 which were fore-runners of the Crazy Gang shows. Miss Mundy died in 1969, but we know little else of these one-time head-liners other than the peremptory comment by WYN CALVIN that Mr Caryll, who died on February 23rd 1939, first 'lost his leg, then his life'.

An act of similar stripe was The Wrangling Raymonds *Domestic Blitz.*

CASEY'S COURT (fl1906-1934 and late 1940s-52)
The Original of all Crazy Shows

a.k.a. The Casey Circus and Casey's Court Nibbs this company of juveniles was established by the comedian Will Murray (b1877) who appeared as Mrs Casey. His youthful support included at various times his son Roy Leo, his grandson Roy jnr, TOMMY TRINDER and Robbie Vincent (see HARRY KORRIS).

Undoubtedly the most illustrious Casey alumnus was Sir CHARLES CHAPLIN who despite making a great success guying Dr WALFORD BODIE later described it as 'an awful show'.

See SKETCH ARTISTES

CASSON, PETER (1921-95)
The Old Master

Having ourself many years ago taken part in a British Medical Research Council project on hypnotism we have some experience of this mysterious phenomenon, and while we are convinced of its therapeutic value we also contend it should only be practised under stringently controlled conditions.

This entry claimed to be the first, in 1946, to present genuine hypnotism on the English stage. This is nonsense; any number of persons had since the middle of the previous century utilised their hypnotic powers for the purposes of vulgar profit, including ARTEMUS, WALFORD BODIE, THE GREAT CARLTON, Kennedy (1855?-94?) *Mesmerist – King Laugh-Maker of the World*, KORINGA, CARROLL LEVIS and Princess RUBIE.

Other manipulators of the twilight zone were Georgina Eagle (see GEORGE BARNARDO EAGLE), Ralph Slater (fl1940s- ?) *The World's Fastest Hypnotist*, and David Wolfe (b1906) *The Hypnotist with a Sense of Humour*.

CASTLE, ROY (1932-94)
Personality Plus

An excellent musician, tap-dancer, singer, and comedian, Mr Castle was surely the last of the all-rounders. He entered Variety when it was on its last gasp, just in time to work with two of the great sketch masters, JIMMY JAMES and FRANK RANDLE, and to gain the experience to work up his own highly original single turns.

It was in *Humpty Dumpty* at the London Palladium in a pantomime in 1959 that this entry enjoyed the great personal success which was to propel him to stardom; we are proud to record that we were a part of that show. We have no truck with those who say this most genuine and charming of artistes should have stuck to one facet of his talents and not muddied his image by showing so much versatility. In our experience people who say that can't do anything.

CAVANAGH, PETER (1914-81)
The Voice of them All

We once heard this entry perform on the radio the most astonishing feat of mimicry; he and ARTHUR ASKEY alternated the lines of a song – *The Busy Bee*, if memory serves – and we could not tell which was which! In his later years Mr Cavanagh was kind enough to undertake the occasional engagement for ourself, the bonus being that not only did this artiste bring his art and experience to the performance but also Mrs Cavanagh, a most attractive singer who accompanied her husband at the piano.

See list of MIMICS in glossary.

CHABERT, IVAN IVANITZ (1792-1859)
The French Fire King

This artiste's demonstrations included 'the forging with his feet of a bar of hot iron; drinking boiling oil; having a wax seal taken on his tongue; bathing his feet in molten lead; and holding his head in a fire of vitriol, oil, and arsenic'.

Of which may we quote the old joke: 'There, you see – too lazy to learn a comic song.'

See CHARLES S BERNARD, THE SALAMBOS

CHAMPION, HARRY (1865-1942)
Quick and Quaint; The Quick-Fire Comedian; Quick, Quaint and Quality

This artiste's grandson assures us that William Henry Crump was born in Bethnal Green in 1865. Originally *k.a.* Will Conray, young Crump's energetic dancing and unrivalled speed of vocalism established his reputation while still in his teens. Becoming Harry Champion in 1887 at the behest of his agent this entry then developed a repertoire of songs which perfectly suited his unsubtle and rumbustious Cockney delivery.

Some of these titles are so deeply embedded in the national consciousness as to be part of our cultural heritage – *Ginger You're Barmy!*, *I'm Henery The Eighth I Am*, and *With The End Of My Old Cigar*. They were hurled across the footlights at breakneck speed, often with a clumping 'clog wallop' or 'big boot *battement*' to enliven the inter-verse symphonies. In the *Royal Variety Performance* of 1935 at the London Palladium the still-energetic performer blasted that stiff-necked audience with *Boiled Beef And Carrots* and *Any Old Iron* and had the place in uproar. The last of the red-nosed comic singers still knew his business.

See GEORGE BEAUCHAMP

CHANEY, LON (1883-1930)
The Man of a Thousand Faces

Born in Colorado Springs, Alonso Chaney earned his soubriquet through a series of powerful and macabre performances in silent films. This gentleman's heavily underlined portrayals as Quasimodo or Phantom of the Opera may be considered over-emphatic in our more sophisticated times, but the actor's emotional strength and sincerity gleam through the patina of melodrama. Mr Chaney's expertise in mime, a pre-requisite for silent screen acting, may, we suggest, be attributable to the fact that both his parents were deaf-mutes.

An earlier *Man with 1,000 Faces* was George Layman (1864-1900), while the vaudevillian Florence Lawrence (1890-1938) described herself as *The Girl with a Thousand Faces*; she was also known as *The Biograph Girl*, a billing more usually associated with MARY PICKFORD.

See list of MIMICS in glossary.

CHANG & ENG (1811-74)
Siamese Double Boys

Though of Chinese origin Chang and Eng (which means left and right) were born in Siam, hence the term 'Siamese twins' for all conjoined siblings. This entry was joined at the waist by nothing more than a band of tissue; no vital organs were shared and separation could almost certainly have been achieved, but having adapted so well to their anomalous condition the brothers declined surgical intervention. They toured the world lucratively under the auspices of an English mercantile opportunist, eventually settling in the United States.

In 1843 the Messrs Bunker, the new name they had chosen for their new life, took up farming in North Carolina; they married sisters and spent alternate weeks with each spouse, an arrangement which produced a total of twenty-two children and so must be deemed conspicuously successful.

In the Civil War the brothers lost much of their fortune (and their slaves) and went back on the road. Chang took to the bottle, much to Eng's discomfort. In 1870, four years after suffering a paralytic stroke, Chang died. Eng expired some three hours later.

In the 1870s Millie-Christine (1851-1912), black American joined sisters, toured Britain billed as *The Two-Headed Skylark* or *The Two-Headed Nightingale*. The original one-headed Nightingale was of course JENNY LIND. On Laloo (b1874), who exhibited himself around the

1900s and whose half-formed twin dressed as a girl protruded from his abdomen, we would rather not dwell.

CHAPLIN, Sir CHARLES (1889-1977)

Sir Charles is better *k.a.* Charlie Chaplin, the stupefyingly famous star of the silent screen. We have no bill-matter for this most distinguished of entries as his Music Hall appearances were within sketch troupes such as CASEY'S COURT, The Eight Lancashire Lads (fl1896-c1930), and FRED KARNO.

But the shadow of the 'little fellow' loomed large, and such is Sir Charles' universality of stature that we felt it would be impertinent to exclude the performer-director whose impact on the inchoate art of film comedy can never be over-estimated.

Just a few of those clinging to the indestructible tramp's coat-tails were Tommy Lorne (1890-1935) *Scotland's Charlie Chaplin*, Mabel Normand (1894-1930) *The Female Chaplin*, Charlie Rivel (1897-1983) *The Chaplin of the Trapeze*, George F Rymer *The Chaplin of the Halls*, Alf Warren *The Australian Chaplin*, and Billy West (1883-1975) *Is He Charlie Chaplin?* It is perhaps not irrelevant to interject here that one evening in 1956 in Valencia we witnessed two Chaplin impersonations in the same *zarzuela*.

See LEO DRYDEN, BILLIE RITCHIE

CHEER, Professor (fl c1950)
The Man with the Xylophone Skull

We never had the pleasure of hearing Professor Cheer play but we have seen similarly talented maestri and can disclose that the technique involves rapping the top of the head sharply with the knuckles while opening and closing the mouth in a fish-like manner; alterations in pitch are achieved by changing the shape of the mouth. By this means a recognisable melody may be discerned though tonal quality leaves something to be desired.

CHERRY SISTERS, THE (fl1893-1903)
America's Worst Act; Something Good – Something Sad

The favourable receptions to which these ladies were accustomed in their home town of Marion, Iowa, persuaded them to accept a scheming manager's offer to perform their homespun recitations, wholesome songs, and improving sketches in the Big City. Predictably the Sisters' hicksville amateurism was greeted with vulgar disapproval, but these spunky gals persisted in their crusade to bring decency, abstinence, and The Word to licentious vaudeville audiences.

This entry's reputation for providing cruel fun spread, and it was at his Broadway theatre in 1896 that Willie Hammerstein wickedly billed them as *America's Worst Act*. The insult to the artistes' *amour-propre* was assuaged by a fee of $1,000 a week and by a net thoughtfully stretched across the stage to catch garden produce hurled by the merciless New York *hoi polloi*. The spectacle was pathetic rather than entertaining, but when 'the vegetable twins' as the last two were known sued a newspaper for a particularly scathing review the judge saw their act and awarded costs to the critic.

CHESTER, 'Cheerful' CHARLIE (1914-97)
Poet Laureate of the Water Rats

The 1915/6 *Era Annual* describes the Grand Order of Water Rats as a society devoted to 'social intercourse and the advancement of the welfare of its members'. 'Cheerful' Charlie was awarded his accolade in 1952 after a suggestion by Bud Flanagan, surely one of that comedian's slyer jokes (see FLANAGAN & ALLEN). During Hitler's War Mr Chester, though only a sergeant, became a power in the Central Pool of Artists (*Stars in Battledress*) and gave important opportunities to many a post-war name.

The performer's predilection for startlingly blue material came as a surprise to those who knew him only as a pontificator of unctuous banalities on his long-running Sunday afternoon BBC Radio 2 record show (*Sunday Soapbox*) which came to a long overdue conclusion in 1996. It was no surprise to those aware that under the *nom de plume* of Carl Noone this entry was the author of a number of unsavoury novels.

CHESTER, (THREE) SISTERS (fl1892-1907)
Grace, Beauty and Banjos

Of all the examples of bill-matter quoted within these covers *Grace, Beauty and Banjos* remains our favourite. It is so redolent of period charm, naïvety, and fragrant femininity; the entire era is summed up in those four words, so artlessly yet so resonantly juxtaposed.

See frontispiece, p.2, BIRDIE BRIGHTLING

CHEVALIER, ALBERT (1861-1923)

The Coster Laureate; The Kipling of the Halls;
The Refined Coster

That Rudyard Kipling (1865-1936) who was sometimes perceived as a poet of the people was flattered by such appropriation of his name and reputation is extremely unlikely.

Mr Chevalier's Welsh and French parentage can be gleaned from his indigestible mix of names: Albert Onésime Britannicus Gwathveoyd Louis Chevalier. The singer-monologuist was a rare instance of an established actor forsaking the theatre and making good on the Halls.

It is often contended that his Coster characterisations were an outsider's sentimentalised view of Cockneydom and that Mr Chevalier regarded the London working-classes as specimens rather than soul-mates. Nevertheless he was hugely popular and was justifiably hurt not to be included in the first *Royal Music Hall Performance* in 1912.

Another *Kipling of the Halls* was LEO DRYDEN, and the American vaudevillian Owen Frawley Kildare (1864-1911) styled himself *The Bowery Kipling.*

See GUS ELEN, ALEC HURLEY, TOM LEAMORE, T D RICE

CHINKO (1880-1943)

(The Eton) Boy Juggler; The Mirthful Juggler;
The Smartest Young Juggler in the World

It is more likely that Thomas Knox-Cromwell came from, rather than went to, Eton. This entry was sometimes billed with his wife Minnie as Chinko & Kaufman. He was the brother of Teddy Knox (see NERVO & KNOX) who was also a juggler and with whom he is often confused by careless commentators.

See JUGGLERS (especially Topper Martyn).

CHIRGWIN, G H (1854-1922)

The White-Eyed (Musical) Kaffir; The White-Eyed
Musical Moke

This artiste's black make-up was relieved by a white diamond across one eye, due to once inadvertently wiping his eye just before going on stage. The audience reaction was so positive that Mr Chirgwin ever after maintained this singularity of appearance. Rarely can a career have been founded on so flimsy a basis, though sometimes he appeared in negative, i.e. in an all-white costume with white make-up and a black diamond.

This entry played the fiddle, after a fashion, and also sang, again after a fashion, two of the most nauseating songs ever penned: *Blind Boy* and *My Fiddle is my Sweetheart.* The lachrymose banality of the lyrics defies belief, but *The White-Eyed Kaffir* was rarely allowed to leave the stage without rendering one or the other, and preferably both. Truly, tastes have changed.

See G H ELLIOTT

CHOCOLATE & CO – see THE RASTELLIS

CHRISTIE, NELLIE (fl c1900)

The Dandy-Coloured Coon; The Original Susie-Tusie; There is None like Her, None (Tennyson)

Miss Christie was what was known as a 'coon-shouter', a term which only seems to have been applied to female white singers who sang what were fondly imagined to be 'plantation' songs.

The first billing refers to a popular song introduced by EUGENE STRATTON as does the second. Notice that for the third Miss Christie helpfully gives its source; a quotation from so illustrious a poet is intended to validate the artiste's claim to inimitability.

See G H ELLIOTT, MAY HENDERSON

CHUNG LING SOO (1861-1918)

Chinese Magician Extraordinary; Has Reached the Highest Pinnacle of Fame; The World's Greatest Conjuror

William Ellsworth Robinson began his career as Robinson *The Man of Mystery*, but it was as Chung Ling Soo that this entry posed a mystery which has yet to be solved. His lavishly mounted show included a Living Target scene in which the magician appeared to catch a rifle-bullet on a plate. At the Wood Green Empire on March 23rd 1918 the trick gun failed to trick; *The World's Greatest Conjuror* received the bullet through the right lung and died a few hours later.

To this day rumours persist that the accident was no accident but a very public suicide. The bereaved widow announced that she would write her husband's life-story and reveal the truth, but she never did.

See CLEMENTINE, MAGICIANS

CINQUEVALLI, PAUL (1858-1918)

The Human Billiard Table; L'Incomparable; The Resourceful Juggler

It is often given that this Polish performer's family name was Paul Kestner or Lehmann; in fact it was Emile Otto Braun. As an apprentice gymnast and trapezist he was billed as *The Little Flying Devil*; when grounded through injury the performer turned to juggling and became the greatest of his day – some say the greatest ever. He left £26,217 17s 9d so he must have been doing something right.

We have seen it stated that 'Chin-kwee-*va*-llee' (for so it was pronounced) was 6ft 6ins tall and wore a wig. We cannot credit a two-metre gymnast and trapezist, though we would not discountenance the rug.

See JUGGLERS (especially Kelly & Gillette) and, for another *Incomparable*, LITTLE TICH.

CLAFF, HARRY (c1880-1943)

Chirrups & Chatter; The Demon and the Fairy; The White Knight

Mr Claff's baritone was an instrument finely wrought at the Royal Academy of Music; after some years in operetta and musical comedy the singer plunged into the waters of Variety and swam like a duck. This entry had the honour of leading the singing of the National Anthem at the first *Royal Music Hall Performance* in 1912, for which epochal event the artiste was dressed Sir Galahad-like as a knight, though the element of mystical saintliness is undermined by his portliness. Frankly, he looks an ass, but the *White Knight* he remained for the rest of his career.

Harry Claff's son, *a.k.a.* Harry Claff, was married for a time to that most breath-takingly beautiful *chanteuse* Joan Regan. But then he fell from grace and lost everything including Miss Regan, so he was an ass too.

CLAPHAM & DWYER (fl1925-43)

A Spot of Bother; Another Spot of Bother

Messrs Charlie Clapham (1884-1959) and Billy Dwyer (1890-1943) were so identified with radio comedy that on the Halls they entered through a giant wireless-set. Both wore white tie and tails with the bull-necked Mr Dwyer as straight man and tall, thin, top-hatted and be-monocled Mr Clapham as silly-ass comic. A feature of their bewilderingly nonsensical cross-talk routines was the introduction, on the thinnest of pretexts, of Cissie, Mr Clapham's cow. Their success was undeniable, but we find Mr Clapham's droll inarticulacy forced. This team made a short film entitled *A Spot of Spring Cleaning*; we do not recommend it.

Humorous representations of the public school nitwit were the stock-in-trade of NORMAN CALEY, Bert Clifford (fl c1915) *The Effervescing Dude*, GEORGE CLARKE, Lord Adolphus Crushington (fl1870s) *The Howling Swell*, Claude Dampier (1878-1955) *The Professional Idiot*, Freddie Forbes (1893-1952) *The Fearfully Awfully Chappie* and *Jest in Fun*, Cardew 'The Cad' Robinson (1917-92) *The Bad Boy of St Fanny's*, Oliver Wakefield (1909-56) *The Voice of Inexperience* – see M Sayle Taylor (MISCELLANEOUS).

The leisured classes at their most languidly superior were guyed by cousins Kenneth (1900-63) and George Western (1895-1969) as The Western Brothers *Those (Old School Tie) Radio Cads*.

Also see MICHAEL BENTINE, RONALD FRANKAU and MALCOLM SCOTT who actually were middle class, and GILLIE POTTER who aspired to that condition.

CLARKE, GEORGE (1886-1947)

The New Car

This entry originally worked with his father as Clarke & Clements, going solo in 1910. His characterisation of a monocled buffoon was, by all accounts, quite priceless, and he 'never resorted', said *The Performer* pontifically, 'to blue material'. The car of the bill-matter was an Austin Seven, with the comedy deriving from Mr Clarke's apparent inability to work the controls. The little motor sped about the stage, bucking and plunging like an untamed horse, which was exceedingly mirthful for the audience and deeply worrying for the pit-band.

See CLAPHAM & DWYER, HARRY TATE

CLAY, ANDREW 'DICE' (b1958)
The Diceman; The Hoodlum of Humour

Andrew Clay Silverstein is an American comedian whose humour is so vituperative, coprolaliac, and offensive to women, minority groups, foreigners, and indeed anyone who isn't Andrew Clay Silverstein that we would rather spend an evening cleaning out the drains.

CLEMENTINE (b1875)
The Queen of Fire Arms

Just before ten o'clock on Monday, November 23rd 1908, at the Middlesex Music Hall in Drury Lane, Signora Clementini Dolcini killed her assistant Howard (or Herbert) Thomas Lees while attempting to shoot a glass ball off his head from 50ft. The distraught performer, a 'short stout woman', was arraigned on a charge of manslaughter by Bow Street Magistrates and remanded on £100 bail; on January 12th 1909 an Old Bailey Grand Jury 'unanimously ignored the bill' and the markswoman faced no further charges.

A similar mishap at the Theatre Royal Brighton some twenty years earlier resulted in the death of a youth sitting in the gallery; see also the strange case of CHUNG LING SOO.

Less unfortunate sharpshooters were ANNIE OAKLEY, CHARLES JOANNYS and Elroy (see UNTHAN), also Mlle Berthe Bordeverry and Company who in July 1906 were advertised at the Palace as *Undressing a Lady with a Repeating Rifle*.

See QUEEN OF...

CLINE, MAGGIE (1856-1933)
The Irish Queen of Vaudeville; Brunnhilde of the Bowery

The Bowery was – and indeed still is – a notoriously unwholesome district of New York; Brunnhilde, as depicted by Richard Wagner in *The Ring* cycle, is a Valkyrie Rhine Maiden of heroic strength and power, characteristics famously exhibited by this artiste.

See QUEEN OF...

CLITHEROE, JIMMY (1916-73)
Small but Pleasing

This entry was a midget who like WEE GEORGIE WOOD appeared as a cheeky, precocious, and mischievous schoolboy – for many years his stage mother was Mollie Sugden. We well recall one occasion during the run of *Tom Thumb* at the Bradford Alhambra when Mr Clitheroe, who had been suffering from influenza, appeared in the wings for his next entrance. Immediately we jumped up to offer him a seat. His response showed him to be a trouper of the old school: 'Oh, I never sit down in me props...'

Other small performers were Wee Georgie Beck *Natural Nugget of Humour,* Henry Bundy (1849-57) *The English Tom Thumb* (an appellation also claimed by Henry Wardle), Caroline Crachami (1815-24) *The Sicilian Fairy,* Dot Delvaine (b1926) *Glamour in Miniature,* Scotch Kelly (1889-1967) *The Miniature Comedy Comet* and *The Tich o' the North,* Mihaly Meszharos (b1939) *The Smallest Man on Earth,* Micro (b1925) *The Miniature Mentalist* who also worked as Prince Tiny *The Midget Magician* and *The Wee Wizard,* Ikey Moe (fl1900s) *The Smallest Hebrew Comedian in the World,* Mlle Nikita (b1872) *The Miniature Patti,* Fred Roper *and his 20 Wonder Midgets* (fl c1930), Tiny Ross *The Mighty At 'Em,* Little Tony (1874-1918) *The Champion Step Dancer in the World* and *The Smallest Clown in the World,* and Mary Jane Youngman (fl c1850) *The Dwarf Princess* who though only 2ft 11ins tall was said to weigh 13st 6lbs which can't have been a pretty sight.

Also see HENRY COLLARD, YVONNE PRESTIGE, Tom Thumb (HENRY COLLARD), LITTLE TICH.

COCHRANE, PEGGY (b c1910)
The Tune a Minute Girl

Miss Cochrane's musical prodigiousness permitted her to play a violin concerto in the first half of a programme and a piano concerto in the second. The Royal Academy of Music must have been chagrined when this entry turned her back on the Classical Masters and headed for the Variety stage. But as the lady herself said 'more money was to be made (and less hard work) playing and singing more popular music!' Could, we wonder, the artiste have been influenced in this pusillanimous decision by her husband, the band-leader Jack Payne (1899-1969)?

See MARGARET COOPER

COGAN, ALMA (1933-66)

The Girl with a Laugh in her Voice

The sudden death of so bubbly and attractive a songstress shocked the nation, for although Miss Cogan's wholesome and uncomplicated style of singing was perhaps becoming passé she did have a considerable following and her fan club remains active and devoted. The artiste was dramatically dark and curvaceous with emphatically arched eyebrows, a beauty spot, and voluminous glitzy frocks destined to have earned her gay icon status.

Typical titles in her repertoire were *Bell Bottom Blues, I Can't tell a Waltz from a Tango* and *Never do a Tango with an Eskimo,* all sung with a squeaky catch in the voice which was infuriatingly lovable. Miss Cogan was never going be any kind of threat to Shirley Bassey but it should not be forgotten that in 1960 her recording of *He Couldn't Resist her with her Pocket Transistor* stood for over a year at No 1 in Japan.

See RONNÉ CONN

COLLARD, HENRY (c1850-88)

The Pocket Sims Reeves

J Sims Reeves (1818-1900) was the leading English tenor of his generation. Although this entry was also billed in 1870 as *The Surprising Dwarf Singer* he would seem to have been a midget, for a contemporary critic observed that 'Mr Collard may be briefly described as Tom Thumb with a voice. He is not taller than the well-known little General but is unquestionably better shaped and much handsomer. Possessed of a fair, frank face, yellow curled hair, and a brilliant complexion, the tiny singer at once prepossesses his audience. But when he begins to sing all sense of the phenomenal is lost in the discovery of the fact that you are hearing an accomplished musician...'

Others to utilise Sims Reeves' great standing were PERCY HENRY and VESTA TILLEY.

General Tom Thumb né Charles Sherwood Stratton (1838-83) was the most celebrated pituitary dwarf in the civilised world. An American, he was brought to Europe by P T BARNUM – who named his charge from the hero of the 16th-century nursery tale – and exhibited to enormous acclaim. A talented artiste, Mr Thumb was a particular favourite of Queen Victoria. For other small people see JIMMY CLITHEROE.

COLLEANO, BONAR jnr (1924-58)

Britain's Favourite American

James Bonar Colleano (1893-1957) and his wife Rubye (d December 25th 1985) with their son Bonar jnr were three of The Colleanos, an extended family troupe of circus aerialists. The most celebrated was Con Colleano (1901-74) who was billed variously as *The Wizard of the Tight Wire* and *The World's Greatest Wire Artist.*

Bonar jnr, after spending his early years aloft began to display marked talent as an actor in revue, films, and plays, and we saw this entry give a very fine performance indeed in an early drug-warning piece entitled *The Man with the Golden Arm.* In 1949 Mr Colleano played opposite the numinous Vivien Leigh in *A Streetcar Named Desire* at the Aldwych Theatre. From the high wire to Stanley Kowalski; what a remarkable career, and how cruelly cut short for he was dead at the age of only 34.

COLLINS, JOSÉ (1887-1958)

The Maid of the Mountains

The daughter of LOTTIE COLLINS was, as might be expected, dynamic, powerful, and wilful, especially after her huge success in *The Maid of the Mountains.* A majestic figure of a woman, Miss Collins found no lasting marital bliss either at her first attempt or her second, but her third husband seems to have suited her very well. He was a medical doctor for whom during World War II Miss Collins abandoned her career to act as his nurse. Dr Kirkland must have loved his wife literally to distraction, for a short time after she died he took his own life.

COLLINS, LOTTIE (1866-1910)

The Flower of Dancers; The Kate Vaughan of the Music Halls

Kate Vaughan (1855-1903) was a much-loved burlesque artiste at the Gaiety Theatre. How many spouses Miss Collins enjoyed is open to debate; certainly there were Stephen Collins who died in 1901 and James W Tate (1875-1922) who after her death married CLARICE MAYNE. It seems that there may have been a shadowy third but at the time of writing we have no firm intelligence on this delicate matter. What is incontrovertible is that Miss Lottie Collins set the Town alight with the unprecedented vivacity and *entrain* of her performance of *Ta-Ra-Ra-Boom-De-Ay*. Also we have discovered that Miss Collins was shrewd enough to acquire the British rights to this American song; every high kick was money in the bank.

Miss Collins was the mother of JOSÉ COLLINS.

COLLINSON & DEAN (fl1920s-c40s)
The Argumentative Comedians; The Pursuit of Knowledge; Still Arguing; Will Argue About 'Ambition'

At some time in the 1940s Mr Collinson split with Mr Dean and took a new partner as Collinson and Breen. This new team burlesqued Army life with the hectoring sergeant and the lame-brained private. Another of their routines involved Collinson endeavouring to teach Bobby Breen boxing, with predictably hilarious results.

The artistes flourished into the 1950s, so far as we can tell, utilising the remarkable bill-matter *Lilies That Fester Smell Far Worse Than Weeds*. While this observation was first made by William Shakespeare in his ninety-fourth sonnet we cannot fathom what attraction it may have had to a potential 20th-century ticket-purchaser.

We have been unable to establish precise information about this entry other than a tentative identification of Will Collinson (1885-1958).

COLVERD, 'Jovial' JOE (d1903)
The Old English Gentleman; The Original John Bull

Mr Colverd was not really the 'Original John Bull', for such a character existed only as a literary device coined c1700 to indicate an Englishman or Englishmen collectively. On the Halls John Bull was interpreted as a bluff, hearty, no-nonsense man who sang aggressively patriotic songs. The American equivalent would be a 'good ol' boy', and we suspect that far from being jovial Mr Colverd was a pain in the neck.

See VICTORIA MONKS, TOM TINSLEY, Verno & Voyce (BICYCLE ACTS)

CONN, RONNÉ
The Girl with the Miracle Voice

Miss Conn's vocal powers must be taken on trust but we have no reason to believe that they were anything other than as the artiste described them.

Other young female artistes to proclaim their charms in similar manner were: Frankie Emmett (1876-1911) *The Little Girl with the Big Voice*, Josie Fearon *The Girl with the Golden Voice*, Cissie Fitzgerald (c1873-1941) *The Girl with the Wink*, Gilda Goulay (fl1900s) *The Girl with the American Beauty Rose*, Gladdy Sewell *The Comedy Girl with the Top Notes*, Ida Shepley (d March 19th 1975) *The Bronze Girl with the Golden Voice*, and Doris York (d1996) *The Girl with the Violin Voice*.

Other ladies 'with' something were ALMA COGAN, Florence Lawrence (see LON CHANEY), TESSIE O'SHEA, Lalla Selbini (BICYCLE ACTS), and NITA VAN BIENE.

COOK, JOE (1890-1959)
A One-Man Vaudeville Show

This performer, whom some consider to have been one of the very greatest of vaudevillians, advertised himself in 1909 thus: 'Master of All Trades. Introducing in a fifteen-minute act, juggling, unicycling, magic, hand-balancing, ragtime piano and violin playing, dancing, globe rolling, wirewalking, talking, and cartooning. Something original in each line – Some Entertainment.' Such was Mr Cook's stature that when he died the doyen of American theatre critics, Brooks Atkinson, referred to him without a trace of irony as 'the greatest man in the world'.

See JUGGLERS

COOPER, JOHNNY (b1908)
Sleightly Inebriated

In his younger days this entry was one of a comedy knockabout dancing act called Lock, Stock & Beryl *They Do Everything*. Later Mr Cooper worked up his well-known drunk magic act, and in his 90th year, we are happy to report, the artiste is still working and working well.

Other pretend Music Hall topers were Foster Brooks (b1912) *The Lovable Lush*, Bert Easley (MAGICIANS), JAMES FAWN, FREDDIE FRINTON, Archie Glen (1889-66) *Blotto as Usual* and *The Inebriated Gentleman*, JIMMY JAMES, George Rissen (fl1940s-?) *Slightly Inebriated*, BILLIE RITCHIE, Bert Weston (1884-1930) *The Idiotic Inebriate*, and Willane (d1955) *The Immaculate Inebriate*.

See Billington (MAGICIANS) for another *Sleightly*.

1. THE THREE ABERDONIANS

2. JULIE ANDREWS
(aged 13)

3. MAX BACON

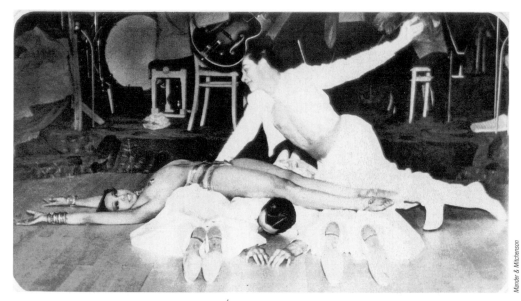

4. JOSÉPHINE BAKER

5. BARBETTE

6. PEG-LEG BATES

7. BILLY BENNETT

LIGHTNING PROGRAMME.

The Non-Stop Show.

The talk of every town visited.

Verdict of the people—

Something New.   Something Refreshing.

Away from all others.

Beautiful plant of own pictorial posters.

No stock stuff.

Over 3 tons of Scenery and Apparatus.

Only VACANT dates this year,

Aug. 24, Midlands.

Sept. 21 & 28.

Dec. 14, 21 & 28.

NOW BOOKING 1926.

Managers write in at once and secure this
great box office attraction, all letters to—

DR. WALFORD BODIE,

This Week: THEATRE ROYAL, LEAMINGTON SPA.

Next Week: EMPRESS THEATRE, GLASGOW.

LEAD ON MACDUFF.

9. WALFORD BODIE

8. BESSIE BONEHILL

10. CAICEDO

11. HARRY CLAFF

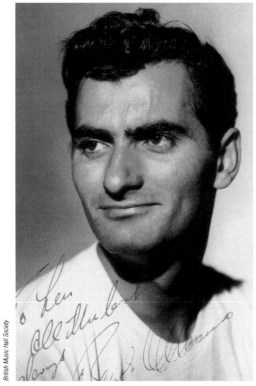

12. BONAR COLLEANO

13. BILLY COTTON & HIS BAND 1930

14. THE DEHL TRIO

British Music Hall Society

15. DELFONT & TOKO

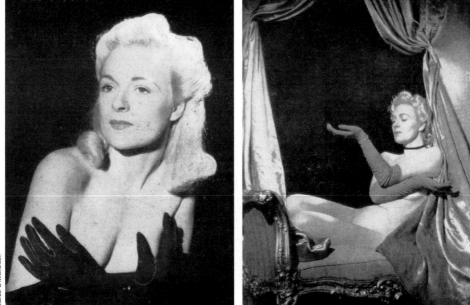

Mander & Mitchenson

Mander & Mitchenson

16. PHYLLIS DIXEY

17. PHYLLIS DIXEY

18. DRUM & MAJOR

19. NORMAN EVANS

COOPER, MARGARET (1877-1922)

The Lady Corney Grain

Corney Grain (1844-95) was a noted piano-entertainer who displayed his talents exclusively to middle-class audiences in middle-class concert halls. Singing at the piano had long been considered too static and anaemic as a Music Hall turn; more than anyone Margaret Cooper helped to change that perception, to be swiftly emulated by the likes of HARRY FRAGSON and Barclay Gammon (1867-1915). In fact there was such a flood of piano-entertainers on the Halls at one time that Foster Kershaw advertised himself as *The Entertainer without a Piano.*

Others in this category were TED ANDREWS, FREDDIE BAMBERGER, VICTOR BORGE, PEGGY COCHRANE, Jack Lane (1879-1953) *The Yorkshire Rustic at the Piano,* Jen Latona (1881-1955) *The Girl at the Piano,* Liberace (1919-87) *The Rhinestone Rubinstein,* NORMAN LONG, SAM MAYO, Little Richard (b1935) *The Bronze Liberace,* Elsie Roby (fl c1910) *The Pianologuedienne* and *The Slavey at the Piano,* Maurice Rocco (1919-76) *Boogie-Woogie Pianist-Dancer,* James Stewart *The Tramp at the Piano;* also Tommy Westwood and Peggy Wilding (both listed under NORMAN LONG).

For pianists pure and unadorned see WINIFRED ATWELL.

COOPER, TOMMY (1921-84)

He's Done It!; Up to his Tricks Again

The following story was related to an acquaintance of ours by this peerlessly funny conjurer in person: 'So I'm at Lime Street station in Liverpool, waiting for the train to London. I'd got a few minutes to spare, I thought "I'll have a cup of tea". I'm sitting in the buffet and this chap sits down at the table. He says, "How'd'you do?" I says, "Fine. How are you?" He says, "Fine". I says, "That's great. Well, got to go. Nice talking to you." I get on the train, we start off for London, and I suddenly realise. It was me brother...'

See WINDMILL THEATRE

CORTEZ, LEON (1898-1970)

Heducating the Higgerant

In his act Richard Alfred Chalkin explained the plots of Shakespeare's plays in broad Cockney, hence the bill-matter. Burlesqueing the Bard was a very popular stand-by on the Halls in the 19th-century, which says something about working-class familiarity with Sweet William's canon. Mr Cortez must have been the last to attempt this line of business, though we do recall Tony Fayne of Fayne & Evans reciting pastiche Shakespearean blank verse at the Ardwick Green Hippodrome in 1956 which went down surprisingly well. Another topic of Mr Cortez' art was the exploration, also in the thickest East End argot, of the world of opera; remarkably, this entry himself sang the explanatory excerpts.

COTTON, BILLY (and his BAND) (1899-1969)
Wakey Wakey!

Born in Westminster, Mr Cotton was a bluff, ill-educated but shrewd man who became a British Institution. His radio show ran for over a thousand editions, and his television show only ceased after twelve years due to his sudden death. This artiste had been an acrobat, boxer, bus conductor, footballer (Wimbledon and Brentford) and a Royal Flying Corps pilot officer. In 1914 he joined up as an Army bandboy and was present at the catastrophic Dardanelles campaign. Despite having been a drummer and bugler he never learned to read music and was but an indifferent player.

But Mr Cotton was an unrivalled showband leader, developing his stage awareness while running a dance band in Stockport, and we recall with huge delight the hearty comic songs redolent of Victorian Music Hall, the slapstick interludes, and thick wodges of sentimentality that characterised his band's hour-long turn (usually the entire second half of a bill). It is surprising to learn that after all his years as a head-liner this entry left only £23,630.

See HACKFORD & DOYLE

COWELL, SAM (1819-54)
The Young American Roscius

Master Cowell was born in England but raised in America where he was thoroughly trained in all the performing arts, hence the soubriquet. The adult Cowell returned to London c1840 and very swiftly established a reputation as a consummate singer of Cockney songs. To put over a comic song against a background of eating, drinking, and gossiping and to an accompaniment of pianoforte and droning harmonium needed enormous power of delivery, strength of personality, and polish of address. All these attributes this entry had in abundance, so much so that when he took his uncompromisingly Metropolitan delineations on a tour of Britain his temerity was met with unanimous acclaim. Mr Cowell even took his repertoire back to the United States where again the excellence of his portrayals was met with ecstasies. In fact the performer was so successful that he came back a wreck, for by the time of his early demise he was knocking back two bottles of brandy a day: his legend remains as the first national and indeed international Music Hall star.

In the 1880s one J W Mann was calling himself *The Modern Sam Cowell.* We wonder whether the similarity was in repertoire or consumption?

See IRA ALDRIDGE; for other juvenile prodigies see Master WILLIAM BETTY.

COYNE, FRANK (1875-1906)
The Realistic Rarity of Rattling Refinement

Bill-matter regularly featured alliteration, a favourite device still mistaken by the ill-educated for wit. Mr Coyne's father Frank snr (1854-82) was also on the Halls, though he did not make such a mark as his son. Frank jnr made his greatest sensation when he took a bath and cut his throat, leaving his wretched wife to make the grim discovery.

There were also two Music Hall artistes named Fred Coyne, the elder of whom lived from c1845 to 1886 and the younger from 1871 until 1943 though we are unsure whether they were related. The elder Fred called himself *The Sterling Comedian*, billing which incorporated a private joke, for Sterling was his family name.

CROCK, DR (fl c1945-c60)
...and his Crackpots

The comedy musical ensemble was always welcome in a Variety bill, especially to one young learner-pianist in the audience. Dr Crock was Harry Hines (b1903); his barmy band purveyed the same kind of cacophonous mayhem as Syd Seymour (1906-58) *and his Mad Hatters* (see DELFONT & TOKO) and Sid Millward (1909-72) *and his Nitwits – Music? in the Millward manner*, though in our experience the funniest of the *genre* were Chocolate & Co., a five-handed troupe which doubled as THE RASTELLIS. It should be noted that the most anarchic comedian of them all, SPIKE MILLIGAN, began his career with the Bill Hall Trio as an unkempt guitarist. But is not the phrase 'comedy musician' an oxymoron? Comedy requires the breaking of rules whereas playing an instrument requires observance of rules. Such an act is only funny if the music is played to professional standard, as was the case with the American drummer Spike Jones (1911-65) *and his City Slickers (Musical Depreciation)* whose tumultuous television shows remain unsurpassed for bizarrie. Watching a Spike Jones tape today is like an acid trip, or so they tell me.

Soloists in this field include Professor Ernest (1865-1907) *The Human Orchestra*, The Geddes Brothers (fl1912-50s) *Putting on Airs*, HACKFORD & DOYLE, ALEC HALLS, HERSCHEL HENLERE, Ray Kay & Betty Bush *Fun in a Music Shop*, TOMMY JOVER, Johnny Laycock *He Plays on Everything Except your Nerves*, J W LISKARD, GEORGE MOZART, Bert Shrimpton (b1893) *Musical K'Nut*, STANELLI, Edwin Styles (1899-1960) *Almost a Musician*, STAN WHITE & ANN, and Vasco (1867-1925) *The Mad Magician* who claimed to play twenty-eight instruments, though not concurrently.

CROWTHER, LESLIE (1933-96)
Come on Down!

An elegant man with the positive style and marked individuality of the star performer, this entry's comedy we always felt to be skilled but mechanical; he always seemed to us slightly out of his *milieu* as a comic. His alleged classical training as a pianist manifested itself in a cabaret act which invariably included an excruciating rock version of Chopin's Nocturne in E♭ (op.9 no.2). The last time we worked with the artiste he included some extremely questionable racist material occasioning complaints to the management of the high-toned London venue.

Having been cured of an addiction to the Demon Drink, Mr Crowther threw himself with redoubled vigour into charitable work only to be severely injured in a motor-car accident in 1992. He never fully recovered, despite a harrowing non-speaking appearance in that year's *Royal Variety Performance*, and his death four years later was deeply regretted but not unexpected.

CRYER, BRIAN (b1935)
It Snows Tha' Knows

Brian Cryer, nowadays universally known and wholly admired by his real name Barry Cryer, once confessed to us that in 1956 for his first week's Variety he had given no thought to bill-matter, and when asked by the theatre manager blurted out *It Snows Tha' Knows*. To this day he has never known why; the provenance of the phrase remains as much a mystery to Mr Cryer as it must have done to his audiences all those years ago. The writer-performer recalls that they did not laugh much; perhaps they were too pre-occupied trying to tease out the significance of *It Snows Tha' Knows*.

This entry is married to the lovely and gracious Terry Donovan who with Jackie Jefferson (later Mrs Edmund Hockridge) were known in the 1950s and 60s as The Taylor Maids *Sophistication with a Difference*.

CUNDELL, PAMELA (b1924)
Cheek, Charm and Chatter

In our opinion this bill-matter is unusually apt; the artiste fills a stage more amply than most, exuding warmth and jollity. For many years Miss Cundell has been a mainstay of the CAA – once the Concert Artistes' Association but now the Club for Acts and Actors. We have had the delight of working with this entry on many occasions, once for two weeks in Stockholm. The Swedes are unaccustomed to funny females, and Miss Cundell was an immense success. They had never seen anyone like her, and it's very unlikely that they ever will again.

CURTIS, SAMMY (1893-1983)
The White Blackbird

For many years this entry – the only artiste we ever met who remembered the authentic Victorian Music Hall chairman – was with the NAT JACKLEY company; he was just under 5ft in height and in tribute to his rôle-model LITTLE TICH described himself as a big-boot dancer. We were told by Dave Jackley (brother of NAT JACKLEY) that in his younger touring days Mr Curtis regularly saved the week's rent by inveigling his landladies to yield the ultimate favour.

D

DAINTY, BILLY (1927-86)
Going Mad – Coming?; Twinkling Feet

Despite a stocky build this entry was fascinatingly light on his feet. His comic dancing was an absolute joy, and we never saw anyone who blended the arts of Terpsichore and Comus so skilfully and so effectively. Not that Mr Dainty was any less successful in patter work, sketches or in pantomime, an assertion attested to by his estate which was valued at a tasty £273,575.

DANIELS, PAUL (b1938)
The Unusualist

This diminutive thaumaturgist at one time appeared with his first wife and his musician brother Trevor (b1943) in an act anagrammatically *k.a.* The Eldanis. Mr Daniels' pretty Mark II wife is Debbie McGee, a magicienne herself who on one celebrated televisual occasion was cruelly asked 'What was it that first attracted you to the millionaire Paul Daniels?'

DANTE (1883-1955)
Sim Sala Bim

We remember this charming Danish baffler well, a distinguished-looking charismatic figure, quite unlike the podgy bespectacled Kalanag (1903-63) to whom he sold his show. When out of funds Dante would sell his show serially, creating several degrees of confusion amongst those who considered themselves to be *Sim Sala Bim's* owners.

A previous Dante (1869-99) billed himself as *The Mormon Wizard*; this gentleman was shot dead in Australia in a hunting accident, his supernatural powers availing him naught.

See RICHARD HEARNE, MAGICIANS, HOWARD THURSTON

DANVERS, BILLY (1884-1964)
Always Funny; Always Merry and Bright;
Cheery & Chubby; The Jolly Jester; The Laughing Fool

Mr Danvers' bill-matter gives a cumulatively clear picture of his style of presentation, and how wearisome it must have been to be 'always' funny and 'always' merry and bright. Did not the comic succumb to the occasional black moment? Did the cheeriness and jolliness never become a touch frayed? It would seem not, for demands for this entry's talents kept him working until only two weeks before his death at the age of eighty.

DATAS (1876-1956)
The Living Encyclopaedia; The Memory Man

This strangely gifted gentleman was a humble gas-works employee when Fate catapulted him on to the stage of the Palace; a week's booking was extended to nine months followed by a tour of all the leading Stoll and Moss Halls. It seems that this entry just could not forget a date, not just the year but the month and day.

More recently the nation was agape at Leslie Welch (1907-80) – also billed as *The Memory Man* – whose recall of sporting events seemed infallible. But with the quantity of information in any sphere growing exponentially by the day it is not surprising that the memory act is no longer encountered.

See THEA ALBA, Elre Cecilia Salambo (THE SALAMBOS)

De BIERE, ARNOLD (1878-1934)
Prince of Entertainers and Entertainer of Princes;
Prince of Jugglers and Juggler of Princes

This artiste's first claim we would deem unexceptional but the second is, we suggest, susceptible to misinterpretation.

See JUGGLERS

De CASALIS, JEANNE (1892-1966)
Mrs Feather

The actress-comedienne was married to the actor Colin Clive (1898-1937) who as the original screen Frankenstein so memorably delivered the line 'He's a-*lieeeve!!!* He's a-*lieeeve!!!*'

Miss Casalis claimed to have introduced Mrs Feather in a sketch at the London Alhambra in 1934, but we have discographic evidence that the garrulous fluffy-brained lady appeared some two years earlier. Whenever it was, the character's misunderstandings on the telephone were very much appreciated by the Great British Public, and indeed the device of the overheard telephone conversation was well suited to the wireless as many other artistes have continued to prove.

De HAVEN & PAGE (fl1920s-50s)

Comix; Much Ado about Nothing; A Pair of Sparkling Gags

The plebeian Birmingham origins of Billy De Haven (b c1895) were no bar to his entertaining – or so he boasted – such eminent personages as President Woodrow Wilson, King George V and Queen Mary, The King and Queen of the Belgians, the Prince of Wales (briefly King Edward VIII), the Duke of Kent, and Field Marshal Lord Haig.

Mr De Haven's partner Dandy (Joseph) Page (1896-1981) could only claim to have diverted the Duke of Kent, but then he was a Russian – Mr Page, that is, not the Duke.

See BILLY SHAKESPEARE

DEHL TRIO, THE (fl1936-9 and 1946-58)

From the Ridiculous to the Sublime

The original three artistes were Freddie Dell (b1905), his wife Gladys (b1917) and Dick Laughton. After the Second World War Mr Dell's partners were Joan Linley and Kevin Nolan (d1997); their repertoire included a *Spider and Fly* routine (see HECTOR NAPIER). The photograph of the Dehl Trio between pp.80-81 was taken at Clacton in 1957, just before the tide came in.

De LEATH, VAUGHN (1900-43)

The First Lady of Radio; The Original Radio Girl

The novelty-value of the new medium and the prestige of association with the BBC prompted increasingly frequent appearances of 'radio' on posters and programmes from the early 1920s. Thirty years later a new novelty rendered the old novelty démodé: the new new novelty was 'television'.

DELEVANTIS, THE (fl c1850-1900s)
Kings of the Carpet

This tumbling act was founded by John Bowden (1825-1908); the troupe included John Allen Whiteley (1843-88) who married the boss's daughter Ellen (b c1845) and founded a dynasty of performers skilled in virtually every circus discipline and which flourishes to this day.

The Delevantis should not to be confused, though they often are, with the contemporary Delavanti Troupe who were also multi-talented circus artistes. Nor must we be ignorant of The Three Delevines, acrobatic brothers who made their début in 1884. In the 1900s they merged with the dancing and musical Sisters Winterton to become The Five Delevines displaying such racy bill-matter as *Flirtations* and *Satanic Gambols*.

See THE FIVE WHITELEYS, ZAZEL

DELFONT & TOKO (fl1930-7)
The Aristocrats of Dance; Syncopated Steps Appeal

As a single act Bernard Delfont (né Barnet Winogradsky 1909-94) billed himself, not unjustifiably, as *Charleston Champion of the East End.* A dancing partnership with HAL MONTY was called The Delfont Boys; Toko (née Judy Miller), a beautiful 16-year-old half-Chinese girl who had once danced for Sid Seymour (see DR CROCK), joined Mr Delfont in 1930 and stayed with him, professionally speaking, for seven years.

Bernard Delfont's rise from poor Russian Jewish refugee background to the House of Lords is remarkable enough, but what makes it all the more astonishing is that Mr Delfont's brother, LEW GRADE, achieved the same eminence. Both men became pivotal figures in all branches of Britain's entertainment industry, from Bingo to feature films, from the London Palladium to television. Even more amazing is that the brothers were so universally liked, respected, and admired. They lived decent honourable lives and contributed greatly to the commonweal of their adoptive country.

See HAL MONTY

DESMOND, FLORENCE (1906-93)
The Hollywood Party; The World's Foremost Impressionist

Miss Desmond's quite exceptional gift of mimicry made her a head-liner on both sides of the Atlantic; her HMV recording *A Hollywood Party* was the 1933 bestseller.

This entry's range encompassed GRACIE FIELDS and JIMMY DURANTE and her ability to assume not just the voice but the features of her subjects was described as nothing less than uncanny. Miss Desmond herself declared 'I don't use wigs or props...it sounds like an exaggeration to say I went into a mental trance, but I did.' Despite international acclaim the artiste announced her retirement at the age of only 49, and was much missed.

See DESMOND & MARKS. Also see list of MIMICS in glossary.

DESMOND & MARKS (fl1940s-70s)
Rising Falling Stars; Fooling & Falling

We had the pleasure of sharing a dressing-room with Frederick George Dawson (b1915) and Jack Marks (b1915) at the Bristol Hippodrome in pantomime. With the collapse of Variety much of their time was spent on the Continent where their services were still in regular demand, but these avuncular knockabouts declared stoutly that wherever they happened to be they never failed to stop the car, switch on the radio, and listen to *The Archers*.

Fred's distinguished sister was FLORENCE DESMOND.

DIXEY, PHYLLIS (1914-64)
The Girl the Lord Chamberlain Banned; A Living Contribution to Art ; The Peek-a-Boo Girl; Queen of Strippers

This West Londoner was an established artiste billed on the Halls with her husband Jack 'Snuffy' Tracey (1903-78) as *The Sap and the Swell Dame*. The febrile atmosphere of war-time London led to a proliferation of ecdysiasts (a coinage of the American littérateur H L Mencken) and in 1940 Miss Dixey joined their ranks by introducing at the Phoenix her celebrated peek-a-boo fan dance. This was by all accounts an extremely artistic display, and we have no reason to doubt the lady's integrity. Miss Dixey was an exceptionally fine-featured and well-formed woman, and a natural blonde.

See Fifi (MISCELLANEOUS), CARRIE FINNELL, Gypsy Rose Lee (QUEEN OF...), WINDMILL THEATRE

DIXON, REG (1915-84)

Confidentially

On one occasion this artiste confided to his audience that as he had a boil up his nose he was feeling poorly. In fact he was feeling 'proper poorly', an expression which raised a big laugh at the time and in the mysterious way of these things became an all-conquering catch-phrase. The performer then composed his signature-tune *Confidentially* of which his own recording rocketed him to top-of-the-bill status. As has been noted under WILKIE BARD Mr Dixon was one of those comedians who enhanced his humorous aspect by wearing a funny hat.

Two other 'confidential' comedians were TONY HANCOCK and ROBB WILTON. Another 'ill' comic was GEORGE WILLIAMS.

DODD, KEN (b1929)

Cock of the North; The Sage of Knotty Ash; The Unpredictable

Apart from being an heroically energetic comedian this entry is notorious for over-running. We have seen with our own eyes the coaches outside the Manchester Palace way after Mr Dodd's show should have finished. In 1989, when HM Commissioners of Inland Revenue hauled the performer before the courts due to some trifling misunderstanding, the joke going the rounds was 'If Doddy gets three years he'll do four.' He was, to the nation's relief, acquitted. A wild, manic, unstoppable force of nature on stage – 'Give up?' – the artiste's technical prowess is unrivalled, and he has become one of the nation's darlings, even if he did keep £336,000 in cash in the attic.

Another *Cock of the North* was Peter Sinclair. Also see HERSCHEL HENLERE.

DRAKE, CHARLIE (b1925)

The Blue-Eyed Boy from the Elephant

The Elephant refers to Elephant and Castle, an area of London just south of the Thames as insalubrious today as it was in Charles Edward Springall's childhood. Another billing used by this entry was his catch-phrase *Hullo, My Darlings!*

In the RAF the future comedian spent much of his service in the guardhouse due to a congenital inability to take orders. Such intemperateness in a man of 5ft 1in resulted in Mr Drake being for a time confined to a mental institution where psychiatrists retired baffled.

After demobilisation the aggressive little reprobate auditioned no fewer than seven times for the WINDMILL, his persistence at this early stage being more apparent than any talent. Access to the world of Variety was finally gained by working as feed to DICK EMERY, and success arrived with an act called Mick & Montmorency in which the cherubic-looking artiste was partnered by the 6ft 3ins Jack Edwardes, a duo particularly popular on children's television.

Turning solo Mr Drake further developed slapstick skills of a high order, his small, rotund body bouncing like a rubber ball through doors and windows. The comic's face was moon-shaped, his ginger hair wispily arranged across his scalp, and his strangely high-pitched speaking voice fought a losing battle with gentility.

Of originality and strength of presence this entry had no lack, though his volatile temperament did not endear him to managements or his fellow-artistes, and his career was effectively ended by injuries sustained in an accident in a television studio.

DREAMS, LYDIA (1869-1949)

The Clown and his Grandma; The Ventriloquial Protean Actor

Walter H Lambert is remembered not so much for his work as a drag vent but for his much-reproduced 1903 painting *Popularity*, a canvas 13ft by 5ft 6ins depicting 226 prominent Music Hall artistes – some deceased. The original is in the Museum of London.

The painting is a lively if crowded scene at the junction of Lower Marsh and the Waterloo Road known in the Profession as Poverty Corner. Here unemployed artistes gathered to chat and gossip and perhaps secure an engagement from one of the many agents located in the vicinity. A later Poverty Corner was by the Hippodrome, Charing Cross Road. As agents moved north of the Thames so did Poverty.

See BARBETTE, BOBBIE KIMBER, OWEN McGIVENEY, VENTRILOQUISTS

DRESSLER, MARIE (1869-1934)
The Ugly Duckling

Like so many whose physical charms are unfashionably wrought Miss Dressler took refuge at an early age in clowning. By the early 1900s the performer was a favourite in burlesque and vaudeville; of her performance at the Palace in New York in 1919 the *New York Dramatic Mirror* stated sententiously: 'Few actresses, even considering those who play Ibsen and other queer fellows' scribbling, are quoted by the transcontinental press as much as she for the reason that she had always something to say that even college professors can understand as well as servant girls.' We are not sure to whom this comment offers the greater insult.

DRUM & MAJOR (fl c1901-26)
A Broker's Man inc. Rose of Palestine; After the Overture

This team, which was sometimes *k.a.* Tom & Kitty Major, comprised Tom Ball (1879-1962) *a.k.a.* Tom Major-Ball and his wife Kitty (Grant) (1874-1928). At a performance of their eccentric clowning and acrobatics in 1926 Mrs Ball was injured so severely that she never trod the boards again; after lingering for two years the unfortunate lady died.

By Mr Major-Ball's second wife Gwen Glen (1905-70) *Dainty Comedienne* he had two sons, the younger metamorphosing into John Major (b1943), Prime Minister of Great Britain 1990-97.

See JIMMY LYNTON

DRYDEN, LEO (1863-1939)
The Kipling of the Halls

Not, we are inclined to think, in the first rank of artistes but this Londoner was fortunate enough to achieve top billing through *The Miner's Dream Of Home*, a fine song still regularly warbled. On the strength of this success Mr Dryden worked up a line of stirring ballads such as *Gallant Gordon Highlanders, God Bless And Keep Victoria,* and *Twixt Love And Duty.* Despite these pious sentiments the singer's private life was highly irregular, and we regret to say that he and Miss Lily Harley (the mother of CHARLES CHAPLIN) indulged in what m'learned friends used to refer to as criminal conversation, to such vigorous effect that not one but two sons inadvertently entered this vale of tears.

See ALBERT CHEVALIER for another *Kipling of the Halls*.

Du CALION (1885-1956)
The Loquacious Laddie on the Tottering Ladder

This artiste was an extremely popular support act during the inter-war years. Mr Du Calion not only tottered alarmingly on his unsupported ladder but told jokes and played musical instruments the while, a style of act we have not seen for many a year. He was said also to have been 'first-class' in pantomime, though in what character we are at a loss to suggest. The Beanstalk?

Other ladder performers were Tom Gilbey *The Fireman on the Ladder* who was killed in action in August 1916, Igor Gridneff (d August 20th 1990) *Have Ladder – Will Travel* and *The Ladder Man*, and Great Scott (fl1910) *The Ladder King*.

DUNVILLE, T E (1868-1924)
The Elongated Lump of Comedy; The Long, Lean, Lorn Loon; The Public Mirth Provoker; Sticking Here for a Week

In the trade press Mr Dunville sometimes put *London Always* under his name, indicating a lofty disdain for provincial engagements. But in the 1920s calls for his services in any part of the country fell away steeply and he drowned himself in the Thames at Reading. The comedian sang nonsensical songs in outlandish clothes, clownish make-up and a fright wig, a get-up which served him well from 1890 until the boys came home in 1918 by which time changing tastes found such freakish figures distasteful. The performer's withered arm accentuated an appearance too bizarre for audiences sated on the real horrors of the Great War.

See BILLY BENNETT

DURANTE, JIMMY 'Schnozzle' (1893-1980)
The Riff-Raff's Caruso

Enrico Caruso was the world's greatest tenor but Mr Durante's singing voice was described, with some justification, by FRED ALLEN as 'a dull rasp calling its mate'. The pianist-comedian first achieved prominence with Clayton, Jackson & Durante *Jest for a Laugh*, an act which from 1923 worked its way up from speakeasy to headlining at the Palace, New York's premiere vaudeville house.

The act split up in 1931 when Mr Durante went solo in response to an offer from Hollywood, the silver screen bringing Schnozzola's warm exuberance to a delighted British public. How we revelled in the delicate artistry of such songs as *Inka Dinka Doo* and *The Guy Who Found The Lost Chord*, and in the jokes about the prodigious size of Mr Durante's beezer. In London, the performer once said, a *Times* journalist 'asks if I minds if he mentions my nose. I'm surrounded by assassins! "If ya don't mention it," I says to him, "you puts me out of business"'.

For other Carusos see BETTY AUKLAND

95

E

EAGLE, GEORGE BARNARDO (c1808-58)

The Napoleon of Wizards; The Royal Wizard of the South; The Wizard of the South

So potent was Napoleon's spell that to this very day his once-dread name is synonymous with superhuman drive and intensity of purpose. Mr Eagle, who travelled a large-scale and extremely elaborate magic show, is the only illusionist we know of to have invoked the Corsican's reputation to amplify his hyperphysical appeal.

Other Napoleons were John W Cooper (see VENTRILOQUISTS), The Great Everhart (1867-1948) *The Napoleon of Hoops* and *William the Conqueror of Hoops*, NAPOLEON, and NAUGHTON & GOLD.

If Mr Eagle was *The Wizard of the South,* 'Lord' GEORGE SANGER and VALENTINE VOX both claimed to be *The Wizard of the West,* while sovranty of the North lay with JOHN HENRY ANDERSON. The Wizardship of the East remained untenanted. Mr Eagle was the father of Georgiana Eagle *The Celebrated Illusionist, Mesmerist and Electro-Biologist.*

See PETER CASSON, Princess RUBIE

EARLE, JACKSON (1902-71)

The Happy Comedian; Let Me Kill It Now

To bill oneself as *The Happy Comedian* may be unimaginative but is at least unobjectionable, whereas *Let Me Kill It Now* would, one might have thought, turned them away in droves. On the other hand the artiste reigned supreme for many years at New Brighton so whatever Mr Earle (*a.k.a.* Jack Cassidy) killed it certainly wasn't the business.

EDWARDS, PERCY (1908-96)

The Pied Piper from Suffolk

This gentleman was a devout naturalist obsessively concerned that his bird and animal impressions should be accurate for the season, the place, and even the time of day. When Variety expired this entry's career disappeared with it and he fell on hard times, claiming welfare payments and cashing in an insurance policy.

A chance meeting with CHARLIE CHESTER led to regular radio work again and the artiste's extraordinary talents were re-discovered; his last years were spent happily making noises for radio and TV drama as well as for feature film sound tracks. Mr Edwards' remarkable range encompassed Orca the Killer Whale and Gregory the Chicken.

Bernard 'Skeets' Martin (1886-1970) *The Animal Mimic who Sings* and *Mimetic Comedian* claimed to have been the youngest bugler in the Boer War.

See WINDMILL THEATRE

ELEN, GUS (1862-1940)

The Inimitable Coster Delineator; The Quaint Comedian

Despite the first billing this scowling beanpole with the singing voice of a rusty hinge was extremely imitable. Mr Elen's markedly individual style and trade-mark squeak on stressed downward intervals have made him popular impressionists' fodder to this very day.

Music Hall aficionados like to contrast the alleged phoniness of ALBERT CHEVALIER's sentimentalising artisans with the genuineness of Mr Elen's rough-hewn diamond geezers. We can only say that for emetic lugubriousness nothing in the Chevalier canon matches Mr Elen's *lentissimo* delivery of *The Coster's Muvver*.

See ALEC HURLEY, TOM LEAMORE.

ELLIOTT, G H (1884-1962)

The Chocolate-Coloured Coon

This artiste's much-parodied bill-matter is nowadays considered impossibly offensive, though it was not so during its bearer's long career nor when one Stanley Richards was billed at the Battersea Town Hall as *The Happy Coon* as late as February 1967.

We had the privilege, on one occasion only, of witnessing a performance of Mr Elliott's most memorable song *Lily of Laguna*; the septuagenarian's fleetness of dancing and certitude of style remain vivid memories.

Other 'negro delineators' entered are BILLY BENNETT, BROWN NEWLAND & LE CLERQ, G H CHIRGWIN, NELLIE

97

CHRISTIE, MAY HENDERSON, Winifred E Johnson (see R G KNOWLES), AL JOLSON, JOE LAWRENCE, E W MACKNEY, J J Mannix *The Coffee-Coloured Coon* (fl c1910), VICTORIA MONKS, TONY PASTOR, The Two Petries (fl1890s) *Singing and Dancing Plantation Cane Dancers*, SAM REDFERN, T D RICE, EUGENE STRATTON, YOUNG TICHBORNE, SOPHIE TUCKER, JAMES UNSWORTH, BRANSBY WILLIAMS, Terry Wilson (1891-1965) *The Entertainer who works like a Nigger*, and CHRIS WORTMAN.

ELRICK, GEORGE (b1903)

Mrs Elrick's Wee Boy; The Man with the Smiling Voice; The Smiling Voice of Radio

This vocalist, comedian, song-writer and bandleader claims to have been born in Aberdeen in 1910, but our intelligence would pre-date this happy event by seven years. Judging by his bill-matter Mr Elrick would seem to have been inordinately proud of his professional rictus, and it is not surprising to learn that his 1948 touring show was called *When You're Smiling*. We are honour bound to record that we always found this entry smug and creepily unctuous.

EMERY, DICK (1917-83)

Talking Turkey

We only once appeared with this popular if over-praised comedian, essaying for his television show the small but telling rôle of Frankenstein's monster. The day did not start well for we became lost in the vast maze that is Shepperton Studios and in consequence arrived in make-up at five minutes past eight. 'You're late,' said Mr Emery without preamble, and so far as we can recollect that was the only remark the artiste vouchsafed us. Despite this unpromising start we consider that we acquitted ourself to general satisfaction.

Our other connection with the performer was on one occasion to accompany his sister Ann Emery *Musical Miss* on the pianoforte at the De La Warr Pavilion, Bexhill, a very select venue. Miss Emery was to give a medley of Old Time Music Hall songs; her music had, it seemed, been hastily scribbled out by a passing bass player and what we were given was a chart of chord symbols with no melody line nor even the titles of the tunes. When therefore Miss Emery dried in mid-medley and asked me what came next I could not advise. I heard a few weeks later that this débâcle was repeated at another venue, news which went some way towards assuaging my feelings of inadequacy.

The father of these siblings was Laurie Howe *The Quaint Comedian.*

See JOE BLACK, CHARLIE DRAKE, WINDMILL THEATRE

EMNEY, FRED (1866-1917)
A Sister to Assist 'Er

The origin of this celebrated sketch was a tea-party scene in the 1906 Drury Lane pantomime *Sinbad the Sailor.* Another pantomime routine was not so fortunate for this entry, for while performing a slosh routine with the Egbert Brothers in *Cinderella* at the London Opera House in Kingsway Mr Emney slipped and fell heavily. Despite finishing the performance the comedian had suffered grave injury and within a fortnight was dead.

We caught a revival of *A Sister to Assist 'Er* in the mid-1960s and despite its legendary reputation the piece was toe-curlingly unfunny.

Mr Emney's son Fred Emney jnr (1900-80) was also a popular comedian who sported the bowler hat, large cigar, mountainous girth and dubious vowels of a turf accountant on the verge of insolvency.

See SKETCH ARTISTES

ENGLISH, ARTHUR (1919-95)
Prince of the Wide Boys

A wide boy or spiv was a sharply dressed, pencil-moustached, kipper-tied, black-marketeering wheeler-dealer who emerged in response to conditions prevailing after the Second World War. It is not generally appreciated today that rationing continued in Britain until the mid-1950s; your friendly neighbourhood spiv was one who could, at a price, supply that extra sugar for a birthday cake or a pair of nylons for that special evening. Mr English exemplified the type in heightened comic form, his rapid huckster's delivery degenerating into total gibberish and invariably ending with 'I dunno what I'm talking about – play the music! Open the cage!' This artiste was one of our favourite comedians.

See SID FIELD, WINDMILL THEATRE

ERNE, MAY (fl1910s)

Ambi-'Pe'-Dexter

Advertised as 'one who uses both hands and feet with equal facility'. We are also informed that 'the act took five years to prepare' and that Miss Erne had two patents to her name, one for a portable glockenspiel and the other a gadget with which to play it. Since a glockenspiel is portable anyway one wonders why a patent was even applied for let alone granted (No. 19014). By 1915 the inventor was billing herself as May Erne and 'He', the latter being the vocalist Erne Chester (1868-1950) for whom Miss Erne obliged on the xylophone. Their billing was *Patched Ballads and Pot Shots*, the significance of which remains obscure.

See THEA ALBA, CLARICE MAYNE

ERROL, BERT (1883-1949)

The Famous Male Soprano and Double-Voiced Vocalist; The Tetrazzini of the Halls

Luisa Tetrazzini (1871-1940) was one of the greatest soprani of her era and it is to be doubted whether the *diva* would have been flattered by Mr Errol's assumption of vocal parity. That being said this entry was unsurpassed in his line as a glamorous female impersonator and though his principal appeal lay in burlesques of musical comedy leading ladies his straight singing (in *falsetto*) was unusually fine.

It is worth recording that Mr Errol's initiation into female impersonation was with Harry Reynolds' Minstrels. Such troupes, unlike concert parties, were almost always male and would therefore include a female impersonator or two to provide musical variety and presentational interest. We note that this performer was married and fathered a daughter, Betty.

See BARBETTE, JESSIE HARCOURT, ST GEORGE HUSSEY, Nellie Richards (MAY HENDERSON)

ETHARDO, Signor (1835-1911)

The Spiral Ascensionist

This artiste's bill-matter describes no more nor less than that which he achieved, which was to stand on a large ball and walk it up a spiral incline to a height of 50ft. Such an act would seem to afford only limited interest but the novelty drew crowds to the Crystal Palace for the entire twelve months of the Ascensionist's engagement. Twenty years later in 1885 an accident put an end to the performer's career, from which time he devoted himself to training a new generation of acrobats.

Signor Ethardo's initial success inspired many imitators, some of whom ascended their ramps *inside* the ball, emerging at the summit in a change of costume.

See EMMELINE EHARDO, OCEANA

ETHARDO, EMMELINE (fl1880-90s)
Mélange Artistique, Jongleuse and Violiniste

We have also seen this lady's bill-matter rendered more demotically as *Juggling, Bending & Violin Playing*, whatever the wording plainly a remarkably varied turn was on offer, though we doubt whether all three of Miss Ethardo's advertised fields of expertise were exercised simultaneously.

This entry was a pupil of but unrelated to the previous entry.

See JUGGLERS

EVANS, NORMAN (1901-62)
Over the Garden Wall

Mr Evans eased himself into the Variety world via after-dinner speaking, smokers, Masonics and the goodwill of fellow-townie GRACIE FIELDS who recommended him to Sir Oswald Stoll (1867-1942), the leading Variety manager of the day.

Although Mr Evans did not turn fully professional until the age of thirty-three this entry's broad boisterous comedy and warmth of personality swiftly elevated him to lasting stardom. *Over the Garden Wall* featured the immortal Fanny Fairbottom standing on an upturned bucket in order to gossip with the next-door neighbour. This quite masterly character study we remember well, and posterity is fortunate in that the performance which includes the priceless moment when Mrs Fairbottom slips off the box and bruises her voluminous bosom is preserved on film.

See BARBETTE

F

FARINI, EL NINO (1855-1939)
The Infant Prodigy

This aerialist was born Sam Wasgate and adopted by William Hunt (1838-1929) *k.a.* Guillermo Antonio Farini. Mr Farini would carry the boy on his back while walking blindfolded along a high tightrope. Did young Sam know, we wonder, that in Cuba in 1862 whilst performing the same stunt Mr Farini's wife had been killed?

In 1870 the lad was billed as Mlle Lu-Lu *The Beautiful Girl Aerialist and Circassian Catapultist* and *The Eighth Wonder of the World.* The *Circassian* may have been bogus but *Catapultist* was real enough, for at the Cremorne Gardens in 1871 Lu-Lu was catapulted to a 25ft high trapeze, turning a triple somersault en route.

When Master Farini's true gender was revealed in 1878 considerable embarrassment was caused to a number of gentlemen of rank and position who had been smitten with the daintily lithe creature. Another protégée of Mr Farini's was ZAZEL, the first human cannonball.

El Nino Farini should not be confused with Lulu the wire-walker (Mrs Winifred Gilbert) who died in April 1929.

See BARBETTE, Master WILLIAM BETTY

FATHER OF...

Philip Astley (1742-1814)
...the Circus

Samuel Foote (1720-77)
...Burlesque
Sometimes called *The English Aristophanes.*

W C Handy (1873-1958)
...the Blues

Robert Houdin (1805-71)
...Modern Magic
See MAGICIANS

FATHER OF... (continued):

Charles Morton (1819-1904)
...the Halls

Some revisionists would deny Mr Morton so exalted a place in the pantheon of British popular entertainment, but we feel that his foresight, integrity, and the esteem in which he was held by all classes justify the tribute. Certainly this was the view of the eminent critic Clement Scott (1841-1904) who first ascribed Music Hall paternity to this entry.

Philip Thomaschefsky (c1844-1913)
...the Jewish Theatre in America

William West (1796-1888)
...the Stage

Soubriquet conferred on Mr West not so much for Thespian distinction as for longevity.

See also entries for: OLIVIER BASSELIN, TONY PASTOR, FRED RUSSELL

FAWN, JAMES (1849-1923)
The Prince of Red-Nosed Comedians

Mr Fawn was an excellent low comic actor who became a finished and well-regarded Music Hall artiste, largely remembered today as the original singer of *If You Want To Know The Time Ask A P'liceman*, although much of his reputation was based on his studies of inebriation. At one time this entry worked a double act with another major comic talent of the era ARTHUR ROBERTS, who wrote that Jimmy Fawn was a bulky man who could never be prevented, even in the awesome presence of Royalty, from sniffing loudly, juicily and constantly.

See JOHNNY COOPER

FEENEY, PAT (1850-89)
The Shaughraun of the Music Halls

The Shaughraun – an impish mischievous little man – was the title of a ragingly popular 1874 play by Dion Boucicault (1822-90). From their inception in the 1850s the English Halls had always given a ready welcome to Irish artistes, so much so that there were not a few ersatz Hibernians cashing in on the vogue such as KATE CARNEY, a very young DAN LENO, G H MACDERMOTT and Whiteman & Thompson (see BILLY MERSON).

It has always struck us as curious that despite the popularity of Irish songs and Irish performers there was no comparable enthusiasm for Scotch or Welsh representation on English stages. Not until HARRY LAUDER came south in 1900 was a Scot to draw the Town so enthusiastically, and we can recall no Welsh Music Hall artiste to occupy so secure a hold on the nation's affections until the emergence of the gentleman who did us the honour to contribute the Foreword to this volume: Sir HARRY SECOMBE.

Mr Feeney was married to the singer Nellie Farrell (1859-89) *The Glittering Star of Erin.*

FIELD, SID (1904-50)
Destroyer of Gloom

This performer evinced the charm and ingenuousness that recall the universal appeal of DAN LENO. After twenty-seven years of languishing in the provinces Mr Field's opening night triumph in the 1943 revue *Strike a New Note* at the Prince of Wales's was so astounding that the eminent impresario Sir Charles B Cochran was moved to write to *The Times.* Sid Field, he stated, 'caused the greatest laughter I have heard in the theatre for many years...' and that the new star '...stood comparison with all the great ones of my crowded memory'.

Later the eminent American entertainer Danny Kaye, then at the peak of his own considerable powers, declared that Sid Field was the greatest comedian he had ever seen.

The vulnerability and feyness of this entry led him inevitably to the rôle of Elwood P Dowd, a man whose constant companion is an invisible six-foot-tall rabbit, in Mary Chase's fantasy-fable *Harvey.* It was while appearing in this play that Mr Field succumbed to a heart attack at the age of only 45. He had enjoyed but seven brief years of fame, in that time making an ineradicable impression on all who saw him and leaving an imperishable legend.

In many of his routines Mr Field's foil was the suavely elegant Jerry Desmonde (1908-67) who was to perform the same office for such as Bob Hope (b1903), NAT JACKLEY, and NORMAN WISDOM. Mr Desmonde, despite the self-confident mien which was his stock-in-trade, took his own life.

See ARTHUR ENGLISH, JACK TRIPP, HARRY WORTH

FIELDS, 'Happy' FANNY (1884-1961)

The American Dutch Girl; The Happy Little Dutch Girl

Miss Fields would seem to have popularised this line on the British Halls, though her claim was disputed by fellow-American May Moore Duprez (1885-1946) who billed herself variously as *Cute and Sassy, The Jolly Little Dutch Girl* and, more contentiously, as *The Original Jolly Dutch Girl.*

We say contentiously because at the Oxford Music Hall in 1899 could be seen *The Unrivalled Dialect Actress* Ada Alexander *The Dutch Girl.*

The Misses Ivy Grant (fl c1920s) *The Jolly Dutch Girl* and 'Happy' Lilian Lee (1900-24) *The Merry Dutch Girl* also cavorted in Dutch clogs, Dutch dresses, and Nederlands caps.

See MACARI

FIELDS, Dame GRACIE (1898-1979)

England's Greatest Comedienne; The Lass from Lancashire; The Queen of Song

This slender Rochdale beauty's remarkably clear and agile soprano was an instrument unique on the Variety stage for tone and quality. Such attributes allied to a spirited sense of fun inevitably indicated stardom, and so it was that in 1925 when the artiste had been touring in *Mr Tower of London* for six years Sir Oswald Stoll booked the revue for a week at the London Coliseum. The morning after it opened the critic of the *Daily Herald* HANNEN SWAFFER wrote that Miss Fields' 'gifts which amount to genius show her as a BEATRICE LILLIE, Florence Mills, an Ethel Levey and NELLIE WALLACE all rolled into one'. From that time on the singer-comedienne's popularity never waned, though it wobbled a little at the outbreak of World War II due to her second husband Monty Banks (Mario Bianchi 1897-1950) being technically an enemy alien.

Dame Gracie was the first female Variety artiste to receive a title, not only for her indefatigable (some would say relentless) touring of service camps at home and abroad during hostilities but as a recognition of the dynamism and vitality of the society from which the performer sprang.

Dame Gracie left £270,513. Her brother was Tommy Fields (1908-1988) *London's Lancashire Comedian* and *The Singing Fool;*

another sibling on the Halls was Betty Fields (d1975) *Gracie's Sister with a Style of her own.*

Other *Queens of Song* were Marjorie Manners, Nellie Melba, Adelina Patti, and Joyce Shock (see QUEENS OF...).

FIELDS, W C (1880-1946)

America's Favorite Comedian; Different from the Rest; The Distinguished Comedian; Greatest of Eccentric Jugglers; The Silent Humorist; Tramp Juggler

This entry's excesses have been so well rehearsed in the public prints that we do not feel it necessary to reiterate the oft-told tales of his excessive drinking, his multiplicity of bank accounts, his Dickensian pseudonyms, his secretiveness, his alleged dislike of children, his cynicism, and general curmudgeonliness. Mr Fields was, it can never be denied, a superb juggler who in 1916 could command $1,500 a week.

When the performer died *Variety's* eulogy concluded 'He has left for the forever land to join the cast of the big show where all good troupers go, and the billing now reads: "Playing at the Eternity Theatre in the Garden of Paradise".'

See JUGGLERS

FINNELL, CARRIE (1893-1963)

The Girl with the Million Dollar Legs

Miss Finnell, whose nether limbs were allegedly insured at Lloyd's of London for $100,000, was the pioneer of American strip-tease and especially of tassel twirling. It was said that the artiste had such muscular control over her bosom that she could make it swivel clockwise and counter-clockwise, and make it pop out of her bra of its own accord. In fact, Miss Finnell could make her breasts 'twitch, jump to attention, and do everything except sing *April Showers* in Swahili'.

An earlier artiste with precisely the same bill-matter was Frankie Bailey, whose legs supported her from 1859 until 1953.

See PHYLLIS DIXEY

FLANAGAN & ALLEN (fl1924-45)

Oi!

Bud Flanagan (1896-1968) and Chesney Allen (1894-1982) originated their much-loved comedy partnership while in *Flo & Co* with FLORRIE FORDE. Mr Flanagan was earlier *k.a.* Fargo *The Boy Wizard* and as Chick Harlem; he was with FRED KARNO and claimed at one time to have once walked from Barnet, North London, to Glasgow for an engagement. Notoriously bumptious and arrogant, this comedian was never above embroidering a story and we give leave to doubt the veracity of this particular Odyssey. We never met Mr Flanagan in person but backstage at the Victoria Palace one morning in 1959 when the Crazy Gang were *in situ* we spotted that his dressing-room door had been left open by the cleaners; we slipped in and for a few breathless moments donned the famous moth-eaten fur coat. We also once met a woman outside the Connaught Theatre in Worthing who alleged that her aunt had been Bud Flanagan's secretary.

Chesney Allen originally went on the stage as a light comedian in the legitimate theatre, crossing over to Variety after the Great War in which he served as an officer in the Royal West Kents. In 1945 arthritis forced this quiet-spoken and unassuming artiste's retirement from the boards; he became the Crazy Gang's agent and, as Fate was to decree, outlived them all.

On the opening night of *Underneath the Arches*, a celebration of the Flanagan & Allen partnership, we were sitting in the Chichester Festival Theatre to review the show for BBC radio. To our amazement and delight Chesney Allen appeared on stage, performing a characteristically bewildering cross-talk routine with ROY HUDD as his old sparring partner. It was intensely moving to see the last of the Crazy Gang who, despite his age of 86 and years of infirmity, seemed chipper and alert. Mr Allen stayed with the show for the season and played in the West End run just for the first few months, a wonderful end to a career which until then had been eclipsed by the ebullient Bud Flanagan and the antics of the rest of the Gang.

Mr Flanagan left £24,000 – a surprisingly large amount considering his life-long affection for lame race-horses – and Mr Allen £92,970.

See CHARLIE CHESTER, ALEC HURLEY

FLETCHER, CYRIL (b1913)

Odd Odes; Dreamin' of Thee

Poems were first heard on the Halls in the 1830s when CHARLES SLOMAN diverted London's song and supper rooms with his rhyming improvisations. At the end of the Victorian age Calliope was represented by the Misses NELLY LENNOX & KATE RALEIGH and in the Edwardian decade by J MILTON HAYES. In the 1920s and 1930s there emerged the incomparable parodies of BILLY BENNETT; in the 1930s Stanley Holloway (1890-1982) made a name for himself with much of Marriott Edgar's (1880-1951) repertoire (*The Lion and Albert, The Runcorn Ferry*, etc) and in the 1940s came the poetic comedian Vernon Watson (1886-1949), whose stage name of Nosmo King was whimsically inspired by seeing No Smoking thus divided on swing doors. In our own day we are fortunate enough to be able to appreciate Pam Ayres, a comic versifier who to our mind is the cleverest of them all.

Mr Fletcher's odes, whose prosodic structure was usually iambic tetrameter, were greatly enhanced by his distinctive cor anglais speaking voice and by a delivery which swooped startlingly from genteel RP to East End grotesque, often to signal the tag line.

Mrs Fletcher was professionally *k.a.* Betty Astell (b1912) *The Girl with the Crinoline Gown*, an exceptionally beautiful woman whose first appearance at the age of two was as an egg.

FORDE, FLORRIE (1876-1940)

Everybody's Favourite; The World's Greatest Chorus Singer

The strapping 21-year-old Antipodean made her début at the London Pavilion in 1897; her magnificent silvery-toned singing voice and charm of manner captivated the Town and Miss Forde remained a favourite until the end of her days. The artiste also had the knack of finding songs with fiendishly singable choruses; her repertoire in this regard is unmatched – *Flanagan, Has Anybody Here Seen Kelly?, Oh Oh Antonio, Pack Up Your Troubles, It's A Long Long Way To Tipperary* and *She's A Lassie From Lancashire* are just a few of the evergreen ditties associated with her name.

In 1990 while researching in the BBC gramophone library we came across the earliest recording Miss Forde made of her best-remembered song *Down At The Old Bull And Bush*, the engineer in attendance gingerly placed the 1904 cylinder on the player whereupon, alas, it fell to pieces.

Miss Forde was, as may be imagined, a popular principal boy in pantomime; the big-hearted *cantatrice* also starred in her own summer show on the Isle of Man for an astonishing thirty-six consecutive seasons.

See FLANAGAN & ALLEN, DONALD PEERS

FORDHAM, FRED
The Man without Talent

All we know of this gentleman is that he was an eccentric comedian who wore a flat cap (see WILKIE BARD); we relish Mr Fordham's bill-matter as an outstanding example of chutzpah. Another in this category is Ernie Gerrard who flourished in the 1930s and whose slogan was *Should be Hanged*. Also throwing hostages to fortune were ALEC HALLS, EDDIE MORRELL, Syd Railton (fl1930s) *He's Dead but He Won't Lie Down* and NORMAN WISDOM.

FORMBY, GEORGE snr (1877-1921)
The Lad from Wigan; The Wigan Nightingale

This entry is principally remembered today as the father of GEORGE FORMBY jnr. Formby snr was a popular figure on the Halls almost as well known for his hacking cough as for his comic songs. 'Ee, Ah'm coughing better tonight,' he would declare to universal mirth, 'Coughing summat champion.' Another quip would be directed to the musical director: 'Come on, I'll cough you for a shilling.' The awful reality was that the man was dying of consumption, and he knew it. But the necessity of providing for his family precluded the artiste from harbouring his waning strength and he literally worked himself to death, at the end having recourse to an oxygen tent in the wings.

Other 'gormless Northerners' were TOM FOY, SYDNEY HOWARD and Jack Pleasants (1874-1923) *The Bashful Limit* and *The Shy Comedian*. For other Nightingales see JENNY LIND.

FORMBY, GEORGE jnr (1904-61)
...and his 'Uke'; I'll Not Be Rushed; An Odd Fellow

Having grown too heavy to continue his apprenticeship as a jockey George jnr followed, *faute de mieux*, in the paternal footsteps. With his father's high-pitched penetrating delivery and broad Lancashire accent the son was to achieve an astonishing degree of popularity. For six consecutive years he was voted the country's most popular British film star; even more remarkable was the finding by Mass Observation that George jnr was preferred to *ITMA* and even Winston Churchill as a war-time morale booster, while in the USSR in 1944 the big-toothed, homely entertainer was second only to Stalin in public esteem.

We saw him but once on stage in an inconsequential domestic comedy in which he was prevailed upon to get out his ukulele ('Come on, Dad, give us a song') but we recall well his clear-cut presence and unforced breadth of personality, two God-given attributes which no amount of cleverness and technical ability can ever outshine.

Eyebrows were raised when within two months of the manically jealous Beryl Formby's death in 1961 her widower announced his betrothal to his long-term covert inamorata, school-mistress Pat Howson (1923-70). But a few scant weeks later Miss Howson was herself bereft, to be consoled (and the performer's family enraged) with a fortune of £135,000.

Other ukulele players – though some say Mr Formby's preferred instrument was the banjulele – were May Breen (1894?-1970?) *The Ukulele Lady,* Mildred Carroll (fl1940s-50s) *The Personality Girl with a Uke,* Cliff Edwards (1895-1971) *Ukulele Ike,* and DONALD PEERS.

FORSYTH, BRUCE (b1928)
The Incredible Character

As a child this entry was *k.a.* Boy Bruce *The Mighty Atom,* but when we saw him in pantomime at the Palace Manchester Mr Forsyth had entered into his adult domain and his accomplished dancing, singing and piano-playing were overlaid with a verve and a dynamism that had audiences eating out of his hand. As Dick Whittington he so enthralled us that by the time he came to propose to Alice Fitzwarren we were positively wriggling with anticipatory delight. How sad then that the artiste should have turned to the house at this most critical of moments with a toothy grin and said 'This is me doing my serious acting bit...' Of course there was a laugh because theatre audiences are polite, but wasn't it a shame that Mr Forsyth did not have the sensitivity or the self-discipline to take the moment?

It is notable that unlike most senior entertainers this performer has not achieved the respect enjoyed by his peers. We suggest that this is not due to any falling off of his powers nor for his having traded in two wives for younger models; no, rather is it that the sniggering classes will never respect a man who sports a whirly.

FORSYTHE, SEAMON & FARRELL (fl1930s-50s)
Get Hot; A Ton of Fun

Charles Forsythe, a generously proportioned Canadian with a rich baritone voice, was the husband of Miss Addie Seamon, an artiste from New Jersey whose acrobatic dancing and humorous non-sequiturs enlivened the proceedings no end. The third member of this bizarre but mightily popular trio was Miss Elinore Farrell whose *embonpoint* presided at the piano. After Miss Farrell's departure Mr & Mrs Forsythe continued as a double, but the magic was lost.

FOSTER, VIVIAN (1868-1945)
The Vicar of Mirth

The Church of England parson was long a figure of fun on the Halls but this entry is the only artiste, as far as we are aware, whose entire career was predicated upon the humour extractable from Anglican clericity. It is true that the customary stage-dress of GEORGE ROBEY was that of a semi-frocked minister of dubious persuasion but Mr Robey's material could never have been described as ecclesiastical. Mr Foster was sometimes billed by his catch-phrase *Yes, I Think So.*

We also list Howard Rogers (d1971?) *Not So Bad* with this entry because alternative bill-matter for Mr Rogers was *The Popular Padre*, but we know no more of him than that.

See GEORGE GRAY

FOY, TOM (1879-1917)
The Yorkshire Lad

Despite his bill-matter Mr Foy was born in Manchester. After the manner of the times the dialect comedian's wife and their three children were pressed into stage service in such sketches as *Fun in a Fiacre* and *Tom Foy and his Donkey*, which latter item utilised an actual ass.

In his solo turns Mr Foy customarily appeared as a gormless, woman-dominated gowk, a character greatly to the taste of North Country audiences at that time. This artiste's final performance was given at the Argyle Theatre, Birkenhead, which was where, thirty-nine years later, we were to commence our career.

Mr Foy was not related to the great American vaudevillian Eddie Foy (1856-1928) whose *Seven Little Foys* were almost as celebrated as their father.

See GEORGE FORMBY snr

FRAGSON, HARRY (1869-1913)

The Caruso of the Halls; Protean; The Singer of the Entente Cordiale

Enrico Caruso (1873-1921) was the greatest tenor of the day; the misleading nature of this billing would have appealed to Fragson's cult following. The word 'Protean' seems odd also, for Fragson had a particularly (some said repellently) idiosyncratic manner whereas Proteus, a mythical Greek prophet, was able to change shape rapidly at will.

Howsoever, this stylishly original artiste was a subtler than usual Music Hall entertainer at the piano with a discriminating following on both sides of the Channel, except for his father, Victor Pott, who shot him dead (see illustration 24).

The American comedienne and siffleuse Helen Trix (1892-1951) was billed as *The Feminine Fragson* and married to Frank Fogarty (c1875-1925) *The Dublin Minstrel*.

By 1931 the Fragson tragedy was sufficiently remote for Tom F Moss (1898-1980) to usurp the billing of *The Caruso of the Halls*; for other Carusos see BETTY AUKLAND; for other piano-entertainers see MARGARET COOPER. Other Proteans are under OWEN McGIVENEY.

FRAME, W F 'Wullie' (1848-1919)

The Apostle of Fun; The Man U'Know

In 1908 at the age of 60 this artiste, unwisely encouraged by Charles (*Two Lovely Black Eyes* and *The Man that Broke the Bank at Monte Carlo*) Coborn, came to London to give the capital a taste of his quality. Alas, the Metropolis could only assimilate one comic kiltie at a time and that was HARRY LAUDER. Mr Frame's accent was too Caledonian and his tam o'shanter too ethnically pawky for effete southern tastes and despite a promising début at the Alhambra the comedian swiftly retreated to the lee of Hadrian's Wall where he was appreciated and intelligible.

FRANKAU, RONALD (1894-1951)

The Aristocrat of Entertainers; The Low High-Brow; ...with Monte Crick at the piano

This entry and MICHAEL BENTINE are, we think, the only two Variety artistes to have been educated at Eton College. In Mr Frankau's case the benefits are evident in the prolificity of his material for concert-party, cabaret and revue, much of it highly sophisticated, i.e. filthy. When fellow-comedian Claude Dampier was banned from the air waves for three months for a remark about having to dash away because he had 'promised to squeeze Mrs Gibson's oranges' Mr Frankau made his celebrated *bon mot* that 'to the pure there's nothing pure'.

In 1930 with TOMMY HANDLEY the performer initiated a popular radio cross-talk duo North & South, in 1934 to become even more so as, respectively, the rapid-fire nonsensical Mr Murgatroyd & Mr Winterbottom *Two Minds without a Single Thought.*

Mr Frankau's accompanist Monte Crick (1908-69) later took over the rôle of Dan Archer from its creator Harry Oakes in *The Archers,* the BBC radio 'everyday story of country folk' which has run since 1950 and in which we ourself have very occasionally been heard.

See CLAPHAM & DWYER, THE ZANCIGS

FRINTON, FREDDIE (1911-68)

Foolish but Funny

It was at the Ardwick Green Hippodrome that we had the fine treat of seeing Mr Frinton's legendary sketch *Dinner for One* in which the old butler becomes progressively more inebriated as he fills and then, at the behest of Her Ladyship (May Walden 1895-1982), empties the glasses of the absent guests. The comedian's lurching from dinner-table to sideboard and his negotiation of the midway hazard of the lion's-head rug were quite wonderfully varied.

Mr Frinton was taken to Las Vegas, but both high and low rollers found the item too tame and his engagement was cut short. In Germany *Dinner for One* has since 1971 been shown annually on New Year's Eve television and has become as much a part of the season's traditions as *gans* and *bleigiessen.* Who says the Germans have no sense of humour?

Another artiste who considered himself *Foolish but Funny* was Tom Fox (d December 12th 1939).

See JOHNNY COOPER, Len Lowe & Audrey May (MISCELLANEOUS), SKETCH ARTISTES

G

GANJOU BROTHERS & JUANITA, THE (fl1929-57)
A Romance in Porcelain

These astonishing artistes were one of the very few speciality acts to achieve Top of the Bill status. They are happily preserved for posterity in the 1943 film *Variety Jubilee* in which Juanita is discovered in an 18th-century ballroom as the gently swinging pendulum of an ornamental clock. The musical intensity increases as her tiny Dresden figure is thrown from hand to hand at a speed which almost defies belief, arching and turning and spinning and whirling in a thrilling display of spectacle and artistry. It was all beautifully executed and hair-raisingly dangerous.

See GASTON & ANDRÉE

GASCOYNE, Mme (fl c1900s)
The Only Clock-Eyed Lady in the World

Bridget Caine was born in Stockton-on-Tees, a town then in Yorkshire. We came across her bill-matter quite unexpectedly in a newspaper report and puzzled as to its import. Then we discovered that Mme Gascoyne was the mother of MACARI who stated that his progenitrix 'showed at Crystal Palace and Reynold's Waxworks, Liverpool, and all parts of the Continent'.

    Mr Macari's son Larry informs us that his grandmother did not really have an act as such but that she displayed 'the whites of her eyes which had markings resembling the Roman numerals on a clock'.

See p.13, Will Atkins (MISCELLANEOUS)

GASTON & ANDRÉE (fl1928-40s?)
Beauty and Rhythm; Dance Artistry

These two superb physical specimens introduced the acrobatic-adagio act to Variety, a novelty so powerfully attractive that the executants were soon Top of the Bill. Jimmy Gaston (d1966) at one time worked with his brother – or possibly his cousin – as Jimmy Wood & Arthur Cragg *Art in Athletics*. Rosemary Andrée (d1974) was also billed as

Britain's Venus, The Pocket Venus and *The World's Most Photographed Girl,* none of which claims would we dispute for the gymnast was a spectacularly beautiful woman.

Though this entry pioneered adagio dancing on the Halls THE GANJOU BROTHERS & JUANITA were the first to feature adagio with one girl and *three men,* a very important distinction in the world of Variety where originality is all.

See The Famous Craggs (SKETCH ARTISTES)

GENEIVE, Mme (1827-63)
The Female Blondin

In private life this tragic lady was Mrs M Edward Powell née Selina Hunt, not to be confused with SELINA YOUNG. Though seven months pregnant Mme Geneive, with a disabled husband and six children to support, was still walking the tightrope.

On July 20th 1863, at a Foresters' fête in Aston Park, Birmingham, the rope broke; the performer fell thirty feet and was killed instantly as was her unborn child. At the inquest her husband deposed that 'it was not uncommon for pregnant women to walk the rope. They considered themselves safer when in that condition than otherwise'.

Mr Powell also said that one Mme Rossini had ascended a very high rope at Vauxhall, Birmingham, some years previously and had been confined the same night. The Park Committee voted the widower and his children £16.

See BLONDIN

GILSON, LOTTIE (1869-1912)
The Little Magnet

Grateful American theatre managers first called this dynamic soubrette *The Little Magnet* because she was such a draw. The performer is also said to have been the first to be paid hard cash to popularise a song.

GITANA, GERTIE (1887-1957)
The Star who Never Fails to Shine

This entry, whose earlier billings include *Dainty Comedienne* and *The Idol of the People,* started her career with Tomlinson's Royal Gipsy Children as Little Gitana. The small, beetle-browed singer with the toothy smile married agent-impresario Don Ross (1902-80) and, according to *The Times*, enjoyed a degree of success with 'the less sophisticated type of audience, especially in the suburbs and provinces'. And indeed the artiste's excruciatingly drawn-out renditions of *Nellie Dean, Never Mind* and *Silver Bell* were very acceptable to many as were her other accomplishments which included step-dancing and playing the saxophone.

See GUS HARRIS, DAISY JAMES

GODFREY, CHARLES (1851-1900)
The Star of All Comic Stars

We find this bill-matter curious for Mr Godfrey was a singer who specialised in 'descriptive' songs, that is to say narrative ditties of a strongly dramatic nature with marked changes of mood and tempo. This entry was also well-regarded for his stridently patriotic effusions such as *On Guard – A Story of Balaclava, The 7th Royal Fusiliers* and *The English Speaking Race Against the World.* If the sun never set on the British Empire it soon set on Mr Godfrey, for he died of general excess at the age of only 48.

GORDON, HARRY (1893-1959)
The Laird o' Inversnecky

This entry was a short bespectacled Aberdonian of astonishing comedic versatility, claiming a repertoire of over three hundred character sketches all penned by himself, besides dozens of radio broadcasts and revue and concert-party items. As a pantomime Dame Mr Gordon was supreme, appearing at the Glasgow Alhambra for no fewer than sixteen consecutive seasons – seven of them with his great friend and fellow comic Will Fyffe (1885-1947).

If the reader will permit a slight digression may we say that we had intended to include a substantive entry on Mr Fyffe, but Will Fyffe jnr informs us that his illustrious father was not known to have had any specific bill-matter. We regret therefore that we cannot dwell upon this fine artiste, for ever remembered as the composer and original performer of *I Belong To Glasgow*, and whose life closed when he accidentally fell from a window of the Rusacks Hotel in St Andrews.

Thus ended with tragic prematurity the career of one whom the eminent theatre critic James Agate unequivocally declared to be a genius.

GOUFFÉ, M.

Man Monkey

John Hornshaw's simian début was made in an 1825 entertainment at the transpontine New Surrey Theatre entitled *Jean Fernandez or The Island Ape*. The performance concluded with the artiste 'running around the Fronts of the Boxes and Gallery, supported only by minute Mouldings'. Such was the appeal of this novelty that Monkey Plays became a popular sub-genre with 'Monsieur Gouffé' their most celebrated delineator.

In 1837 Mr Hornshaw retired, to be replaced by one Sam Todd, a subterfuge which seems to have passed unremarked. Mr Todd lacked his predecessor's finesse, however, for of one of his early performances *The Times* thundered that 'the manager would do well to restrain some of the liberties this gentleman occasionally takes with the audience or get rid of him altogether; the indecencies of a monkey may be copied too closely to be tolerated.'

See CHARLES LAURI jnr, Hervio Nano (Mlle ALMA), Olmar (KING OF...)

GRAD & GOLD (fl1927-8)

The Charleston Champions; The Lightning Strutters; The XN Trick Dancers

These two hoofers were LEW GRADE and Al Gold (1905-88).

GRADE, LEW (Lord) (1906-98)

Charleston Champion of London; Charleston Champion of Great Britain; Charleston Champion of the World; The Dancer with the Humorous Feet; The Man with the Musical Feet

This entry was the brother of Leslie Grade (1916-79) and Bernard Delfont (see DELFONT & TOKO); their sister was briefly a singer *k.a.* Rita Gray (b1925) *Sweet Sophistication*. After hanging up his pumps (see GRAD & GOLD) Mr Grade became Britain's most powerful and ubiquitous entrepreneur. Like brother Bernard he achieved both knighthood and peerage, and also like Bernard he married out, his wife being Kathy Moody (b1921) *The Singing Starlet.*

Mr Grade was once twitted with scheduling too much trivial light entertainment on his television station at Christmas. 'I put on an hour of Gilbert and Sullivan!' expostulated the indignant impresario. 'No one can call *that* entertainment...'

See Eddie Gordon & Nancy (BICYCLE ACTS), DELFONT & TOKO, VICKI LESTER

GRAY, DUNCAN (1893-1969)
Accused of Being Funny – Found Guilty

Whether this was the correct verdict we do not know but we can produce this quote from the artiste's own *curriculum vitae*: 'When 17 joined Chris Baker as assistant, singing and playing the graduated bottles in a number *Doh Ray Me* and other songs until 1914.'

GRAY, 'Monsewer' EDDIE (1898-1969)
Juggler-May-Be

This bespectacled, red-nosed, handlebar-moustached artiste was long acknowledged as the comedian's comedian and though never a star was a particular favourite with Variety-goers. Mr Gray's insouciant style of jugglery while pattering in Franglais – '*Moi* is going to throw the hoop and *vous* is going to catch it' – remains unapproached.

Despite his reputation for practical jokes both on and off stage the performer was a quiet-living and unclubbable man, ever resentful of the scale of his 'remuneration' and the fact that despite his personal stature and his many years' service as a member of the Crazy Gang he was always the lowest-paid of the team.

See JUGGLERS

GRAY, GEORGE (b c1863)
The Fighting Parson

Although we stated earlier that VIVIAN FOSTER was the only clergyman on the Halls we should more accurately have said that Mr Foster was Variety's only *comic* cleric, for George Gray's melodrama sketch *The Fighting Parson* toured the Halls for some ten years from 1903. The Reverend's fist-fight with an unrepentent sinner in the fifth and final scene was invariably received with roars of approval, for there was nothing your British Music Hall audience liked more than a robust exhibition of muscular Christianity.

See CHARLES AUSTIN, JOHN LAWSON, SKETCH ARTISTES

GRAYSON, LARRY (1923-95)
He's Priceless!

Apart from female impersonators this entry (originally *k.a.* Billy Breen) was the first overtly homosexual entertainer. There had been other limp-wristed, lisping comics – Ray Martine, for instance, was a regular television face in the late 1950s and early 1960s – but not until 1970 did the West End experience the epicene hypochondria with which Mr Grayson convulsed his admirers. The nation's sitting rooms had to wait until 1972, a full five years after the Sexual Offences Act had helped to soften attitudes (and *fifteen* years after the Wolfenden Committee had reported). It must be admitted that not all gays appreciated this performer's emphatic projection of the undiluted quean.

GREEN, HUGHIE (1924-97)
...and his BBC Gang; Britain's 14-year-old Broadcasting Wonder

'Uncle Hughie' as this entry liked to be known ran his talent show on radio and television for nearly thirty years, giving a useful boost to the careers of, *inter alia*, Russ Abbot, Pam Ayres, Frank Carson, Mary Hopkin, Bonnie Langford, Little & Large, Tom O'Connor, Peters & Lee, and Freddie Starr.

Mr Green was a compulsive talker, a tiresome, difficult man of rolling-eyed insincerity and paranoid disposition whose feuds with the BBC led to bankruptcy and visits from the bailiffs. His funeral was enlivened by revelations that at one time the deceased had run a wife and four mistresses simultaneously.

Hughie Green's godfather was HARRY TATE.

GRIFFITHS, BROTHERS (fl1876-1937)

The Safe Men on a Silver Bar and Magical Hatters; We're the Only Two that's Left in All the Family

These two acrobatic knockabouts were originally Fred Delaney (1856-1940) and Joe Ridgeway (1852-1901); after Joe died Fred was joined by his son Fred jnr and occasionally his daughter Lutie (d1945). The act's two most celebrated routines were *The Blondin Donkey* and *Pogo the Performing Horse,* both of which by common consent represented the pinnacle of animal burlesque. The act worked the Halls for over sixty years, a remarkable and unique record.

See BLONDIN, SKETCH ARTISTES

H

HACKFORD & DOYLE (fl1945-50s)
Wood & Wind – Mostly Wind

The bill-matter of this comedy musical duo is fondly remembered by Variety buffs, though all we have been able to discover about the artistes is that John Doyle was born in Newcastle in 1908, that he spent five years with BILLY COTTON and six with the Royal Air Force before teaming up with Hackford in 1945.

Details of his partner have resisted research though we can reveal that this team invariably finished their act in time-honoured fashion with a dance.

See DR CROCK

HAIG, JACK (1913-89)
The Life of the Party; Nutty but Nice

Born in Wigan, Mr Haig was a diminutive comedian with a large ego. Belated recognition came with his rôle as M. Le Clerc in the long-running television situation comedy *Allo! Allo!* An artiste of our close acquaintance who had the misfortune to share a dressing-room with Mr Haig informed us of his habit of urinating in the wash-basin without rinsing it out afterwards.

MORRIS & COWLEY also considered themselves to be *The Life of the Party*, whereas George Doonan (1897-1973) went one better as *The Life and Soul of the Party*.

HALA (fl c1880-1908)
The Shooting Star

Bristol-born trapezist Robert Barton suffered for his art with one accident leaving him with a severely broken leg and another with a silver plate in his head. But as is so often the case with these hardy folk the artiste remained undaunted by misadventure or the rigours of 19th-century surgery.

HALL, ADELAIDE (1910-93)

The Brown Venus; The Crooning Blackbird; Singing Songs – and How

The Brooklyn-born artiste was one of the finest jazz singers of her generation. After running a night club in Paris Miss Hall chose in 1938, like her friend and fellow American Elizabeth Welch before her, to settle in England, and we count ourself fortunate to have seen and worked with both these legends.

We are happy to report that at the time of writing Miss Welch (b1908) *Syncopating Songstress*, with whom we have had the pleasure of speaking at Denville Hall, is as sharp and spiky as ever.

HALLS, ALEC (1904-84)

The Big Stiff; A Cavalcade of Junk

This comedy musician earns his entry as the only performer to be appointed MBE for his work with ENSA (Entertainments National Service Association) in the Middle and Far East. Mr Halls, who was professor of the accordion, the piano, the trombone, the trumpet, drums and bagpipes, is also inexcludable because he was Dame Marie Tempest's second cousin.

See DR CROCK. Also see EDDIE MORRELL for identical bill-matter.

HANCOCK, TONY (1924-68)

The Confidential Comic

Mr Hancock worked his way through Ralph Reader's RAF Gang Shows to concert-party to the WINDMILL THEATRE, a not unusual route taken by aspiring post-war entertainers. The comedian's big break was as tutor to Archie Andrews in the hugely popular radio series *Educating Archie*. We saw him on the boards more than once and were greatly struck by this artiste's massive presence and large features which so clearly registered from the farthest seats. Mr Hancock's personal and professional worries led him to take his own life in his hotel room in Australia, a melancholy exit also taken by his predecessor as Archie Andrews' tutor, ROBERT MORETON.

See PETER BROUGH & ARCHIE ANDREWS, REG DIXON, BILL KERR, PETER SELLERS, ROBB WILTON. Also see Mrs SHUFFLEWICK.

HANDLEY, TOMMY (1894-1949)

The Disorderly Room

This musical skit on an Army court martial arose from experiences of World War I service life and was still being worked by Mr Handley during the Second Unpleasantness. The original script was by Eric Blore who went to Hollywood in 1923 and made a corner in snooty butlers.

Tommy Handley is principally enshrined in broadcasting legend and in the hearts of the British people as the pivotal figure in the comedy series *ITMA* ('It's That Man Again' - a reference to one Adolf Hitler) which ran from 1939 until the comedian's unexpected and much lamented death ten years later.

Radio used to revel in voices which had authority, pungency, resonance, and clarity; voices which seized and held the attention. Mr Handley, a Liverpudlian like so many entertainers, had just such a delivery and remains to this day the pre-eminent radio comedian.

We were surprised to discover that this entry also made a brief *sound* film for the British Empire Exhibition in 1924, as did TOMMY TRINDER.

See RONALD FRANKAU, SKETCH ARTISTES

HANLON-LEES, THE (est c1860)

Entortillationists

This descriptive slogan is derived from the French for entwined or entangled, but in 1876 the six Hanlon brothers (protégés of John Lees) announced that they were 'no longer in the arena of Gymnastic and Acrobatic art'. From then on the troupe presented elaborately mounted comedy mime sketches, the most celebrated being *A Journey to Switzerland* (*Voyage en Suisse*). Hanlon-Lees troupes were performing in the 1920s and doubtless are to this very day.

See SKETCH ARTISTES

HARCOURT, JESSIE (1876-1900)

The Child Baritone

Since the poor lassie departed this life at the age of only 24 we have no information to impart other than to record Miss Harcourt's bill-matter which reflected the curious popularity on the Halls around the turn of the century of freak vocalists, e.g. Bobbie Cook (1905-81) *Boy Contralto*, Ella Dean *Double-Voiced Vocalist*, BERT ERROL, Nellie Gertine *Lady Character Baritone Vocalist*, PERCY HENRY, Alberta Laine *One Girl Two Voices*, and Alice Lloyd *England's Only Female Tenor*. This last artiste fl1870s and should not be confused with the ALICE LLOYD entered *infra*.

HARLOW, JEAN (1911-37)
The Platinum Blonde

The forward modernity and blatant sexuality of this film player thrilled women and intimidated men the world over. The stridency of her image was matched by her private life for in a tragically short life Miss Harlow was married three times, her second husband killing himself within a few months of their nuptials. Nonetheless this entry did not deserve her awful fate: an agonising and unnecessary death of uraemic poisoning. Her mother was an adherent of that Christian cult which considers it impious to consult medical practitioners, and so her wretched daughter was condemned to perish in the stench of her own urine at the age of 26. It is said that at a Hollywood party attended by Margot Lady Asquith (1864-1945) the actress enquired as to the pronunciation of her first name. 'The T is silent,' came the reply, 'as in Harlow.' We believe this story to be a myth, for we cannot accept that any English lady, especially the widow of a Prime Minister, would ever be so gratuitously offensive.

HARMER, DOLLY (1867-1956)
The Rum 'Un

A favourite in musical comedies of the 1890s, Miss Harmer has her place in Variety history as WEE GEORGIE WOOD's stage mother. The artiste essayed the character from 1917 until her death at the astounding (and carefully hidden) age of 89. Prior to Miss Harmer the rôle was briefly sustained by IDA BARR.

During World War II the act toured widely under the auspices of ENSA entertaining Allied troops, earning Miss Harmer the title *Mother of the Forces*.

HARRIS, GUS (fl c1890s-30s)

Entertainer and Elocutionist; The Great Versatile Hebrew Comedian; The Only Yiddisher Scotsman in the Irish Fusiliers; The People's Popular Chorus Idol

This artiste was never as popular as his wife, the statuesque IDA BARR, and his resentment of her greater success destroyed their marriage. The second instance of his various billings indicates the basis of Mr Harris' style, the third derives from his best-known song.

This entry must not be confused – though it is exceedingly unlikely that he ever would be – with Sir Augustus Harris (1852-96), manager of Drury Lane Theatre.

For other artistes who worked Jewish see ISSY BONN. Other 'Idols' were James Bland (1854-1911) *The Idol of the Halls*, Arthur Corney *The London Idol* also *The Unobtrusive*, GERTIE GITANA, Harry Linn *The Idol of the North*, EUGENE STRATTON, Jenny Valmore (b c1865) *The People's Idol*, and VESTA TILLEY.

HAY, WILL (1888-1949)

Britain's Master of Comedy; The Eccentric Comedian; The Schoolmaster Comedian

Will Hay, whose early career was like so many others with FRED KARNO, also used as bill-matter the titles of his sketches such as *The Fourth Form at St Michael's* and *Inkstain's Theory*, the latter inspired by the work of the great physicist Albert Einstein. It was Mr Hay's good fortune to light upon an untapped vein of humour: the inadequate dominie. The comedian's shifty, seedy, ignorant, pince-nez'd minor public schoolmaster was forever one of life's remittance men, a second-rate con-artist always out of his depth but somehow just keeping his head above water. The character was original and well-founded, for this entry's repertoire of bafflement, bemusement and affronted outrage as the boys scored one over him yet again was unceasingly entertaining, especially if one happened to be a schoolboy oneself.

Off-stage Mr Hay was an amateur astronomer of considerable stature – having written a book on his discovery of a white spot on Saturn he was elected a Fellow of the Royal Astronomical Society.

The performer's most celebrated foils were Graham 'fat boy Albert'

Moffatt (1920-65) and Moore 'senile Harbottle' Marriott (1885-1949); from 1925-33 the 'Cheeky Boy' was his son Will Hay jnr (b1913).

See SKETCH ARTISTES

HAYDN, RICHARD (1905-85)
The Only Living Fish Mimic

In 1938 Mr Haydn, whose unique piscine talents were first exhibited under the name of Professor Edwin Carp, went to the United States in a revue with (Sir) Noël Coward and BEATRICE LILLIE; from Broadway the artiste gravitated to Hollywood, there to carve out a second career which reached its apogee with the rôle of Max Dettweiler in *The Sound of Music.*

HAYES, ELTON (fl1930s-50s?)
He Sings to a Small Guitar

The rhythm of this artiste's bill-matter (derived from Edward Lear's poem *The Owl and the Pussy-Cat*) lent itself all to readily to parody including such unkind versions as *He Coughs to a Slight Catarrh.* Mr Hayes' songs were of the 'too-ra-li-oo-ra-li' *faux naïf* folk-song variety and it was no surprise to see him in green tights adorning a film version of Robin Hood as the outlaw minstrel Alan-a-Dale. On the wireless this entry's voice was reedy and quavery and we were always relieved when he finished.

HAYES, J MILTON (1884-1940)
The Laugh-Smith with a Philosophy

Of all the songs and sketches and recitations which flowed from this entry's fertile pen only one dating from 1911 was ever likely to survive: *The Green Eye of the Little Yellow God,* a poem whose parodic and burlesque possibilities were eagerly seized upon by the likes of BILLY BENNETT (*The Green Tie on the Little Yellow Dog*) and Leslie Henson (1891-1957), a very popular pugfaced revue artiste whom we once saw in an uproarious sketch version of the poem called *Pukka Sahib.* Even we ourself must confess to having published a two-handed version for 'reciter and gesticulator'.

See BIG BILL CAMPBELL, CYRIL FLETCHER

HAYMAN & FRANKLIN (est 1899)
The Gossips from the Ghetto

Joe Hayman was an American Jewish comedian whose stage partner Mildred Franklin (1875-1954) also shared his life. The Jewish experience of East European persecution and Russian pogroms was very much part of the New York ethos; in London it barely impinged upon traditional East End Cockney life which is perhaps why the novelty of this entry's act made them so successful when they first appeared in Britain in 1904. And in Britain they remained, with Mrs Hayman surviving long enough to see a terrible renewal of the word which she and her husband had long before used so light-heartedly: Ghetto.

See ISSY BONN

HAYNES, ARTHUR (1914-66)
A Good Boy in Bad Company; Keeps Things Moving

The first billing was for a *Stars in Battledress* production, the second for a Forces' show in which this entry was listed as Sapper Arthur Haynes. The comedian's forte was the exudation of a slyly malicious insolence which baffled, infuriated and finally defeated those icily superior bureaucrats which were perhaps more prevalent in the days of jobs-for-life than now.

One of the very earliest occasions on which we had the nerve to impose ourself upon the nation's television screens was in a two-handed black-out sketch with Mr Haynes. We do not recall any notes from the star but we do remember being given minute directions by his feed, one Nicholas Parsons.

HEARNE, RICHARD (1909-70)
Mr Pastry

This entry was trained in acrobatics by his father, Richard Hearne snr, a background which accounts for the physicality of much of Richard jnr's comedy. The artiste's national celebrity was founded upon his eccentric old gentleman *Mr Pastry* in which guise we once saw him dance his famous one-man Lancers, a routine originated by the comedian Tom D Newell who appeared in it as a woman.

The business was passed on to Mr Hearne by Mr Newell's grieving widow – her husband, while out hunting in 1935, had been inadvertently shot to death. But, as we've said, the solo Lancers made Mr Hearne's fortune so every cloud has a silver lining.

See DANTE

HEMSLEY, HARRY (MAY) (1877-1951)
Child-Life

No artiste achieved such prominence in so narrowly specialised a field as this entry, for Mr Hemsley was that *rara avis* a child imitator. In fact we know of only one other, Wilson Hallett, whose career remains shadowy. Mr Hemsley's Radio Family included his 'daughter' Winnie who alone was able to understand the babblings of baby Horace. 'What did Horace say, Winnie?' became a catch-phrase of the day, making the lives of real Horaces and Winnies a misery.

HENDERSON, DICK (1891-1958)
The (Yorkshire) Comedian who Sings

This entry was a fat bowler-hatted cigar-chewing comic who, according to his son DICKIE HENDERSON, was the first to finish with a straight song. We saw him but once and found the blueness of his material and lack of charm quite repellent.

HENDERSON, DICKIE (1922-85)
A Smile, a Song and a Dance; Nonchalant Nonsense

Originally *k.a.* Dick Henderson jnr this artiste was an extremely attractive, skilful and multi-faceted light entertainer whose Variety work we greatly savoured, especially his inept would-be Sinatra, falling off the bar-stool and being sabotaged by an unhelpful stage-hand on the other end of the microphone cable. Mr Henderson spoke with a slight American accent (acquired from a seven year sojourn in California at a tender age) which added to his appeal, for in the post-war years everything American was redolent of sophistication and glamour.

The performer's sisters Winnie (1920-c55) and Triss (Theresa) (b1920) worked as The Henderson Twins *Singing and Swinging* and *A Song, a Smile and a Dance.* Their father was DICK HENDERSON.

In the 1950s Joan Price & Barry Speed were also displaying *With a Song, a Smile, a Dance,* bill-matter construction which would appear to have been pioneered by NORMAN LONG and much copied, *viz* Syd Jackson (c1920-98) *A Song, a Smile and an Accordion.*

HENDERSON, EDDIE (fl1930s-60s)
Alive – Alive – O!

The only reason we include this comedian is that we once were in a play he wrote and starred in on the south coast called *Summer Laughter.* It wasn't very good and neither was he. Nor, for that matter, were we.

HENDERSON, MAY (1885-1937)
The Dusky Queen

As her bill-matter indicates this comedienne worked in black-face, one of the very few lady artistes to do so. There were other female 'coon-shouters' as they were called, such as NELLIE CHRISTIE, VICTORIA MONKS, ELLA SHIELDS (before her male-impersonation days), the erratic May Yohé (1869-1938), and the pioneer of the *genre* Bessie Wentworth (1874-1901), though these ladies eschewed the traditional burnt-cork make-up.

Nellie Richards (1864-1932) *America's Pride* and *The American Violet* came over with Haverly's Minstrels, which makes the artiste one of the few ladies to appear in a Minstrel Troupe. Whether Miss Richards blacked up or not we cannot say for sure, but on the balance of probabilities we would say that she did. Another visitor to our shores was Winifred E Johnson, whose details are listed under the entry for her husband R G KNOWLES.

Lastly under this entry we draw attention to Syd Wickard *The Dusky Kid* who flourished in the 1920s and 30s.

See BERT ERROL, G H ELLIOTT, T D RICE

HENLERE, HERSCHEL 'Jizz' (1888-1968)
The Famous Canadian Composer; The Mirthful Music Master

This artiste was an eccentric but extremely clever and deservedly popular novelty pianist, known and feared throughout the Profession for grossly over-running. Finally Moss Empires took to putting him on last so the house curtain could be dropped in on him. One must assume that, like KEN DODD, this entry loved his work and never liked to leave the shop. Mr Henlere specialised in breath-takingly swift switches from one melody to another, also in playing popular tunes in incongruent styles.

For other purveyors of musical humour see DR CROCK; for other pianists see WINIFRED ATWELL.

HENRY, PERCY (1874-1953)

Champion Boy Tenor of the World; The Pocket Sims Reeves; The Wonderful Infantine Tenor

It was while this entry was appearing in Paris in 1883 with Virto & Thompson *The Musical Savages* that a French printer first rendered Percy Henry Thompson's middle name as Honri. The young artiste decided he liked the Gallicisation and kept it, hence the separate entry for PERCY HONRI. (Virto's daughter, born c1888, achieved modest eminence as Mlle Renée *The Greatest Ocarina Player in the World*, bless her.)

Others to compare themselves with J Sims Reeves were HENRY COLLARD and VESTA TILLEY. For other juvenile prodigies see Master WILLIAM BETTY and for freak voices see JESSIE HARCOURT.

HERTZ, CARL (1859-1924)

The King of Cards

This magician's reputation lost some of its lustre when it was rumoured that his Flying Birdcage effect necessitated the squashing to death of a canary at each performance. The artiste denied the calumny and the British public accepted his word. In fact the rumour was true but the wizard abandoned the illusion and did not perform it again. In 1914 Mr Hertz was obliged to issue another denial, that he was an American and not a filthy Hun.

Other monarchs of the paste-boards were HOUDINI and HOWARD THURSTON, whereas Charles Ovalden (fl c1910) aspired only to be *Knave of Cards*.

See ANIMAL & BIRD ACTS, KING OF..., MAGICIANS

HILL, BENNY (1925-92)

Ribbing the Hipps

After demobilisation this artiste underwent a lengthy and frustrating Variety apprenticeship, unable for some years to unlock his comic potential and failing even to secure an engagement at the WINDMILL. From 1948-50 he was feed to REG VARNEY; *Ribbing the Hipps* derives from an act during this period in which Mr Hill parodied the kind of tired old Variety turns still regularly to be seen in the High Street Hippodromes in most major cities.

Despite many set-backs the comedian persevered; his provincial reputation grew and by 1952 he was a major television star. But the unabashed seaside-postcard bawdiness which was this entry's stock-in-trade became increasingly offensive to the feminist lobby and after more than twenty years the show was scrapped by Thames Television. But by then it was too late: Hill was an international star and a multi-millionaire. His will was proved at £7,548,192.

HILL, JENNY (1849/50-96)

The Vital Spark

This entry was first billed as *Comédienne* but it was Dan Saunders, manager of the Star Music Hall Liverpool, who around the year 1877 suggested *The Vital Spark*. Miss Hill's cards in *The Era* sometimes declared that *None but Herself can be her Parallel*; we have also seen the artiste referred to as *Queen of the Halls*, a billing more usually associated with BESSIE BELLWOOD.

VESTA TILLEY wrote of this performer, 'If I were asked who, in my opinion, was the greatest artiste we ever had on the Variety stage, I would unhesitatingly plump for Miss Jenny Hill.' Alas, early privations had undermined her health and *The Vital Spark* was extinguished at the age of only 46 or thereabouts.

Miss Hill's elder daughter originally went on the Halls as Letty Pasta *Unapproached and Unapproachable*; in her teens Miss Pasta (b1869) abandoned her father's stage-name and took the name by which, although only lightly touched with her mother's genius, she became a popular and respected singer-dancer: Peggy Pryde *Jenny Hill Number 2*.

For other 'Sparks' see LILY LANGTRY. Also see MARIE LLOYD, QUEEN OF..., ELLA RETFORD.

HOGAN, ERNEST (1865-1909)

The Unbleached American

Mr Hogan was a black singer and song-writer whose popular song *All Coons Look Alike To Me* (1896) haunted him to the grave.

HOLLIDAY, MICHAEL (1925-63)

Television's Friendly Voice

This singer employed a relaxed, intimate style perfectly suited to home viewing, hence his billing. Mr Holliday's singing voice startlingly resembled that of arch-crooner Bing Crosby (1903-77), which in the late 1950s and early 60s did him no harm at all. What did harm him were HM Commissioners of Inland Revenue who drove the poor man literally to suicide. This entry left £9,796 and a family; also a manager, HAL MONTY, who should perhaps have taken better care of his client.

HONRI, PERCY (1874-1953)

The World's Greatest Concertinist

Mr Honri made his professional début as a clog-dancer at the age of five under the name of PERCY HENRY; while still in his teens he was producing his own elaborately mounted full-length revues and burlettas. Although skilled on a variety of musical instruments the artiste eventually focused upon the concertina, hence the designation *A Concert-in-a-Turn* for an act which he worked with his daughter Mary (1910-88) from 1935 until his retirement in 1951. This entry's grand-son Peter Honri proudly bears this bill-matter to this very day, as we ourself know from personal experience.

See BETTY AUKLAND, Professor MacCann (KING OF...)

HOOPER, HILDA (fl1940s)

Ilford's Own Opera Star

But how much opera was there in Ilford in the 1940s?

HOUDINI, HARRY (1874?-1926)

The Demon of the Cells; The Impossible Possible; The King of Cards; The King of Handcuffs; The Marvel of the Age; The Modern Jack Sheppard; The Mystic of the World; The Wizard of the Chain; The World Famous Self-Liberator

Erik Weisz took the stage-name of Houdini in tribute to the much-respected Jean Robert-Houdin (see Robert Houdin, MAGICIANS). The Six Brothers Luck (SKETCH ARTISTES) worked an item called *The Demon of the Cellars* which may have been a spoof on the first example given above of Mr Houdini's many different billings. *The Impossible Possible* dates from the escapologist's early years with his wife Wilhelmina Rahner (1876-1943) *k.a.* Beatrice or Bess as his assistant. Other *Kings of Cards* were CARL HERTZ and HOWARD THURSTON. Jack Sheppard (1702-24) was a petty criminal whose four spectacular escapes from various London prisons made him a folk hero.

Harry Houdini's feats were so astounding that many who should have known better were convinced he had access to the supernatural. This was particularly irritating to a dedicated debunker of the paranormal in general and spiritualism in particular, but even when Mr Houdini declared publicly that all his escapes and illusions were plain old-fashioned trickery there were those who insisted that, whether he knew it or not, the performer possessed powers denied ordinary mortals. One was none other than Sir Arthur Conan Doyle who created Sherlock Holmes and believed in fairies.

See THE THREE KEATONS, KING OF..., MAGICIANS, THE ZANCIGS

HOUSTON & STEWART

Variety's Sweethearts

The slightly over-ripe swains were Renée Houston (1902-80) and her third husband Donald Stewart (1909-66). Prior to this personal and professional partnership Miss Houston worked with her sister Billie (1906-55) from 1920-35 as The Houston Sisters *The Irresistibles.*

On tour in her early days Miss Houston once arrived in Manchester where she shared a bedroom with two other young ladies. During the night one of them needing to answer a call of nature felt under the bed for the customary chamber-pot; to her unbridled horror her hand met a cold human face. It was the corpse of her landlady's freshly deceased husband.

See REVNELL & WEST, ELSIE & DORIS WATERS

HOWARD, SYDNEY (1883-1946)
The Slow-Witted Droll from Yeadon

Yeadon is a place in Yorkshire one goes through *en route* to Leeds and Bradford airport. Sydney Howard's daftness, eccentric walk and catch-phrase 'What's to do?' were meat and drink to impressionists, though for a comedian who enjoyed a meed of fame he is curiously little remembered and seldom features in reference books or memoirs. We knew him as a cartoon character in the children's comic *Radio Fun* which for an hour or so each Thursday inspired us to walk around stiff-armed with our knuckles sticking out, hoping we would be found amusing.

See GEORGE FORMBY snr

HOWERD, FRANKIE (1917-92)
The Borderline Case

A tall bulky individual with the features of an anxious *putto* Mr Howerd was riven by insecurities which despite (or perhaps because of) swift early success undermined his confidence. In the early 1960s the comedian's career was revived by appearances at The Establishment, a Soho night-club specialising in political satire, and by his now-legendary routine on the 1963 Budget for BBC tv's *That Was The Week That Was.*

We had the pleasure of working with Mr Howerd on radio and in two pantomimes (at the Coventry Theatre and the London Palladium) and we recognised how intensely nervous and stress-ridden he was. His introspection sometimes gave offence - 'I said hello to Frankie and he just ignored me!' - but we never knew him to be deliberately unkind.

When it was announced that Mr Howerd was to star in *A Funny Thing Happened on the Way to the Forum* we happened by chance to be having luncheon with him that very day and enquired as to the nature of the show. 'Ooh, it's *filthy...*!' leered this entry as only he could. 'I'm the only virgin *in it!*'

See p.15, DEREK ROY

HUDD, ROY (b1936)
The Peculiar Person

This comedian gives unstintingly of his time and considerable talents for charitable causes, as we can personally vouch. The affection Mr Hudd inspires in the bosom of the Great British Public no less than his compeers is vast, and his strong ebullient personality and deep interest in the history of his Profession have, with the passing of the years, turned this entry into a National Treasure.

See FLANAGAN & ALLEN, MAZDA & OSRAM

HUGHES, THE GREAT (1890s-1900s)
Codology

Magician Hughes claimed to have invented the word 'codology', meaning trickery or deception. There must have been merit in his claim for on June 24th 1894 a High Court judgement was given in his favour over his bill-matter's copyright. However, the word 'cod' meaning to chaff or to humbug was in use at least twenty years earlier, so perhaps it is time that judgement was reversed.

See MAGICIANS (especially Billington and Arthur Dowler).

HUGHES, TOM E (d February 13th 1938)
The Ragbag of Vanity

This wistful billing gives some slight indication of the nature of Mr Hughes' show for the titles of some of his songs *Can London Do Without Me?, I Don't Think I'm So Busy After All, I Wonder What It Feels Like To Be Poor?* suggest that his was an ironical, even cynical, entertainment.

HUNTER, G W (1850-1936)
The Mark Twain of the Music Halls; The Quintessence of Quaintness; Raconteur

Mr Hunter was a second-rate Music Hall performer whose repertoire, largely written by himself, consisted largely of laboured topical songs and feeble parodies of songs by abler hands. For this entry to associate his meagre talents with those of the illustrious Mark Twain (1835-1910), the revered humorist, lecturer, and novelist-chronicler of backwoods America, is arrant vanity.

See GEORGE BEAUCHAMP

HURLEY, ALEC (1871-1913)

The Coster King

A major head-liner in his own right Mr Hurley is also noted for being the second husband of MARIE LLOYD. The comedian-singer was a quiet-living man, too much so for Our Marie who liked noise, parties, people and fun.

More authentic than ALBERT CHEVALIER and less grotesque than GUS ELEN Mr Hurley delivered his coster songs in a confidential unforced style which greatly influenced the young Bud Flanagan (see FLANAGAN & ALLEN) – it is no coincidence that the latter's *Underneath The Arches* shares the same slow sauntering 4/4 tempo as this entry's best-remembered number *I Ain't Nobody In Perticuler*. Alec Hurley died a bitter man, still half in love with the wilful, phrenetic woman who deserted him for a man seventeen years younger.

HUSSEY, ST GEORGE (d1881)

The Female Irishman

Irish singers were standard fare on English Halls from the 1850s and it may be that Miss Hussey was the first female artiste to exploit the vogue, possibly in male attire which at that time was a rarity. But note that a contemporaneous performer, Miss Kate Clifton, billed herself as *The Only Female Irishman*. Or did she only do so after Miss Hussey's demise?

Star male impersonators like BESSIE BONEHILL or VESTA TILLEY were yet to emerge; ladies wishing to suggest the opposite sex would merely don an accessory like a man's hat or jacket or scarf (though see NELLIE POWER).

A similar approach to Miss Hussey's is detectable in Nellie Coleman's billing *The Only Female Comedian in the World*, though this artiste was flourishing thirty years later by which time full male impersonation was well established. Miss Coleman also attempted to exploit the popularity of Britain's favourite comedian by calling herself *The Only Female Dan Leno*.

We cannot leave this *genre* without listing May Levey *The Adonis of Vaudeville*, also see BERT ERROL, HETTY KING, Fanny Robina (FLORRIE ROBINA), ELLA SHIELDS. For female impersonators see BARBETTE.

J

JACK & EVELYN (fl1903-23)
Growing Older Every Day

Although the melancholy bill-matter of Jack O'Connor (1886-1923) and his sister Evelyn (b1888) may have been factually accurate it belied an extremely lively and finished comedy singing act which, while never a topper, was always welcome at the best Metropolitan Music Halls.

JACKLEY, NAT (& CO) (1909-88)
The Original Rubberneck Comedian

This entry was a class comedian of the old school – original, and above all, funny. Mr Jackley had a very long neck which, due to his years as a speciality dancer, he was able to capitalise on to great effect. The performer was also one of the sweetest-natured men we have ever encountered. How sad it was, during our pantomime run at the New Cardiff, to see the distress and embarrassment caused the artiste by his abusive and violent first wife, Marianne Lincoln, who at the Palace Pier Theatre Brighton pushed her husband down the stairs.

Eventually the ex-soubrette's alcoholic disruptiveness caused her to be banned both from the theatre and the local hostelry, a not infrequent occurrence wherever her unfortunate spouse was playing. One management wouldn't even have Mrs Jackley in the same *town*. Nat Jackley was the son of another fine performer George Jackley (1884-1950) *The Indignant Comedian*.

See SAMMY CURTIS, Jerry Desmonde (SID FIELD)

JAMES, DAISY (c1885-1940)
The Dainty Comedienne

As well as singing and being funny and dainty at the same time Miss James was notable for her skipping-rope dancing. In 1915 the artiste was residing at 65 Sudbourne Road, Brixton Hill, London SW and her telephone number was Brixton 2115.

We have located three other ladies who advertised themselves as *Dainty Comedienne*: GERTIE GITANA, Gwen Glen (see DRUM & MAJOR), and Lucy Weston. Of similar kidney were Belle Avalon *The Dainty Skater*, Mrs Coleman (fl11900s-10s) *The Dainty Canadian Widow*, Dainty Doris Dormer (1883-1947) *An Artiste to her Finger Tips* and ALICE LLOYD.

JAMES, JIMMY (& CO) (1892-1965)
First Night; The Shoebox; Sober as a Judge; The Spare Room

Originally *k.a.* Terry *the Blue-Eyed Irish Boy* Mr James built up a repertoire of beautifully crafted and superbly executed sketches, the titles of which comprised his bill-matter. The comedian's company always included Hutton Conyers (a village in Yorkshire), the best-known of whom was ROY CASTLE, and Bretton Woods (the New Hampshire venue for the 1944 United Nations financial conference). This entry was a greatly respected professional whose drunkenness displayed consummate technical mastery, all the more remarkable in a teetotaller. Or perhaps not.

Mr James's sketches are, we are pleased to observe, kept alive by Eli Woods whose years of working them with his uncle are a guarantee of quality and authenticity.

See JOHNNY COOPER, SKETCH ARTISTES

JESSEL, GEORGE (1898-1981)
Toastmaster General of the United States

This billing was conferred upon the comedian by Harry S Truman, the second instance noted in these pages of Presidential interest in such matters. Mr Jessel's partnership with Lou Edwards in an act billed as *Two Patches from a Crazy Quilt* brought the pair to the Victoria Palace during the Kaiser's War, though they were not too well received outside London. Due to a disagreement over his emolument Mr Jessel spurned a rôle in the landmark sound film *The Jazz Singer*, thus ceding his place in the pantheon of motion picture legends to one AL JOLSON. Later this entry created his own unique if sombre legend as America's finest elegist.

See THEA ALBA

JEWEL & WARRISS (fl1934-66)

Gems of Comedy

We can understand a Jewel being a Gem but what is a Warriss? Of this thirty-year partnership Jimmy Jewel jnr (1909-95) was the simpleton and Ben Warriss (1909-93) the aggressive straight man. The difference between the cousins was pointed up by their stage dress, with the former in baggy trousers and a funny hat (see WILKIE BARD) and the latter in very natty gents' suitings indeed. Their cross-talk routines were, even to young ears, irritatingly inane and their slapstick without warmth or finesse. These performers were, we would say, the last top-of-the-bill exponents of a style of comedy which was old-fashioned even in the 1940s.

Similar bill-matter was displayed by Ada Lundberg (1850-99) *The Gem of Comedy*.

JOANNYS, CHARLES (b1886)

Although we have no knowledge of this Swiss artiste's bill-matter we cannot exclude one whose stupefying versatility permitted him to perform as athlete, juggler, conjurer, lightning sketch artist, transformist(?), imitator, trapezist, musical clown and sharp-shooter 'but since 1910 has specialised in shadowgraphy'. As late as 1950 Mr Joannys was, assisted by his wife and son, still demonstrating his umbrageous skills.

See THEO BAMBERG. Also see list of MIMICS in glossary.

JOLSON, AL (c1885-1950)

The World's Greatest Entertainer

Harry Jolson (c1882-1953) was so well-established as *The Black Faced Singing Comedian* that when he took his younger brother into a sketch called *The Hebrew and the Cadet* the word was that it was good of Harry to give the kid a break. Who could have foreseen that within ten years young Al would be Broadway's most incandescent star?

Given this artiste's vocal talents his rise was inevitable, for he possessed a voice that was flexible, ultra-rhythmic, and whose uncannily compelling timbre gripped his auditors like a grapnel. Add to that a dynamism as powerful and unstoppable as a Sherman tank (and an ego to match) and it becomes clear that Mr Jolson's oft-quoted bill-matter was nothing more than plain fact.

For other black-face entertainers see G H ELLIOTT. Also see BILLY MERSON, GEORGE JESSEL, and CHRIS WORTMAN.

JOVER, TOMMY (NENA & RAF) (fl1940s-50s)
Burlesque in Rhythm; Musical Comicalities

Florencio Tomas Jover (1895-1983) was a third-generation circus artiste; Nena and Raf were his children – Raf also worked a similar act with his brother called Raf & Julian *Two Wrongs Making a Riot*. Señor Jover is the only entry herein who, in his own words, 'did some bull fighting when his family hit hard times'.

See DR CROCK

JUGGLERS

Joe Devoe
Juggling Jester

Roy Dove (fl c1920s)
Garrulous Juggledian

Boy Foy (b1918)
England's Youngest Juggler; The Wonder on One Wheel
See BICYCLE ACTS

Gicardo (fl c1910)
The Cleverest Backward Juggler in the Profession

Lucy Gillet (fl c1910)
The Greatest Lady Juggler on Earth

Tom Hearn (1879-1954)
The Laziest Juggler on Earth; The Sleepy Juggler

Kelly & Gillette (fl1900s)
The Human Billiard Table
See CINQUEVALLI

Johnny Lamonte & Suma (fl1944-5)
Juggling for Pleasure
Son and daughter of Masu & Yuri. After Johnny's call-up Suma (b1927) worked solo into the 1950s. Her husband is Victor Seaforth (see PAUL J BARNES).

JUGGLERS (continued):

Eddie Le Roy (fl1930s-50s)
Juggling Humorist; Laughter Let Loose

Topper Martyn (b1923)
Juggling on Ice Skates
Originally *k.a.* V C Martyn *The Eton Topper.*

Mr & Miss Nemo (fl1870s)
Impalement Act

Franco Piper (1881-1933)
The Man with the Spinning Banjos
Depressed at wife's illness and lack of bookings killed himself.
See BIRDIE BRIGHTLING

Enrico Rastelli
See THE RASTELLIS

Rebla (fl1910s-30s)
The Doleful Juggler; The Unconcerned Juggler

Jimmy Savo (1896-1960)
*The Boy Wonder Juggler; Juggles Everything from
a Feather to a Piano*

Severus Schaeffer (b1867)
The Prince of Jugglers
Brother Sylvester (b1859) and nephew (1885-1949) also jugglers.

Henry Sparrow (1860-1905)
The Mad Juggler

Ollie Young & Miss April (fl c1900)
Soap Bubble Jugglers

Zellini (1887-1953)
The Human Chimney; Comedy Juggler

See also entries for: FRED ALLEN, THE GREAT ATROY, THEO BAMBERG, CHARLES S BERNARD, CHINKO, PAUL CINQUEVALLI, JOE COOK, ARNOLD DE BIERE, EMMELINE ETHARDO, W C FIELDS, 'Monsewer' EDDIE GRAY, ANNETTE KELLERMAN, TOM MENNARD, NERVO & KNOX, GASTON PALMER, Professor RISLEY, FELICIEN TREWEY

JUMEL, BETTY (1901-90)
The Bundle of Fun

This lady was small in stature, jolly of grin, and one of the few tolerable female pantomime Dames. When understudying (Sir) HARRY

SECOMBE as Humpty Dumpty at the Manchester Palace the artiste only had to take over on one occasion – the first half of a Monday matinée when her principal's aeroplane flight from Heathrow was delayed by snow – and what a grand job Miss Jumel made of winning over a disappointed audience and delighting them with her own strong and individualistic interpretation of the rôle.

JUMPIN' JAX (fl1953-81)

Fun on a Trampoline

This oft-repeated bill-matter was also displayed by Billy & Bob, a team of which we know nothing whatsoever. Jumpin' Jax comprised Bob Johnson and a succession of no fewer than thirteen lithesomely winsome partners, including Terrie Lomas (see illustration 31) and Dawn Sinclair (the second Mrs Johnson).

Ernie Dillon (b1900) *On the Bounce* also crowned himself as *The King of 'Bounders'* (see KING OF...) and we would surmise that *Beauty on the Bounce*, the bill-matter displayed by Paulette & Renée in the 1950s, similarly indicates a trampoline act. And if not, what?

JUNA (b c1890)

The Human Gasometer

It seems that M. Juna could ingest butane gas which when exhaled and lit with a match enabled the artiste to illuminate gas-lamps, brackets, street lights and so on. He could even ingest sufficient fuel to fry an egg. This does not sound like much of an act, and having seen a photograph of this entry in action we suspect that it wasn't.

K

KANE, HELEN (1908-66)
The Boop-a-Doop Girl

A petite hazel-eyed brunette from New York, Mrs Kane earned her soubriquet through her quaint style of singing, so redolent of the 1920s Flapper era. The artiste gained her first stage experience working two seasons with the Marx Brothers, a baptism of fire which, in our book, entitled the lady to call herself whatever she chose.

This entry tripped down the aisle on three occasions, firstly with Joseph Kane (1894/7-1975), secondly with Max Hoffman jnr (1903-45), and thirdly with fellow-performer Dan Healy (1888-1969) who styled himself *Broadway's Boy* and, less appealingly, as *The Night Mayor of Broadway*.

KARDOMA (1891-1959)
Fills the Stage with Flags; Magic at its Best

This gentleman originally appeared under his family name Leon Clifford *Britain's Youngest Illusionist*. In the Second World War the magician filled the stage with flags of the Allied nations and billed himself as *The Patriotic Illusionist*. His post-war bill-matter, *Fills the Stage with Flags*, was the inspiration for this present volume as outlined in the Introduction.

The artiste should not be confused with the once-popular chain of Kardomah coffee-houses.

KARNO, FRED (1866-1941)
...and his Speechless Comedians; Celebrated Company of Comedians

Frederick John Westcott made his professional début c1881 in an acrobatic act, experience which was to stand him in such good stead when devising and directing the manic slapstick sketches which with his name has become synonymous. It was with his most celebrated sketch *Mumming Birds* that those two filmic immortals first set foot on God's Own Country: Stan Laurel (1890-1965) and CHARLES CHAPLIN.

The reason Mr Karno's original sketches were 'speechless' is that until 1911 plays were prohibited in Music Halls, though from the turn of the century this restriction was more honoured in the breach than the observance.

While granting this gentleman his pre-eminence in the Comedy Hall of Fame we regret to say that Mr Karno's private character was utterly despicable, for he offered his blameless first wife little but sexual perversion and violence. Once when Mrs Karno was *enceinte* her husband knocked her down and stamped on her face, leaving a permanent heel-shaped scar.

Other alumni of this vile man's companies mentioned in these pages are CHARLES AUSTIN, Bud Flanagan (FLANAGAN & ALLEN), WILL HAY, JAY LAURIER, Jack Melville (SKETCH ARTISTES), Jimmy Nervo (NERVO & KNOX), DONALD PEERS, SANDY POWELL, and BILLIE RITCHIE.

KAUFMANN'S TRICK CYCLISTS (fl1880s-1910s)
Twelve Cycling Beauties

From 1899 Nick Kaufmann (b1861) and his troupe were regular visitors to the Alhambra, Leicester Square, where they were always assured of a hearty welcome from the bucks of the Row and men about Town. Only six of the company are shown in the illustration between pp.160-161, possibly because the photographer found the full complement of pulchritude too overwhelming.

See BICYCLE ACTS

KAYE, DAVY (1916-98)
The Heart-Throb

In the 1950s, with the demise of Variety increasingly apparent, this small-statured but energetic and incomparably dapper comedian followed a well-beaten trail by becoming an agent and small-time management. We ourself once gave our Little John in *Robin Hood* under Mr Kaye's benign aegis; rehearsals took place in the Max Rivers Studios in Great Newport Street where *The Heart-Throb* was directing two other pantomimes simultaneously.

On arrival at the Pavilion Liverpool we were chagrined to discover that we had not been provided with a single stitch of costume. A pleaful telephone call to the Clarke brothers at the Argyle Theatre Birkenhead for whom we had obliged a year or two earlier resulted in a fetching combination of knee-length suede boots, jerkin, tights, and one of those saucy little Sherwood Forest hats rakishly adorned with a feather: in the clubs and pubs of Lodge Lane our performance is still talked of.

With a partner in the 1930s this entry was billed as Kaye & Vale *The Only Two Jewish Cowboys in Captivity.*

See ISSY BONN

KEAN, KEMBLE (b1899)
Public Nuisance No 1

Despite a stage alias derived from two of the most illustrious names in English drama – John Philip Kemble and Edmund Kean – this comedian's career was largely spent in variety and revue. In 1950 Mr Kean claimed to have 'compèred from the stage the world's first dictoniatic picture *We've Got to Have Love* for B and N Films. Characters in the film spoke to the compère on the stage and eventually brought him into the story. He...in the finish was shot by one of the characters in the film'. The eerie blurring of image and reality must have been perturbing and we are not surprised that 'dictoniatic' pictures did not survive.

KEATONS, THE THREE (fl1900s)
The Human Mop; The Man with the Table

The trio consisted of Joe Keaton (c1867-1946), his wife Myra Cutler (c1880?-1955) and their son Joseph jnr (1895-1966). Family friend HARRY HOUDINI was so impressed by the youngster's tumbling ability that he gave him the nickname by which posterity remembers him: Buster.

The boy's *sang froid* while being savagely hurled around a table by his father with wince-making speed is evident in the mature comedian's films, where his apparent lack of expression earned him the soubriquet *The Great Stone Face.* But to those with eyes to see, the beauty and expressiveness of the performer's mask are very apparent and Mr Keaton is now rightly regarded as a very great film actor indeed.

KELLERMAN, ANNETTE (1887/8-1975)
The Divine Venus; The Million Dollar Mermaid

Quite why the little Australian lady's swims in the Seine, the Rhine, the Rhône and the Thames attracted such notice we are at a loss to fathom; we can only state that on both British and American stages Miss Kellerman's aquatic demonstrations in a glass-sided tank created a furore. This entry's non-natatorial talents, which included diabolo throwing, tightrope walking, and singing and dancing were decidedly not of the first water, so we must assume that Miss Kellerman's very considerable drawing-power had much to do with her clinging one-piece swimming-costume.

Part of the performer's act was to eat a banana while submerged, a feat which pales beside the achievements of Blatz *The Human Fish* who while underwater could eat, read a newspaper and play the trombone. Nor can we omit Enoch *The Man Fish* who not only played the trombone *sub aqua* but also sang and *smoked.*

In private life *The Million Dollar Mermaid* was the wife of comedian James E Sullivan (1863-1931) *The Polite Lunatic* – see STAN STENNETT.

KERR, BILL (b1922)
The Lad from Wagga Wagga; The Voice of Gloom

An Australian comedian, Mr Kerr always started his radio spots by saying apologetically 'I'm only here for four minutes.' As his bill-matter indicates the artiste was a practitioner of the dimwit school of comedy, principally remembered today as a foil to TONY HANCOCK in the *Hancock's Half Hour* radio series.

Wagga Wagga (pronounced 'Wogga Wogga') lies on the Murrumbidgee River in New South Wales some 230 miles south west of Sydney. Its secondary industries include a rubber-goods factory.

KIMBER, BOBBIE (1918-93)
(It) Speaks for Itself; With Augustus Peabody

Miss Kimber's appearance was so matronly and unglamorous that her entrance regularly evoked titters of derision. But sneers soon vanished as this entry displayed the ventriloquial powers which for over thirty years made her a welcome visitor round the nation's Number One Halls.

The artiste invariably concluded her act with Augustus singing *Popeye the Sailor Man.* The abyssal bass notes with which the dummy ended his rendition astounded all who did not realise that off stage Bobbie Kimber was Ronald Victor Robert Kimberley.

See BARBETTE, LYDIA DREAMS, HANNEN SWAFFER, VENTRILOQUISTS

146

KING OF...

Harold Alanza
...the High Wire
See CAICEDO

Reuben R Brooks
See BIRDIE BRIGHTLY

Ernie Dillon
See JUMPIN' JAX

Lonnie Donegan (b1931)
...Skiffle

T Nelson Downs (1867-1938)
...Koins

Gus Fowler (fl1920s)
The Watch King

Benny Goodman (1909-86)
...Swing

Grock (1880-1959)
...Clowns
See CHARLIE CAIROLI & CO, Dan Rice *infra*, NONI & HORACE

Professor John Holtum
See ZAZEL

Scott Joplin (1868-1917)
...Ragtime Writers

Bert Leslie (1873-1917)
...Slang

Max Linder (1884-1925)
...the Kinema

Herbert Lloyd (1872-1936)
...Diamonds

Professor MacCann (fl850s-1900s)
...the Concertina
See BETTY AUKLAND, PERCY HONRI

Nevada Ned (fl 1870s-80s)
...Gold

KING OF... (continued):

Olmar (c1835-85)
...Gymnasts
Possibly *a.k.a.* Olma The American Gorilla whose partner was *Man Monkey* Le Main.
See M. GOUFFÉ

Al Reeves (1865-1940)
...Burlesque
See Sam Rice *infra*

Dan Rice (1823-1900)
...Clowns
See Grock *supra*

Sam Rice (1874-1946)
...Burlesque
See Al Reeves *supra*

Harry Richman (1895-1972)
...Broadway

Selbo (fl1920s)
...Clubs

Nat Travers
...the Coster Comedians

W H Vane
See BIRDIE BRIGHTLING

W F Wainratta
See CAICEDO

Fred Walmsley (1879-1943)
...Pierrots

Bert Weedon (b1920)
...Guitar

Paul Whiteman (1890-1967)
The King of Jazz

Harry Wulson
...Yodellers
See ALEC PLEON

Henny Youngman (1906-98)
...the One Liners

See also entries for: ATLAS & VULCANA, HARRY BAILEY, IRVING BERLIN, CAICEDO, CARL HERTZ, HARRY HOUDINI, ALEC HURLEY, BERNARD MILES, GEORGE F MOORE, EUGENE SANDOW, HARRY TATE, HOWARD THURSTON

KING, HETTY (1883-1972)
The Immaculate (Man)

Miss King was the original singer of *Ship Ahoy! (All the Nice Girls love a Sailor)* whose rendering we twice had the privilege of witnessing. An eminent thespian once told us that the artiste's performance of this song so affected him that he always watched it 'through a mist of tears'. The octogenarian's minutely observed stage business, executed with breath-taking precision, gave a brief glimpse into past glories, now all departed. Miss King was the last of her kind, and we shall not see her like again.

See ST GEORGE HUSSEY, Ernie Lotinga (SKETCH ARTISTES)

KIRKWOOD, PAT (b1921)
The Schoolgirl Songstress

This artiste remains unquestionably the finest pantomime Principal Boy we have ever seen with a singing voice, looks, slim figure, long legs, and swash-buckling dash that, in our lengthy experience, remain unequalled. In *Chrysanthemum* at the Prince of Wales's in 1958 we had the intense pleasure of seeing Miss Kirkwood displaying considerably more of her person than we had a right to expect. The memory is still a thrill.

KITTY, JOYCE (1874-1915)
Suicide Kitty

If the artiste lived up to her bill-matter Miss Joyce can have given but a single memorable performance.

KNOWLES, R G (1858-1919)
The Very Peculiar American Comedian

Mr Knowles was in fact a Canadian whose early attempts at comedy earned him more kicks than ha'pence. Telling a rowdy Chicago house that if they didn't laugh they'd better ask for their money back endeared him neither to audiences nor managers.

At his 1891 London début at the Trocadero this entry's dry originality was greeted with 'enthusiastic silence' for the first ten minutes but then with such delight that the artiste was held over for over a year.

R G Knowles was the husband of Winifred E Johnson (c1871-1931) *Coon Singer and Past-Mistress of the Banjo*, the highlight of whose turn was a twangy *Home Sweet Home*.

See G H ELLIOTT

KORINGA (1913-76)
The World's Only Girl Fakir

Renée Bernard presented an unusually varied turn in which two crocodiles would be hypnotised into immobility; then the artiste would be placed in a coffin and buried in sand without suffocating, walk up and down a ladder of demonstrably sharp swords, and be stretched across two of these swords while two assistants broke paving stones on her bare midriff with sledge-hammers. At the conclusion of all this dubious spectacle the two crocodiles would be awakened and off the *Fakir* would skip, to repair her make-up for the next house.

In the 1960s there flourished Rahnee Motie *The Youngest Girl Fakir in the World.*

See Mlle Betra (ANIMAL & BIRD ACTS), Mlle Paula (ANIMAL & BIRD ACTS), PETER CASSON

KORRIS, HARRY (1888-1971)
The Falstaff of the South Pavilion

This particular South Pavilion was in Blackpool, a Lancastrian seaside holiday resort always highly appreciative of Mr Korris' drolleries. The highlight of the well-padded comedian's career was his seven-year run on stage and radio as Mr Lovejoy, the manager of a variety house, with Cecil Frederick as Ramsbottom the stage-manager and Robbie Vincent (1895-1968) as the dim-witted call-boy. How wistfully we recall the lyrics of their gently rocking theme-song, so evocative of the 1940s:

> *We three in 'Happidrome',*
> *Working for the BBC;*
> *Ramsbottom and Enoch and me.*

See CASEY'S COURT, ALBERT MODLEY

L

LABURNUM, WALTER (b1847)

The Star of the East; The Longest Living Lath of Laughter

Few Music Hall artistes in the 1860s-70s displayed any bill-matter worth the mention so this comic singer is a rare exception. Mr Laburnum's first billing refers to the East End of London where he was especially popular; the performer specialised in topical songs and in Cockney rhyming slang, an obscure but interesting instance of which may be discerned in his second billing, *i.e.* lath = lath and plaster = master.

See HYRAM TRAVERS

LACY, GEORGE (1904-89)

The Ace of Jokers

This comedian was particularly venerated as a pantomime Dame. We saw him in skirts twice, at the Leeds Grand and the Cardiff New, and found him disappointingly salacious. In 1982 we were asked to transport Mr Lacy to the De La Warr Pavilion, Bexhill, for an Old Time Music Hall show in which he topped the bill and we were 'Your Worthy Chairman'.

For the two-and-a-half-hour journey from his flat in Hammersmith to the seaside the veteran comic regaled us with his triumphs, and we were happy to hear the highlights of a distinguished career. That evening, in the star spot at the end of the show, Mr Lacy's performance was a total frost. The audience sat and stared at him for twenty minutes of cringe-making embarrassment. In the motor-car on the return journey the Fallen Star was subdued, saying little other than to ask us, pathetically, 'Do you have to make a report on the show...?'

LAFAYETTE, THE GREAT (1871-1911)

Dr Kremer – Vivisectionist; The Lion's Bride

A few days after the death of his adored dog Beauty the celebrated illusionist was killed in a fire at the Empire Edinburgh. Ten of Lafayette's troupe were also killed, one of whom was the magician's stage double who, it was soon realised, had been cremated in his master's stead. The correct corpse was rushed to the flames and a swift substitution of urns effected.

Lafayette had bought a plot for Beauty and it was decided to place his ashes in the dog's coffin. But the local rabbi refused to attend because of the presence of the embalmed pooch; a Church of Scotland minister was found to do the needful. The show, or what was left of it, passed to Lalla Selbini (see BICYCLE ACTS).

See MAGICIANS

LANGTRY, LILLIE (1877-1965)

The Electric Spark; The Versatile Comedienne

Miss Langtry should not be confused, though she often was, with *Mrs Langtry* (1853-1929) whose appellative *The Jersey Lily* was journalistic rather than theatrical. To confuse the picture even more both ladies appeared on the Halls, though the latter only in one-act plays whereas the former worked soubrette songs.

In the 1890s Signorina Galimberti not only also billed herself as *The Electric Spark* but warned off would-be imitators that her title was 'registered number 23,839'. This did not daunt Daisy Jerome (b1881) who flaunted an identical caption. But then she also sometimes called herself *The Little American Girl* so perhaps she didn't know about Signorina Galimberti's register.

Nita Mayhew was *The Vocal Spark* but of this artiste we know no more.

See JENNY HILL

LASHWOOD, GEORGE (1863-1942)

The Beau Brummell of the Halls

Despite this singer's noted immaculacy of dress his Victorian beefiness was far removed from your dandified Regency exquisite. Public tastes changed so sharply after the Great War that the artiste's style of patriotic bombast *(The Death or Glory Boys, The Last Bullet)* was no longer acceptable and he retired to a Worcestershire farm. Prinny's arbiter of fashion died in miserable debt-ridden exile, but the *Beau Brummell of the Halls* died in the bosom of his family worth £131,328.

LAUDER, Sir HARRY (1870-1950)

The Laird of the Halls

No Scotch artiste had ever made good in the Metropolis but this entry decided to *changer tout çela*. In 1900, with twenty gold sovereigns in his sporran, the comedian-singer advanced upon the Metropolis having promised Mrs Lauder that if he had not established himself by the time the money was spent he would return home. Booked by TOM TINSLEY as an extra turn at Gatti's in Westminster Bridge Road the performer created a furore; by the end of the week, besieged by agents and managers, he had signed contracts for six years' work.

In 1919 Mr Lauder became the first Variety artiste to be knighted, having raised over a million pounds for War charities in the United States. His son, an only child, was killed in action. Sir Harry's fame and popularity, at least with the public, never waned though he was not much liked within the Profession for his meanness and aloofness.

At the Empire Inverness in 1935 the local manager was so overcome by the magnitude of the Lauder name and reputation that he billed his star with the apoplectically tautologous *As Ever, New – This Time Newer Than Ever*.

The bill for the week commencing August 21st 1911 at the Grand Theatre Chorley included Jessie Star *The Female Lauder*, *The Pocket Harry Lauder* was Alec Finlay (1906-84).

See PAT FEENEY, W F FRAME, ALICE LLOYD, TOMMY MORGAN, MUSAIRE, BILLY WILLIAMS

LAURI, CHARLES jnr (1848-1904)

The Garrick of Animal Mimes

David Garrick (1717-79) was the great English actor – some say the greatest ever – renowned for an uncanny ability to alter completely his appearance and manner.

The Lauri family were primarily a knockabout sketch troupe and it was in panto that this entry established his reputation as an animal mime. His repertoire encompassed parrot, goat, goose, cat, cow, donkey, monkey, opossum, and alligator. In one sketch the faunal artiste's death scene as a dog caused such serious distress amongst his audiences that the plot had to be re-written to allow him to survive.

See M. GOUFFÉ, SKETCH ARTISTES

LAURIER, JAY (1879-1969)
The Farmer's Boy

As did so many comedians of his generation Mr Laurier served an apprenticeship with FRED KARNO. The comedian's principal line of business was as a country bumpkin, wearing a red wig and a costume of Tate & Lyle sugar sacks. Shrewd enough to see that in a post-War world that kind of grotesquerie was played out, this entry switched to the legitimate theatre – including Shakespeare – with surprising ease and success. His Dogberry was particularly admired.

See BERNARD MILES

LAWRENCE, JOE (1849-1909)
The Double-Headed Nondescript; The Upside-Down Comedian

The word nondescript nowadays signifies mundane or uninteresting, a reversal of its original meaning of unclassifiable and thus novel or odd, e.g. Julia Pastrana (1832-60) who suffered from severe facial deformity and billed herself as *The Nondescript*. Mr Lawrence was a black-face performer famous for siring VESTA VICTORIA and for performing comic songs while standing on his head.

See G H ELLIOTT, J H STEAD

LAWSON, JOHN (1865-1920)
Humanity

This entry starred in his own lurid one-act melodramas with such titles as *The Shield of David* and *The King of Palestine*. Far and away the most popular – and sensational – was *Humanity* (1904) in which the artiste sang *Only a Jew* very badly and fought a set-smashing duel with his unfaithful Gentile wife's lover, ending with the two of them falling through a staircase and expiring. One would have needed a heart of stone not to laugh.

See CHARLES AUSTIN, ISSY BONN, GEORGE GRAY, SKETCH ARTISTES

LEAMORE, TOM (1866-1939)
The Daddy of Them All; The Wrinkle Wrecker

This gentleman was, it would seem, the first Music Hall artiste to make commercial recordings. Others such as GUS ELEN and ALBERT

CHEVALIER had dabbled in the new medium but Mr Leamore was the first to make records that were actually released for public sale. In London on September 1st 1898 the performer's high-pitched tones singing *Mary Ann* (E-2017) and *I've Been Left in Charge* (E-2022) were recorded by Berliner. It is several years since we heard this entry's 1903 pressing of *I Used to be Poor Myself* but his weirdly haunting voice lingers in the mind's ear.

LEARMOUTH, JIMMY (1891-1921)
The Comic whose Smile Never Wears Off

One whose smile never wore off would surely make an uneasy bedfellow. We would prefer the company of Sober Sue (fl c1900s) *The Girl who Never Smiles.*

LENA, LILY (b1877)
The Princess of Comediennes

Miss Lena, née Alice Archer, was cousin to MARIE LLOYD, and from 1893-6 was teamed up with Miss Lloyd's sister Rosie Wood as The Sisters Lena. This entry did not, it must be confessed, enjoy a particularly distinguished career and her bill-matter represents a triumph of wishful thinking.

LENNOX, NELLY & RALEIGH, KATE
The Original Music Hall 'Sapphos'

This was a late-19th-century act which was surely offered with a pure mind and an innocent heart. Sappho was the Greek poetess of Lesbos from which we may surmise that these ladies recited odes of their own devising. Further speculation might lead into realms of prurience and so is best avoided.

See CYRIL FLETCHER

LENO, DAN (1860-1904)
The Chief of Comedians; The Grand Comic Vocalist and Champion Clog Dancer of the World; Monarch of All Comedians

After a private Command at Sandringham in November 1901 this entry was also billed as *The King's Jester.* As a child Mr Leno appeared as

Little George, *The Infant Wonder, Contortionist and Posturer* (see Master BETTY) and at the age of nine as The Great Little Leno, *The Quintessence of Irish Comedians* (see PAT FEENEY). In New York the performer was puffed provocatively as *The Funniest Man on Earth* - WILKIE BARD, TOM BURKE and ROBB WILTON also suffered from their entrepreneurs' over-enthusiastic billing.

Indisputably the greatest Music Hall comedian of his day Dan Leno died insane at the age of only 43. A few days later Sir Max Beerbohm wrote 'He had, in a higher degree than any other actor that I have ever seen, the indefinable quality of being sympathetic. I defy anyone not to have loved Dan Leno at first sight,' and MARIE LLOYD said 'He had the saddest eyes in the whole world. That's why we all laughed at Danny, because if we hadn't we'd have cried ourselves sick'.

Also see BARBETTE, HERBERT CAMPBELL, Nellie Coleman (ST GEORGE HUSSEY), SID FIELD, VALENTINE, HENRY WRIGHT.

LÉOTARD, JULES (1838-70)

Although better known today for introducing the close-fitting one-piece garment which bears his name M. Léotard was the inventor of and pioneer performer on the flying trapeze. GEORGE LEYBOURNE'S song *The Man on the Flying Trapeze* was inspired by this entry's second visit to London in 1866 though the athlete does not seem to have used the phrase as bill-matter. We have often wondered whether it was this song which established the tradition that aerial acts should always be accompanied in 3/4 time.

Many different dates have been given for M. Léotard's birth; we can confidently assert that the Frenchman first drew breath at 6.00 a.m. on August 1st 1838, for these are the details given on our copy of his birth certificate obtained from the *mairie* at Toulouse.

Among many to utilise the trapezist's name were Azella (fl1868-80s) *The Female Léotard* and Master Alfred Corello (see BLONDIN). Nor should we overlook Pfau *The Russian Léotard.*

LESLIES, THE TWO (fl1935-49)
Britain's Brightest Entertainers

The original Two Leslies were Leslie Sarony (1897-1985) and Leslie Holmes (1901-61). Graduates of concert-party (with the former on the piano and the latter skipping brightly about), these artistes were teeth-grindingly avuncular; if they really were *Britain's Brightest Entertainers* then the state of British comedy in the 1930s left much to be desired.

In 1949 Mr Sarony reverted to a single act, his bill-matter averring him to be *As Clean as a Whistle and as Broad as a Bean*. This musical entertainer also wrote a number called *Mucking About the Garden* under the witty pseudonym of Q Kumber.

See BOB & ALF PEARSON

LESTER, ALFRED (1872-1925)
The Melancholy Comedian

This entry was celebrated for his lugubrious manner, displayed to advantage in such sketches as *A Restaurant Episode* and *The Scene-Shifter's Lament*. One of his most successful songs was *I Gotta Motta* from the original 1909 production of *The Arcadians*; another, from *Round the Map* (1917), was *The Conscientious Objector's Lament* which suggested that Conchies were little better than homosexuals, than which there could be no greater insult.

See SKETCH ARTISTES

LESTER, VICKI (fl1940s-50s)
Scotland's Judy Garland

Judy Garland (1922-69) was described by LEW GRADE as 'the greatest female performer of her time'. We never experienced Scotland's Judy Garland and so can offer no opinion on the artiste's talents which is a pity because at Caesar's Palace in Las Vegas in 1967 we did see Judy Garland's Judy Garland.

LEVIS, CARROLL (1910-68)
Every Discovery is a Star of Tomorrow

The Canadian son of a murdered police officer began his performing life as The Great Richelieu *Magician, Eminent Hypnotist and Necromancer*. At the age of 26 but already silver-haired and weighing 23 stone this entry, having established himself on radio, undertook his first British tour with his Discoveries augmented by local talent. Very few of Mr Levis' protégés ever actually reached stellar status, but the presenter's popularity kept his show on the road until the 1950s, proving if proof were needed the limitless self-delusion of the amateur artiste.

See PETER CASSON

LEYBOURNE, GEORGE (1842-84)
The Lion Comique; The Longitudinal Lion of Laughter

Some chroniclers have stated that George Leybourne, a Newcastle mechanic who started on the Halls as Joe Saunders but reverted to his family name, was the greatest Music Hall artiste of them all. The performer was 6ft 4ins in height, well-proportioned, blond, and 'the handsomest man on the Halls'. Add to that a fine voice and a splendid address and you arrive at a singularly, perhaps even uniquely, impressive figure. Mr Leybourne was also fortunate in acquiring such excellent songs as *Up in a Balloon* (see NELLIE POWER), *The Man on the Flying Trapeze* (see LÉOTARD) and the 1867 number with which he is most closely associated *Champagne Charlie*.

This entry's magisterial appearance and all-embracing personality prompted J J Poole, manager of the huge South London Music Hall, to describe him as a Lion of a Comic; the Victorian habit of frenchification led to *Lion Comique* which soon became a generic term for all such Music Hall magnificos as ARTHUR LLOYD, G H MACDERMOTT and ALFRED VANCE. There were even those gentlemen who tried to out-Leybourne Leybourne by calling themselves Mammoth Comiques but these upstarts were never of any consequence.

LILLIE, BEATRICE (1894-1989)
Serio Comic Singer with a Refined Repertoire

Of genteel Canadian origin – a background which may go some way to explain this entry's eccentricity – Miss Lillie was often described as the funniest woman in the world, and having seen her versions of the Japanese Tea Ceremony and the ballad *Come into the Garden Maud* we would not disagree with that assertion.

The misery of an unhappy marriage to Sir Robert Peel was compounded by the loss of her son, an only child, in World War II. The funniest woman in the world took to drink, and though her talent was never quite extinguished she became unreliable and only survived in the film *Thoroughly Modern Millie* through the kind intercession of JULIE ANDREWS.

In old age Miss Lillie fell under baleful influences and her sizable fortune, if not her person, seemed in danger. The Peel family recognised the tragedy of her twilit existence and had the once-great artiste brought back to England where she was cared for until her death at the age of 94.

For other serios see ANNIE ADAMS. Also see GRACIE FIELDS and RICHARD HAYDN.

LIND, JENNY (1820-87)
The Swedish Nightingale

This bill-matter was devised by P T BARNUM, and a hugely successful advertising wheeze it became for the whole Western world soon associated singer and slogan – even today one is rarely mentioned without the other. In London Miss Lind crossed swords with the impresario Alfred Bunn, a man of notoriously choleric disposition, causing the distinguished soprano to refer to him as Hot Cross Bunn. Not a bad joke for a Swede.

The singer's renown persuaded Jeannie Bishop to call herself *The Black Jenny Lind*; other imitative songbirds were GEORGE FORMBY snr, Catherine Hayes (1820/25-61) *The Irish Nightingale* and *The Swan of Erin*, Helen Hill (1904-83) *The Nightingale of Radio*, Edna Lyall *The Australian Nightingale*, Millie-Christine *The Two-Headed Nightingale* (see CHANG ENG), TRULY SHATTUCK, Florence Smithson (1885-1936) *The Nightingale of Wales*, Rennie Stallard (fl1920s-30s) *The Welsh Nightingale*, Rachel Walker (fl1890s) and Margaret Wing (fl1920s-30s) who both described themselves as *The Creole Nightingale*, and Lydia Yeamans (1866-1929) *The Australian Nightingale*. This last artiste also billed herself as *The Original Sally in our Alley*, which if true would have made her age at death as nearly 200.

LISKARD, J W (fl1860s-70s)
The Musical Momus

Such bill-matter shows a presumption of knowledge of classical myth amongst the *hoi polloi* surprising in an age still wrestling with compulsory education. How many of the GBP today, we wonder, could tell you that Momus was the Roman god of ridicule? To be brutally frank, we had to look him up ourself.

See JOHN HENRY ANDERSON, DR CROCK, 'Jolly' JOHN NASH

LISTON, HARRY (1843-1929)

The Stage Struck Hero

This billing was the title of Mr Liston's one-man show, a *genre* of which he was an early proponent. The dialect comedian was also a concert-party pioneer, touring his *Merry Moments* show round the provinces for many weary years.

LISTON, VICTOR (1838-1913)

The Robson of the Halls

Frederick Robson (1821-64) was a burlesque artiste renowned for his ability to switch from broad farce to high tragedy with astonishing facility.

Mr Liston achieved celebrity in 1868 with his powerfully pathetic rendering of *Shabby Genteel*, a song which drew the Town – including that stout champion of the underclasses the Prince of Wales – to the unfashionable Philharmonic Hall in Islington for seven months. That Mr Liston was unable to sustain this career impetus is evinced by his acceptance, some years later, of the managership of the Bon Accord Music Hall, Aberdeen.

William (*a.k.a.* Billy) Randall (1830-98) also freewheeled in the slipstream of a superior talent by styling himself *The Robsonian Comedian* or *Comique*.

LLOYD, ALICE (1873-1949)

The Ideal Daintee Chanteuse

In 1907 the Broadway manager Percy Williams engaged MARIE LLOYD for his Colonial Theatre. Inadequate communications resulted in the arrival not of the famous comedienne but of her unknown sister Alice. Mr Williams was not best pleased, engaged another star and gave his unwelcome import fifth spot.

It is heart-warming to record that by the end of the week the wrong Miss Lloyd's triumph was so complete that she was Top of the Bill, her name was up in lights, and her salary raised from $300 to $1,500 a week. *Variety* wrote enthusiastically if clumsily of her rendition of *Who Are You Looking At?* 'No more dainty, artistic bit of song acting has been given on the American stage and there is not an American actress who

20. SID FIELD

21. GRACIE FIELDS

22. FLANAGAN & ALLEN

23. MAX MILLER, GEORGE FORMBY Jnr & BERYL FORMBY

24. VICTOR POTT (aged 83)
Under arrest for killing his son, Harry Fragson.

HARRY FRAGSON

25. GASTON & ANDRÉE

26. TOMMY HANDLEY   27. JENNY HILL

28. HERSCHEL HENLERE

29. NAT JACKLEY

30. BETTY JUMEL

31. JUMPIN' JAX

32. KAUFMANN'S LADY CYCLISTS

33. KORINGA

34. LUCAN & McSHANE

35. DAN LENO
"...the saddest eyes in the whole world."

36 DAN LENO

37. MARIE LLOYD
Two of this artiste's famously prominent teeth were
punched out by her third husband,
jockey Bernard Dillon.

38. MARIE LLOYD

could not benefit by listening to this number.' For over thirty years Miss Lloyd remained a major vaudeville attraction, second only in celebrity and popularity to HARRY LAUDER. Her husband was Tom McNaughton (see SKETCH ARTISTES).

The performer was also at one time puzzlingly billed in the United States as *The Bonnie Belle of Scotland*, but then outside his own country your average American's grasp of geography tends to the woolly.

See JESSIE HARCOURT for an earlier Alice Lloyd, also DAISY WOOD and, for other 'dainty' artistes DAISY JAMES.

LLOYD, ARTHUR (1840-1904)

The Royal Comique

This entry's billing arose from his having shared with 'Jolly' JOHN NASH in 1863 the honour of being the first Music Hall artistes to perform before Royalty, *viz* the Prince of Wales. Like his fellow *Lions* Mr Lloyd possessed a commanding manner and a flamboyant personality, and it was his drawing-power which saved the fortunes of the newly opened London Pavilion Music Hall in 1866.

By the 1890s the artiste was billing himself as *The Last of the Lions Comiques*; whether he really was the last of his stripe is debatable, though after the death of the old Queen there cannot have been many still performing 'swell' songs of the 1860s and 70s. But the veteran was true to his code and never abandoned either his repertoire or his old-style heavy moustache.

See GEORGE LEYBOURNE

LLOYD, MARIE (1860-1922)

Queen of (All) Comediennes; Queen of Comedy; Queen of Serio-Comediennes

Marie Lloyd's tragical-comical life and career were the stuff of legend. With three unhappy marriages and an army of spongers and hangers-on bleeding her dry it is not surprising that the artiste died, physically and emotionally spent, at the age of only 52. Miss Lloyd – toothy, short and plump – possessed an earthy exuberance which in combination with a wretched private life has left a folk-memory of a great-hearted, impulsive, vital woman whose breadth of personality and huge unforced talent gave her performances a distinction rarely seen on the Halls, even if her reputation for indecency did preclude the artiste from ever appearing in a Royal Variety Performance. But Our Marie's spell retains its potency, and even today mention of her name brings a lift to the heart and a smile of affectionate half-remembrance to the lips.

Although often referred to as *Queen of the Halls* we find no evidence that this entry ever used such bill-matter, probably because of its association with BESSIE BELLWOOD and JENNY HILL. The myth that she was billed as *The Sarah Bernhardt of the Halls* arose from the inscription on a photograph from the great tragedienne who claimed to have enjoyed Marie's impersonation of her. Mme Bernhardt may also have been amused by the English Music Hall star's choice of stage name, the same as that of a distinguished French actress.

ALICE LLOYD and DAISY WOOD were Matilda Alice Victoria Wood's sisters; LILY LENA was her cousin, ALEC HURLEY her second husband and GEORGE W WARE her first agent. MAX WALL was her godson.

For other *Queens of Comedy* see HYLDA BAKER; for other serios see ANNIE ADAMS. Also see p.14, FRED BARNES, DAN LENO, MARIE LOFTUS, NELLIE POWER, QUEEN OF..., THE TILLER GIRLS, VESTA VICTORIA.

LLOYD-PARKER, HENRY (1891-1967)
The Burlesquedian; E Nose, Detective!

In the 1960s this gentleman, having dropped the Lloyd, was still on the road with what must have been the very last of the fit-ups. With his wife Mary Kinloch (1890-1995) and a clutch of tiros Mr Parker barnstormed the braes of Scotland performing a different play each night and a musical on Saturdays. The Kinloch Players' repertoire included such grand old favourites as *Maria Marten* and *East Lynne* plus scratch dramatisations of Sir Walter Scott. In 1956 we ourself were offered our first engagement by Mr Parker but were advised by an ex-pro family friend to wait for something less Dickensian to turn up. In some ways we regret having accepted that advice.

It will be noted that Mrs Lloyd-Parker died in her 105th year, thus making this lady the longest-lived entry in these pages.

LOCKE, JOSEF (b1918)
Britain's Greatest Tenor

The Londonderry tenor did indeed possess a fine organ ruined by undisciplined bawling and a delivery drenched in sentimentality.

Nevertheless, this entry was a broth of a bhoy whose singing gave great pleasure to the musically undiscerning. In the 1950s after a number of well-publicised skirmishes with the Revenue the performer suddenly disappeared, rumour said to Eire where his varletry was much admired.

There was a curious sequel some twenty years later when a singer whose voice was astonishingly like that of Mr Locke's appeared on the London club and theatre circuit. This gentleman was billed as Mr X and performed in a mask, so was this *Britain's Greatest Tenor* making a covert come-back? After a further twenty years the story surfaced yet again in that most appealing of films *Hear My Song* – the title of Mr Locke's theme song. There remains one unanswered question: who was the real Mr X?

Joseph M White (1891-1959) *The Silver Masked Tenor* might have been a candidate except that he died too soon.

See HAROLD BERENS

LOFTUS, MARIE (1857-1940)
The Sarah Bernhardt of the Halls

Miss Loftus was a woman of stately mien; Mme Bernhardt (1845-1923), the world's most renowned tragedienne, was famously wraith-like so it is puzzling to understand why the former took the latter as her artistic template, unless it be that both ladies were Jewish.

The singer's earlier bill-matter – *The Hibernian Hebe* – also raises queries for we may search through her repertoire in vain for any reference to country or race. Miss Loftus seemed more to specialise in 'motto' songs such as *A Thing you can't Buy with Gold* and *To Err is Human, To Forgive Divine*. Not that the less ennobling passions were ignored in *He Kissed I Once* and the still regularly performed *He's Going There Every Night*. This entry's claim to be the first female Music Hall artiste to top bills is unlikely to withstand scrutiny.

Others to nibble at The Divine Sarah's colossal celebrity were Mona Garrick *The Sarah Bernhardt of the Variety Stage*, Yvette Guilbert (1865-1944) *The Sarah Bernhardt of the Café Concert*, and Gerda Lundequist (1871-1959) *The Swedish Bernhardt*.

Miss Loftus' daughter, Cecilia or Cissie Loftus (1876-1943), enjoyed a career even more distinguished than her mother's, for the daughter not only worked the Halls as an acclaimed impressionist but also acted in plays for the Elevator of the Stage, Sir Henry Irving himself.

See ISSY BONN, MARIE LLOYD

LONG, NORMAN (1893-1950)

A Song, a Smile and a Piano

Mr Long's bill-matter was much parodied and its rhythmic construction much copied with at least three artistes – Richard Liszt, Tommy Westwood (fl c1950) and Peggy Wilding (fl1950s-60s) – displaying identical devices. By 1949 Mr Long wrote that he had 'virtually retired from the Profession to devote his attention to his Bolt Head Hotel, Salcombe, Devon' and therefore probably wasn't over-bothered.

See MARGARET COOPER, DICKIE HENDERSON

LOOSE SCREWS, THE THREE (fl1940s-50s)

Just 'Nuts'

The comedy act was run by Jack Farr and his dog Lulu; other Screws were MIKE & BERNIE WINTERS (who were with Mr Farr 1953-5 and later shamelessly plagiarised his bill-matter) and Cannon & Ball (Tom Cannon b1935 and Bobby Ball b1944).

A comic called Alf Bolony was using *Just Nuts* in the 1930s as were Syd & Max Harrison though these last two gentlemen, so their sons Hope & Keen have informed us, also displayed *Nuts in May, June and July*. As a solo performer Mr Farr billed himself as *It's in the Bag(pipes)*, which gave fair warning.

Arthur Worsley (VENTRILOQUISTS) had a similar notion.

LORRAINE, LILLIAN (1892-1955)

Queen of Venuses

The exceptionally beautiful San Franciscan vocaliste rose swiftly from the chorus to become a major Broadway musical comedy and revue star while still in her teens. Florenz Ziegfeld (1869-1932) was especially susceptible to her manifold and manifest charms, and it was in various editions of his legendary Follies that the artiste sang such immortal ditties as *By The Light Of The Silvery Moon, Row Row Row*, and the mysteriously entitled *Ballin' the Jack*.

See QUEEN OF...

LOSS, JOE (AND HIS BAND) (1909-90)

Radio's Kings of Rhythm

The favourite society maestro used to say waggishly that his most frequent request was 'Where's the gents?'

LUCAN & McSHANE (fl1913-52)

Old Mother Riley and her daughter Kitty

The team's best-known sketch by far was *Bridget's Night Out* in which the bony Miss McShane played an unlikely colleen with Mr Lucan in fustian drag as her widowed mother, an Irishwoman of febrile temperament whose limbs whirled and twirled in direct ratio to their owner's irritability. As the dialogue heightened tempers and crockery began to fly; the sketch ended, gloriously and most satisfyingly, only when every single plate, cup and saucer in the kitchen had been smashed to pieces.

Few who watched the slapstick antics of Arthur Lucan (1885-1954) and his wife Kitty McShane (1897-1964) realised the extent to which their on-stage battling spilled into their private lives. The relationship deteriorated to such an extent that for the last of the fifteen Old Mother Riley films their scenes had to be spliced together from single shots, for they could not bear being on set together. The bankrupt Mr Lucan carried on touring with a new partner until he literally dropped, dying in his dressing-room at the Tivoli, Hull. A sad, bitter end.

See SKETCH ARTISTES

LUNE, TED (1921-68)

The Lad from Lancashire; They Sent for Me So I 'Ad to Cum

Though we do recall very clearly how Mr Lune's tights flapped round his meagre shanks we were shocked to realise in the course of our researches that at expiry this entry was only 47, for his tubercular gauntness made him seem much older. This was at the Liverpool Empire where we were working with the comedian in pantomime when illness overwhelmed him and an ambulance took him home to Blackpool. He never worked again.

One of Mr Lune's routines in the show was the Letter from Mum ('I've just had all my teeth taken out and a new fire-place put in') which, with additions and refinements, we ourself are still working to this very day. Thank you, Ted.

Jack Warman (b1887) *The Lean Rasher of Mirth* also played on an anorexic physique with an advertisement in 1922 which billed him as *The Stick of Mirth – It's Sickening.*

Another *Lancashire Lad* was Morny Cash (1872-1938), nowadays remembered solely for the song *I Live In Trafalgar Square.*

See WILL OLIVER

LUPINOS, THE (fl since c1600)
The Wreckers

This illustrious family ran like a silver thread through the tapestry of British performing arts for four hundred years. *The Wreckers* was but one of many sketches worked on the Halls by 19th-century representatives of the line; in the 20th century the Lupino heritage nurtured such comedian-pantomimists as Arthur (1864-1908) and Harry (1865-1925) with *The Monkey & the Sailor* and Barry (1882-1962) with *One Good Turn.* Arthur was personally chosen by Sir James Barrie to play Nana the dog in the original production of *Peter Pan,* the boy who wouldn't grow up.

Their niece Ida (1918-95) took the Lupino name to Hollywood where her sultry mouth and edgy personality were particularly suited to the *films noirs* of the 1940s. Now the Queen of Smoulder is dead and the line is played out; Lupinos are no longer seen on our stages and we are all the poorer.

See REVNELL & WEST, SKETCH ARTISTES

LYNN, Dame VERA (b1917)
The Forces' Sweetheart; Radio's Sweet Singer of Sweet Songs

In the early 1940s a certain Eric Lloyd also called himself the *Forces' Sweetheart;* whether this gentleman's billing pre-dated Dame Vera's we do not know, nor are we aware of the nature of his entertainment though female impersonation would seem a likely bet. But impersonate Vera Lynn? Surely no one would have dared.

LYNTON, JIMMY (1887-1970)

We have no bill-matter for this artiste other than *The Boy with the Silver Notes* (from his time with Professor O'Dell's Royal Juvenile Pierrots) but we cannot forbear from entering the grandfather of a Very Important Personage indeed.

It is the most improbable coincidence that two successive British Prime Ministers should have been directly descended from Music Hall artistes, but such is the case. John Major's connection is entered under DRUM & MAJOR; Tony Blair (b1953), who took office in 1997, is the paternal grandson of singer-dancer-mentalist-escapologist-comedian Jimmy Lynton and singer Celia Ridgeway (1888-1969).

We worked with Mr Lynton at the Players' Theatre, where with a partner he performed two excellent comedy mime routines. We also trod the boards with this entry in *Jack & the Beanstalk* at the London Palladium in which Mr Lynton most ably sustained the front half of Daisy the Cow.

LYONS, ESTHER (1864-1938)

The Klondyke Girl

In similar vein was Kitty Rockwell (1876-1957) *Klondyke Kate*. What did these ladies do to divert their audiences? Prospect?

LYTTON & AUSTIN (fl1896-c1900)

The Stage-Struck Waifs; Two Plants Just Budding

Of CHARLES AUSTIN details may be seen *supra* but of Will Lytton we have no divulgations whatsoever. Another two-hander using the bill-matter *The Stage Struck Waifs* was Spencer & Marks. Were these gentlemen Lytton & Austin? If so, why did they change their names? Did Messrs Marks & Spencer, the popular clothiers, threaten interdicts? These are deep waters.

Mc

McCORD, CAL (1906-83)
Entertaining All Ways; Noted Cowboy

Sometimes billed *with Ladybird.* In 1930 this entry was advertising himself as Cal McKord *The Kordial Kowboy* which is, in our considered opinion, the cheesiest bill-matter of all time.

See TEX McLEOD, THE MIKE-ROGUES

McCORMACK, Count JOHN (1884-1945)
The English Caruso

This billing is wildly misconceived on two counts: firstly the great singer was not English at all but a most fervent son of Erin, and secondly his un-Italianate lyric tenor was patently unlike Caruso's uniquely weightier timbre.

We feel sure that Count John would have been flattered by Princess Lei Lani who flourished on the Halls c1910 and who described herself as *The McCormack of Hawaii.*

For other Carusos see BETTY AUKLAND, TOM BURKE.

MACDERMOTT, G H (1845-1901)
The Statesman of the Halls

In his early days on the Halls this entry jumped aboard the bogus Irish band-wagon and proclaimed himself Gilbert Hastings *Irish Comedian and Champion Policeman.* Later as G H Macdermott he was billed as *Champion Spot* and *The Covent Garden Bluebeard,* but it is as The Great Macdermott *The Statesman of the Halls* that the singer is best remembered.

The soubriquet arose from the True Blue hue of many of Mr Macdermott's songs which made managers whose licences were issued by Liberal benches reluctant to engage him; the artiste's tendency to leaven his material with salacity also contributed to an increasingly thin diary and so the *Lion Comique* became an agent, the last resort of so many performers unable to find a shop.

Unquestionably the most notable song of the robust performer's career was that known variously as *We Don't Want To Fight* or *The Jingo Song,* or, as our copy has it, *Macdermott's War Song.*

It may be an over-statement to say that this ditty changed the course of history, but not by much. The British public's attitude to Russo-Turkish sabre-rattlings in 1877 was certainly polarised in favour of the Turks by G W Hunt's lyrics; Gladstone had his windows smashed, Disraeli came back triumphant from the Berlin peace conference to be offered a dukedom by a besotted Queen Victoria, and Britain got Cyprus. Such is the potency, as was later observed, of cheap music.

See PAT FEENEY, GEORGE LEYBOURNE, J H MILBURN

MacDONNELL, LESLIE (1903-78)
Mr Sunshine

Mr MacDonnell's soubriquet was awarded by virtue of his tremendous work for the Variety Club of Great Britain. After succeeding Val Parnell as managing director of Moss Empires this entry became Chief Barker of the club, and it was largely Mr MacDonnell's energy and vision which brought into being the Sunshine Coach programme for transporting handicapped children, a worthy activity now also undertaken by Variety Clubs International.

McGIVENEY, OWEN (1884-1967)
The World's Greatest Quick Change Artiste

While still damp from the printers Charles Dickens' vividly theatrical novels were ruthlessly plundered by actors and Protean artistes and reciters. Mr McGiveney was not guiltless in this regard, having concocted a scene in which he portrayed Bill Sikes and four other rôles 'with record-breaking changes'. We are not sure what this means.

Chanti (fl1900s-1910s) was the self-styled *World's Great Master of Protean Science*; Mlle Von Etta (fl1906-14) was *The Only Lady Illusionist, Protean and Quick Change Artiste*; R A Roberts (1866-1932), perhaps the most distinguished in this category, contented himself with *The Protean Actor*.

Finally and reluctantly we list Oliver & Twist *A Dickens of an Act* – if these artistes were as feeble as their bill-matter it is no wonder we know no more of them.

See Adelina (GEORGE F MOORE), LYDIA DREAMS, HARRY FRAGSON, BRANSBY WILLIAMS

McLEOD, TEX (1890-1973)

The Cowboy Humorist; Spinning Ropes & Yarns; The Will Rogers of England

Mr McLeod must have billed himself as *The Will Rogers of England* in a fit of extreme abstraction because he was in fact a Texan.

See CAL McCORD, WILL ROGERS

M

MACARI (1896-1971)
...and his Dutch Serenaders

The Serenaders were founded by Anthony Macari in 1931; by the 1950s the troupe included his children Joe (1924-90), Rosa (1923-92) *Princess of Pep* who sang, and Larry *Europe's Greatest Accordionist.* In 1949 the show was called *Dutch Mill*, a colourful and lively presentation with Dutch scenery and costumes and featuring Billy Reed whose klompen dansen was much admired.

Mr Macari, who at one time 'performed in front of his father's booth to draw crowds', was the son of Mme GASCOYNE *The Only Clock-Eyed Lady in the World.*

An earlier Nederlander on the British Halls was Jake Friedman *and his Dutch Hussars* (fl c1910); was this the same Jake Friedman (b1867) whose bill-matter was *The One-Man Opera?*

See 'Happy' FANNY FIELDS for other Low Country artistes.

MACKNEY, E W (1825-1909)
Negro Delineator

Often billed as *The Great Mackney* or *The Inimitable Mackney* this Londoner was the first solo black-face star in Britain. From the 1840s 'Nigger Minstrel' troupes had become increasingly popular but it was Mr Mackney's powerful talents as singer, dancer, fiddler, banjoist and bones player which popularised the notion of a *single* 'Darkie' on the Halls, so much so that by the end of the century no bill was complete without one, two, or even three such acts.

So well-integrated into the warp and woof of light entertainment had the black-face artiste become that it was not unknown for actual black performers to wear white make-up round their mouths and eyes, thus presenting the bizarre spectacle of a black man pretending to be a white man pretending to be a black man.

See G H ELLIOTT, T D RICE also YOUNG TICHBORNE

MADISON, JAMES (1871-1943)
The American Joe Miller

The year after the death in London of 'witty actor' Joe Miller (1684-1738) John Mottley brought out his compilation of *Joe Miller's Jests - The Wit's Vade-Mecum*. It is curious that although in the United States Joe Miller's name is still synonymous with weak and venerable humour, in his native Britain the 'favourite low comedian' has quite passed from general ken.

MADRALI, AHMED (fl1900s)
The Terrible Turk

In the imagination of the GBP Turkish men were unspeakably cruel, had filthy habits and indulged in thrillingly exotic depravities in the privacy of their own harems.

Almost as beastly were the Greeks, hence the appearance on our Halls of Antonio Pieri (fl1900s) *The Terrible Greek*. But all was not necessarily what it seemed for Ted Pablo (1855-1937), another *Terrible Turk*, was in reality Edward Charles Darby, a name more redolent of the Home Counties than the Golden Horn.

MAGICIANS

Roger Barkin (1914-95)
The Poetic Magician

James Bassett (1854-1907)
The King's Conjuror

The Great (Edgar) Benyon (1902-78)
Bam-Boozalem

David Berglas (b1926)
Man of Magic
See WINDMILL THEATRE

Ali Bey (b1905)
Quick as Lightning – Startling as Thunder

Billington (fl1940s)
Slightly Different Codologist
See JOHNNY COOPER, THE GREAT HUGHES

MAGICIANS (continued):

Jimmy Binnie (fl1950s-60s)
The Magical Funatic

Ali Bongo (b1929)
The Shriek of Araby

George Braund (1904-69)
The Biggest Thing in Magic

Fred Brezin (b1890)
The Boy Magician

Cardini (1895-1973)
The Ace of Conjurers
a.k.a. Valentine, Val Raymond, and Professor Thomas

The Great Carmo (1881-1944)
Australia's Wonder Worker; The Master Phantasist;
The World's Colossus of Mystery

The Great Carter (Charles J Carter) (1874-1936)
Boy Magician

Cellsus (fl1920s)
The Whirlwind Illusionist; The White Wizard

The Great Cingalee (1901-66)
...and his Company of Skilled Mystifiers;
The Silent/Yellow Man of Mystery

Cire (b1895)
The Emperor of Mystery
From 1936 ran a robot act – see AL CARTHY.

Leon Clifford
See KARDOMA

Mystic Craig (1900-87)
Fashions in Magic

Howard De Courcy (1914-90)
Debonair Deceiver
See Leslie Lester *infra*, WINDMILL THEATRE

Jack Demain (fl1930s-50s)
The Ace of Manipulators

MAGICIANS (continued):

Deveen (b1890)
...and his New York Blondes; The Distinguished Deceiver (with 100 Lighted Cigars)
See LYDIA THOMPSON

Arthur Dowler (1896-1953)
The Wizard of Cod

T Nelson Downs (1867-1938)
The King of Koins

Roy Earl (fl1950s)
The 'Dance Mad' Magician

Bert Easley (1904-87)
The Tipsy Trickster
See JOHNNY COOPER

Emerson & Jayne (fl1960s-90s)
The Magic Carpet
Husband & wife team: Ted and Hilda

Erikson (fl1930s-40s)
The Official Deceiver
See WINDMILL THEATRE

Fargo
The Boy Wizard
See FLANAGAN & ALLEN

The Amazing Fogel (1911-81)
The World's Greatest Mind Reader
See THE ZANCIGS

Frakson (1891-1981)
...with his Cigarettes

Horace Goldin (1873-1939)
The King's Magician (from 1902)
The Peerless Illusionist
The Royal Illusionist (from 1902)

Freddie Harris (1908-92)
There's a Trick in It

MAGICIANS (continued):

Terry Herbert
Master of Disaster
a.k.a. Mr Woo the Wizard

Professor Eugene Hermann (fl1850s-60)
American Wizard & Ceiling Walker
See Mlle ALMA

Charles Hoffman (b1896)
The Highest Paid Bartender in the World
From 1938 *k.a.* Charles 'Think-a-Drink' Hoffman

Professor Hoffmann (1839-1919)
Wizard of the City of the Golden Gate

Robert Houdin (1805-71)
The Father of Modern Magic; The Sole Monarch of the World of Wonders

Paul Howard (d1958)
Just Tricks and Things

Ionia (b c1885)
The Goddess of Mystery

Joseph Jacobs (1813-70)
The Wizard of All Wizards

Al Koran (1916-72)
*Television's Man of Magic;
The World's Fastest Mind Reader*
See THE ZANCIGS

Jack Le Dair (1880-1958)
The Amusing Trickologist;The Survival of the Slickest

Servais Le Roy (1865-1953)
The World's Monarch of Magic
Married Mlle Talma *infra*

Leslie Lester (1906-68)
The Debonair Deceiver
See Howard De Courcy *supra*

The Great Levante (1892-1978)
How's Tricks?

MAGICIANS (continued):

Levantine (1851-1929)
The American Wonder; ... with his Magic Barrel

The Great (Cecil) Lyle (1889-1955)
The Magic Milliner

Malotz
The Singing Telepathist
See THE ZANCIGS

Jasper Maskelyne (1902-73)
The Royal Command Magician
Grandson of J Nevil Maskelyne – see next entry

Maskelyne & Cooke
The Royal Illusionists and Anti-Spiritualists
J Nevil Maskelyne (1839-1917) and
George A Cooke (1825-1904)
See previous entry

June Merlin
The Bewitching Witch

Orville Meyer (b1911)
The Wizard of Ah's

Clement Minns
See VENTRILOQUISTS

E J Moore (1881-1957)
The Talkative Trickster

Charles Morritt (1860-1936)
The Yorkshire Conjurer

Rahnee Motie
See KORINGA

Murray (1901-88)
Round the World in Magic

N'Gai (fl1930s-50s)
Magic in his Words
First name: Ronald

MAGICIANS (continued):

David Nixon (1919-78)
It's Magic
See NORMAN WISDOM, WINDMILL THEATRE

Billy O'Connor (c1895-1974)
...and his Fifty-Two Assistants; A Pack of Humour

Charles Ovalden
See CARL HERTZ

Vic Perry (1919-74)
*Boy Pickpocket Magician; The World's
Greatest Pickpocket*

Channing Pollock
America's Foremost Prestidigitateur
Nephew of the American artist Jackson Pollock (1912-56)

Glen Pope & Ann (fl1930s-40s)
A Magic Flirtation
Glen Pope (1910-c1950s)

The Great Ramses (1876-1930)
The Eastern Mystic

Raoul (b1897)
To Amuse and Confuse; Wonders Without Words
Family name: Ralph Chart

Rayanne & Partner (fl1938-50s)
Mind Over Matter; The World's Wonder Girl
Husband and wife team: Winifred L (b1918) and Jack P L Martens-Moore (b1897)
See THE ZANCIGS

The Great Richelieu
See CARROLL LEVIS

Robinson
See CHUNG LING SOO

Ben Said (fl1900s-30s)
The Algerian Funjuror; The Egyptian Funjuror
a.k.a. Amasis (1909-25), Professor Hottoff, and Li-Sing-Poo

MAGICIANS (continued):

Saphrim (fl c1900)
The Gay Deceiver

Cyril Shields
See SIRDANI

Sorcar (1913-71)
The World's Greatest Magician

Mlle (Mercedes) Talma (1861-1944)
Queen of Coins
Married Servais Le Roy *supra*

Harold Taylor (1913-93)
Wit & Wizardry; The Witty Wizard
See WINDMILL THEATRE

The Great Tomsoni (b1934)
Poland's Finest Magician; The Wizard of Warsaw
From 1976 reverted to family name and worked with wife
Pam as John Thompson & Co.

Van Hoven, Frank (c1887-1929)
The Dippy Mad Magician; The Mad Magician;
The Man who Made Ice Famous

Anne Vernone (fl1840s-?)
The Only Female Professor of Modern
Magic in the World

John Wade
Magically Yours; The Patter of Magic Feats
See WINDMILL THEATRE

Princess Wah-Letka (fl1920s-30s)
The Psychic Marvel

Francis Watts (fl1926-60s)
Magic in Everything

Claud 'Medals' Williams (1891-1972)
Almost a Magician
a.k.a. The Great Claud. Brother-in-law of DENNY WILLIS

Vic Wise (1900-76)
The Youngest Magician in the World
Later with Campbell & Wise *The Weak Guy and his Weakness*.
In the 1950s took a new partner as Vic Wise & Nita Lane.

Zahla (fl1949-50s)
The Blindfold Intuitionist
Sometimes worked as Stan Aces and from 1925-43 also as
Zada *The Blindfold Mystic*.
See THE ZANCIGS

Mlle Zara (fl1900s)
*Florentine Society Magician and Magnetic Queen
of Second Sight*
See THE ZANCIGS

The Bewildering Zodias (fl1950s-60s)
Mystifying Mentalists; The World's Fastest Mentalists
See THE ZANCIGS

See also entries for: ANNIE MAY ABBOTT, SHEK BEN ALI, JOHN HENRY ANDERSON,
ARTEMUS, LARRY BARNES, Dr WALFORD BODIE, KUDA BUX, THE GREAT CARLTON,
CHUNG LING SOO, JOHNNY COOPER, DANTE, GEORGE BARNARDO EAGLE, CARL HERTZ,
HARRY HOUDINI, THE GREAT HUGHES, KALANAG, KARDOMA, THE GREAT KOVARI, THE
GREAT LAFAYETTE, THE GREAT NIXON, Dr JOHN HENRY PEPPER, SANDY POWELL, ARTHUR
PRINCE, PAUL RAYMOND, ROVI, 'Lord' GEORGE SANGER, SIRDANI, VALENTINE VOX

MAJOR, TOM & KITTY – see DRUM & MAJOR

MATTHEWS, JESSIE (1907-81)
Dancing Divinity

On discarding her dancing shoes Miss Matthews launched a career as
a cabaret singer, but with her once svelte figure now bloated and
ungainly and with vocal resources not of the highest order this enterprise
did not thrive; an unexpected offer in 1963 to take over as Mrs Dale in
The Dales (originally *Mrs Dale's Diary*) came opportunely.

But this entry had had a miserable private life and her reason began
to totter. We ourself flitted in and out of the long-running BBC radio
serial during the 1960s and can bear witness to Miss Matthews' erratic
behaviour which became more marked as the decade progressed –
the Royal Family was in danger and only she could save them. By
1969 the actress had become too irrational to sustain her central rôle
and the BBC decided to wind the serial up. Perhaps Mrs Dale had had
her day anyway, but it was all desperately sad.

MAYNE, CLARICE (1886-1966)
...and That (Fellow)

Considered one of the best principal boys of her day Miss Mayne was a witty, pretty and glamorous singer, though in the style of the time perhaps a touch arch. *That* was her first husband James W Tate (1875-1922) who supplied his wife with much of her Music Hall repertoire and accompanied her from a piano Up Centre. His first wife had been LOTTIE COLLINS, a lady ten years his senior. Miss Mayne was ten years his junior, and he must have found the change invigorating – perhaps too much so for he was dead at the age of 47.

By chance Miss Mayne's second husband, Teddy Knox of NERVO & KNOX, was ten years her junior, a disparity of which the ageing ingenue was always acutely conscious, and not without reason. As she lay dying the wronged wife's thoughts were not on her Maker but on how to stop the mistress getting her jewellery.

See MAY ERNE

MAYNE, ERNIE (1887-1937)
The Simple One; Sitting on 't Fence

Mr Mayne was an extremely corpulent comic singer who specialised in ditties concerned with the ingestion of comestibles such as *A N'Egg And Some N'Ham And A N'Onion, No We Don't Keep Fish Only Kippers, Plenty Of Pudden, I Like A C'Hup Of C-Hocoa, I Can't Do My Bally Bottom Button Up*, and the immortal *You Can't Get Many Pimples On A Pound Of Pickled Pork*. The artiste retired to become a publican at Shoreham-on-Sea, a small town on the Sussex coast where we spent an inglorious eighteen months clerking in the local Barclays Bank.

MAYO, SAM (1881-1938)
The Immobile One

This strange comedian, customarily clad in an old brown dressing-gown and a yellow scratch wig, sometimes sang from the piano with a face almost devoid of expression and sometimes standing Down Centre, motionless, with his hands between his knees.

Mr Mayo was a prolific writer for others as well as himself, though the droll peculiarity of his songs has not ensured their survival in today's Old Time shows. The performer's lugubrious, slightly sinister style was not to all tastes though he claimed to hold the record for multiple Metropolitan engagements, having for four weeks played twelve Halls a night! A less enviable record was his three bankruptcies.

Of similar conceit to Mr Mayo was Alf Gibson (1860-1920) *The Comedian who Never Moves.*

See MARGARET COOPER

MAZDA & OSRAM
Two Bright Sparks

We have no documentary evidence to support the *actualité* of this entry but as it was supplied by ROY HUDD it must be valid.

MENDELSSOHN, FELIX (1911-81)
...and his Hawaiian Serenaders

The musician was born in Brondesbury Park, an undistinguished but not unpleasant inner suburb of North West London in which we ourself resided for some years.

Before forming his *Hawaiian Serenaders* Mr Mendelssohn had been a stock-broker's clerk, a sailor in the Royal Navy, an actor and a 'high pressure publicity agent for a number of well known variety and night club personalities'. But when this entry claimed to be 'a descendant of the famous composer of the same name' the pressure must have been turned too high for his alleged ancestor died childless.

MENKEN, ADAH ISAACS (1835-68)
The Naked Woman

Fresh, or fairly fresh, from a New Orleans orphanage Dolores Adios Fuertes married Alexander Isaacs Menken whose name she bore through sundry alliances both regular and irregular. Mrs Menken was the greatest star the hippodrama ever knew, her international notoriety being founded upon but one rôle: Mazeppa.

In a dramatisation of Byron's poem the well-rounded actress was strapped, apparently unclad, to a horse which galloped off on an epic ride from the Dnieper to Tartary. The artiste was in fact comprehensively covered in pink fleshings; in those large, dimly lit circus arenas the lady's 'magnificent audacity' was taken on trust even though it was not unknown, if the performer were out of sorts, for her place to be taken by a male double with no one the wiser.

This entry was also of a literary bent, publishing a slender volume of verse and sleeping with Alexandre Dumas *père*, A C Swinburne, and, just to show her versatility, George Sand.

MENNARD, TOM (1918-89)
Juggles with Live Geese

In his latter years Mr Mennard became a celebrity in *Coronation Street* playing the rôle of Sam Tindall (with his dog Dougal). As a young comedian this entry exhibited a penchant for hilarious practical jokes – hence his bill-matter – such as advertising in his parish magazine for an underwater wood-burning stove, placing a card in his local newsagents announcing that the local Claustrophobia Society were forming a potholing section, and driving a bus in Brighton dressed as a nun. What a card!

See JUGGLERS, WINDMILL THEATRE

MERMAN, ETHEL (1909-84)
The Golden Foghorn

A press nickname rather than true bill-matter – *cf* Mel Tormé (1925-99) *The Velvet Fog*. We experienced Miss Merman's tremendous personality in a television studio in Elstree, though we must confess we were fascinated not so much by her performance as by her radio microphone, such contrivances being then new to Britain's shores.

MERRICK, JOSEPH CAREY (1862-90)
The Elephant Man

The tale of the grotesquely deformed Leicester boy is harrowing beyond belief, with much credit due to the eminent surgeon (Sir) Frederick Treves who first saw him exhibited in a Whitechapel Road shop near the London Hospital. Both Treves and the Board of the Hospital behaved commendably in providing Mr Merrick with the privacy and security he so desperately needed.

Although this entry remains by far the worst recorded case of multiple neurofibromatosis known to medical science, the melancholy fact is that the disorder is still incurable and hardly any more treatable that it was a century ago.

See SAM TORR

MERSON, BILLY (1881-1947)
London's Favourite Comedian

Before becoming established as a soloist Mr Merson worked c1901-8 with Bernard Whiteman under various stage names including Whiteman & Thompson *Irish Comedians and Trapeze Performers*, Snakella & Travella *Eccentric Equilibrists and Gymnasts*, and Keith & Merson; in the Antipodes the artiste was briefly Ping Pong *Australia's Greatest Clown*, odd bill-matter for a Nottingham boy.

In 1909 this entry produced his greatest hit *The Spaniard That Blighted My Life*, a song pirated by AL JOLSON in 1913 though litigation afforded the hapless Mr Merson only ruinous expense.

See PAT FEENEY

MIKE-ROGUES, THE (fl1940s-50s)
Discords in Harmony

If CAL McCORD gets the wooden spoon for Worst Bill-Matter this entry takes the biscuit for Worst Act Title.

MILBURN, J H (1848-1923)
The Noisy Swell

A swell was a swaggering, over-dressed, would-be toff. Jem Milburn's songs – *Come Along Boys, Let's Make A Noise, Pull Yourselves Together Boys, On The Beach At Brighton* – give the general flavour of a middle-rung artiste too modestly talented to be numbered among the *Lions Comiques*, that august group of which his son-in-law, G H MACDERMOTT, was so illustrious an ornament.

MILES, BERNARD (Lord) (1907-91)
The Uncrowned King of the Chiltern Hills

For years the actor-comedian worked his Variety act to raise funds for the Mermaid Theatre at Puddle Dock, Blackfriars Bridge, the first theatre to be built in the City of London for three hundred and fifty years.

We can still chuckle at the memory of Mr Miles leaning over a large cart-wheel and slyly regaling us with stories of rural life, often of a nature unsuitable for a vicarage tea. This entry received a peerage for services to the theatre, only the second actor (after Laurence Olivier) to be so honoured.

MILLER, MAX (1895-1963)
The Cheeky Chappie

Born in Brighton, Thomas Henry Sargent was by common consent the greatest front-cloth comic of his era. This magnificent performer could light up those huge Variety auditoria to a greater extent than we have seen before or since. Another billing, *The Pure Gold of the Music Hall*, was coined by Lionel Hale in the *Daily Mail*, and no one who ever saw the comedian would disagree with that encomium. Mr Miller's material concentrated almost exclusively on the grosser passions, and how we loved him for it. A quiet-living man despite his public persona as a joyously unquenchable philanderer, this entry's reputation for meanness is belied by his unsung generosity to St Dunstan's home for blind ex-Servicemen. The smile in the artiste's voice is so irresistible as we listen to his recordings that even the surliest of today's adolescents cannot forbear to respond, a phenomenon we have seen with our own eyes.

'When I'm gone,' Maxie would assert, 'the game's over.' And how right he was. The great comedian left an imperishable reputation, £27,377 and a yellow Rolls-Royce.

See p.15, WILKIE BARD, JIMMY WHEELER, MIKE YARWOOD

MILLIGAN, SPIKE (b1918)
Late of the Human Race

The influence of this entry on British humour in the second half of the 20th century cannot be over-estimated. *Beyond the Fringe, Monty Python's Flying Circus* and the so-called Alternatives all owe their existence to the zaniest of them all. Mould-breaking, anarchic, iconoclastic, timeless – the writer-comedian was all that young comics still strive to be, though rarely evincing a fraction of his wit, originality or compassion.

The pressure of writing more than 200 episodes of *The Goon Show*, BBC radio's most successful comedy show ever, wrecked both Mr Milligan's marriage and his health – '...and I've been a neurotic ever since. I gave my sanity to that show'. But even in his frail and wispy old age the spark of irreverence still smoulders, as when at an award ceremony in 1995 the honorand was heard to refer to his life-long admirer the Prince of Wales as 'that little creep'.

See Foreword, DR CROCK, HARRY SECOMBE, PETER SELLERS

MILLS, NAT (& BOBBIE) (fl1923-55)
The Rare Pair

Just as we feel cheated when insanity turns out to be the rationale of a hitherto interestingly plotted thriller so are we dismayed when imbecility is made the premise for humour. With Nat Mills (1900-93) and Bobbie Macauley (1905-55) the fault was compounded by both artistes appearing to be what used to be termed Educationally Sub-Normal. For this reason we never warmed to this husband and wife team, a couple whose patter was studiedly stupid and whose appearance was the stuff of nightmares.

MILO, LA (fl1900-1910s)
The Inimitable Breathing Marble

Snug-fitting pink costumes and subdued lighting persuaded wide-eyed audiences they were seeing more than was proper, and Mrs Eggena (née Pansy Montague) was not the only one to take advantage of the seething prudishness of the times. According to Ernest Short the costume worn by this beautiful young woman as Velázquez' Venus 'consisted of a thick plaster preparation which covered the figure from top to toe, but Johnnydom was deceived'.

The eminent man of letters Keith Waterhouse recently wrote in a programme note that the poseuse was billed as La Milo *Wearing only a Smilo* but we think this is a joke-o.

A decade or more earlier at the Palace the Viennese showman Edward Von Kilyany (1852-95) caused hushed whispers and mordant sighs with his representations of great masterworks called *Living Pictures*, most of which, by an odd coincidence, displayed much naked – or seemingly naked flesh.

Of The Three Olympiers *Living Bronzes* an overheated reviewer in *The Era* wrote in June 1906 'They pose in the nude, and their artistic realisations of bronze groups are admirable. They are fine, powerful, muscular fellows...the illusion being aided by a secret process whereby the naked bodies of the performers are coated with a preparation of bronze.'

MISCELLANEOUS

Abadaroffs, The
Prehistoric Mountebanks

MISCELLANEOUS (continued):

Hadji Ali (1892-1937)
The Egyptian Enigma
Regurgitator of rodents and fish.
See HARRY NORTON

Allen & Lavoie (fl1930s)
Just Let Loose for This Show Only

Jack Anthony (1900-62)
Jack's The Joy; Nae Bother at A'

Edgar Atchison-Ely (fl1890s)
The Future Dude

Will Atkins
The Clock Face
See Mme GASCOYNE

Charlie Baldwin's (fl c1920)
...Bank Clerks

Susanah Bale (1877-1943)
Simosa San

Barclay Sisters (fl1940s)
Melody from Shoes

Barrett & Knowles (fl1920s)
Comedians (The Green Lizard and his Friend)
with Piano Attached

Harry Bass (fl1880s)
Champion Bottle Carrier and Pedestrian of the World

Countess Bekoffska (fl1910s)
The Lightning Flower Painter

Willie Best (1916-62)
Sleep'n' Eat

Burdon, Bryan (b1934)
The Chance of a Laughtime
Regularly misprinted as *The Chance of a Lifetime* prompting
the artiste to change to *Following in Father's Fingerprints* after his
celebrated comedian father Albert Burdon (1900-81).
See WALLY STANLEY & EDITH LESTER

MISCELLANEOUS (continued):

Carla
As a singer Kathleen McDonough's bill-matter was *With a Song in my Heart*, as a contortioniste it was *Danseuse Extraordinaire*, as an exotic dancer it was *Tassles & Twirls*, and as an erotic dancer it was *My Lady's Boudoir*.

Fred Carr
The Giant Electric Chicken
See Walter Stanton *infra*

The Carson Sisters (fl1930s)
The Neighbours are Glad They're On Tour

Jack Carter (b1923)
Jack of all Tirades

Ciselatus (fl1900s)
The Scissor King

Eddie Clark (fl c1910)
...and his Merry Kiddos
In the US billed as Eddie Clark with his *Six Winning Widows*.

Jack Clifford (1880-1956)
The Man with the Infectious Smile

Josephine Clofullia (b1831)
The Bearded Lady of Geneva

Mrs Coleman (fl1900s-10s)
The Dainty Canadian Widow

Arthur Corney
The Unobtrusive
In 1885 billed as *The London Idol*, perhaps abandoning this cognomen to the far better known VESTA TILLEY.

James H Cullen (1872-1925)
The Man from the West

Will Cummin (fl1910s)
The Mad Hatter
Chapeaugraphist?

M. A De Bessell (fl1900s)
Lightning Clay Modeller
See Yost & Partner *infra*

MISCELLANEOUS (continued):

Mlle De Dio (fl c1900)
In Search of Faith
This artiste in 1906 at the Palace presented 'a sensational series of dances with fire and water effects'.

Dorrie Dene (d March 1966)
The Indescribable
Comedienne

Laurie Devine (1905-36)
Meg o' the Halls

Demaris Dore (fl1930s)
Hotsy Totsy

Bunny Doyle (1896-1955)
The Minister for Idiotic Affairs

Patsy Doyle (1866-1930)
The Big Sad Man; The Sad Fat Man

Renée Dymott (1922-81)
The Unusual Girl

Jimmy Edmondson (1911-76)
Professor Backwards

Maudie Edwards (1907-91)
The Voice of Wales

Joan Elliott & Billie Roche (fl1940s)
2 Girls 2 Good 2 Miss
See Len Howe & Audrey Maye *infra*

Evangeline Florence (1873-1928)
The New Eiffel Tower Soprano
Possessed phenomenally high notes.

Fifi
...and her Panoramic Nudes
Appeared at the Granville, Walham Green, West London, in 1962.
See PHYLLIS DIXEY

Gertrella (fl1890s)
The Phanto-Gymnast

MISCELLANEOUS (continued):

Carroll Gibbons (1903-54)
...and his Boy Friends; ...and his Savoy Hotel Orpheans

Marie Gilchrist (fl1880s-90s)
Congress of Nations

Jackie Gleason (1916-87)
The Great One

Leslie Gould (d1969/70)
The Man in the Straw Hat

Esmé Hand
On her Electric Organ

Rich Hayes (1890-1933)
Exploring with Man Friday on Crusoe Island

Len Howe & Audrey Maye
The Fool and the Foil; Just for Laughs; 2 Funny 4 Words
Husband (b1919) and wife (b1930). Mrs Howe's mother was May
Walden (see FREDDIE FRINTON).
See Joan Elliott & Billie Roche *supra*

Walter Jackson (d1977)
Uranium in the Cranium

Jo-Jo (1868-1904)
The Dog-Faced Boy/Man
né Fedor Jeftichew; suffered from hypertrichosis.

Sissieretta Jones (1868-1933)
The Black Pearl

Young Josephs (fl1900s)
The Fighting Actor
A boxing champion of sorts; toured sketch called *Brother
against Brother.*
See GEORGE GRAY

Emmett Kelly (1898-1979)
The American Hobo Clown; Weary Willie

J W Kelly (1857-97)
The Rolling Mill Man

MISCELLANEOUS (continued):

Neville Kennard (fl1920s-50s)
Red, Bright & New

Johnny Lockwood (b1920)
Born to be Happy

Lock, Stock & Beryl
They Do Everything
Comedy knockabouts including JOHNNY COOPER

Len & Bill Lowe (fl1938-50s)
Hi-Jinks
Len Lowe (b1923) – brother of Don Smoothey *infra*

The Four Sisters Lund (fl c1900)
Cute! Clean! Clever!

Jack Mack (1873-1943)
Pro-Pella

Cliff Martell
Borstal's Gift to Variety
Borstal institutions: juvenile prisons.

Horace Mashford (1908-85)
But of Course!

Stephen C Massett (1820-98)
Jeems Pipes of Pipesville

Ronnie Moon
Always a 'Fool Moon'

Syd Moorhouse
Nature's Gentleman

Alex Munro (1911-86)
The Size of It!

Max & Harry Nesbitt (fl1920s-60s)
The South African 'Pep' Boys
Brothers Max (1903-66) and Harry (1905-68) Horvitz

Jimmy O'Dea (1899-1965)
Ireland's King of Comedy

MISCELLANEOUS (continued):

E J Odell (1834-1928)
The Last of the Bohemians

Bobby Olrac & Lillian
In Spasms of Tomfoolery

Kate Palmer (fl c1870)
The Umbrella Belle

Orville Parker (fl1860s-70s)
The Great New York Squash Swamp Dancer
a.k.a. Boss Parker

Graham Payne (1877-1951)
No Pleasure without Payne

Eddie Peabody (1902-70)
Stringing Along

The Three Phoites (est 1874)
American Elastic Kickapoo Dancers
Kickapoos: Algonkian-speaking indigenous North Americans.

Pop, White & Stagger (fl late 1940s-50s)
Half Dancers – Half Crackers

Louise Pyne (1832-1904)
The English Sontag
Henriette Sontag (1806-54): the great German soprano.

Michael Ray (fl c1950)
The Singing Politician

Billy Rhodes (1914-67) & Chika Lane (1915-96)
Anything for a Laugh

James Richmond (1859-1907)
The Man with the Green Gloves
a.k.a. James Richmond Glenroy

G J Ritz (fl1860s-70s)
North American Indian Tamburinist

Rochefort (fl1920s)
The Singing Phonofiddlist

MISCELLANEOUS (continued):

Mr Ryley & Miss Barnum (fl c1900s)
The Dancing Quakers
James Ryley (c1841-1922?)

Don Smoothey (b1919)
What a Life!
Brother of Len Lowe *supra*. Originally with Tom Layton as
Smoothey & Layton *Laughing at Life*.

Jack Stanford (1900-68)
The Dancing Fool

Walter Stanton (1855-1943)
The Giant Rooster
See Fred Carr *supra*

Teddy Stream (fl1920s)
The Part Worn Actor

Taceto (d November 4th 1940)
Painting without Paints

M Sayle Taylor (1889-1942)
The Voice of Experience
See Oliver Wakefield (CLAPHAM & DWYER)

Vic Taylor (b1900)
Smart, Clean and Clever

Van Der Koors
Quack Illusionists, with Felix the Mind-Reading Duck
See THE ZANCIGS

Rusty Warren (b1930)
The Knockers Up Gal

Warren, Latona & Sparks (fl1946-50s)
Killing Work
Australian comedy acrobats: Leslie Warren (1920-94), wife
Maisie Sparks (b1922) and Joseph Latona (1920-89).

Lovelace Watkins (1938-95)
The Black Velvet Sledgehammer
This artiste was a singer.

MISCELLANEOUS (continued):

Billy Whitaker & Mimi Law
In Clown Tonight
Husband and wife team. Whitaker's father was The Great Coram
(see MAGICIANS). Bill-matter derives from a popular BBC
radio programme *In Town Tonight* (1933-60). Billy died
November 16th 1994 *aetatis* 80.

Dawn White (fl1940s-50s)
...and her Glamazons
Fat, Funny but Not Forty

Robert Wildhack (1882-1940)
Professor of Sound Phenomena

Clarence Willard (d August 2nd 1962)
The Man who Grows

York & King
Tin Types
US vaudevillians Chic York (1887-1970) and wife Rose King.

Yost and Partner (fl1930s)
The World's Best Clay-Modeller
See M. A De Bessell *supra*

MODLEY, ALBERT (1901-79)
Lancashire's Favourite Yorkshireman

In the early 1930s this entry was the original Enoch to HARRY
KORRIS's Mr Lovejoy; in the late 1940s he toured with his own show
On with the Modley and achieved national recognition as resident
comedian on *Variety Bandbox*, a BBC radio show which helped so many
talents up the ladder of fame. Mr Modley claimed Barnsley as his
birthplace, though this happy event actually took place in Liverpool.

The performer's brother Allen Modley (1902-76) *I Know Thee* was
also a comic, some thought finer than Albert. Isn't it always the way?

MONKHOUSE, BOB (b1928)
Britain's Latest Thrill

Oleaginous charm and an over-glib facility for accessing jokes denied
the writer-comedian, at least until recently, totemic status. But Mr

Monkhouse's staying-power and essential decency are at last winning him a place in Britain's affections and grudging respect from the Fourth Estate.

MONKS, VICTORIA (1883/88-1927)
John Bull's Girl

Miss Monks was a small vivacious singer of coon songs, the most popular of which, *Bill Bailey, Won't You Please Come Home?*, hurtled her to prominence in 1905. The artiste's nervous instability led to a tempestuous private life; divorce and bankruptcy were followed by sundry irregularities and brushes with the law. This fascinating but notoriously difficult performer died in her early forties of a combination of influenza, bronchitis, pneumonia, and most probably consumption. She was much mourned.

Others to invoke the name of the mythical archetype were JOE COLVERD, Richard Garnsay (b1831) *The Miniature John Bull*, TOM TINSLEY and Verno & Voyce (BICYCLE ACTS).

Also see G H ELLIOTT and MAY HENDERSON.

MONTY, HAL (d c1975)
Laugh and Be Happy

Sometime in the 1920s Albert Sutan, at that time calling himself Albert Sutton, teamed up with Barnet Winogradsky in a dancing act *k.a.* Grade & Sutton and later as The Delfont Boys. After they split up Mr Sutton became Eddie May but it was as Hal Monty that the artiste, now a comedian, reached national prominence. He also became manager to the popular songster MICHAEL HOLLIDAY; this was not a good move, especially for Mr Holliday as may be seen under that gentleman's entry.

See DELFONT & TOKO

MOORE, GEORGE F (1850-1890)
The Facial King

What a facialist was we are not entirely sure, though we suspect mimicry may have been involved. Others similarly endowed were Neal Abel (1882-1952) *The Man with the Mobile Face*, Adelina *Female Facialist and*

Quick Change Artiste, Amann (fl c1900) *Facial Artist & Impersonator*, and John Cronow *The World's Greatest Facial Expert.*

See OWEN McGIVENEY, FELICIEN TREWEY, KING OF...

MORECAMBE, ERIC (1926-84)
He's Not All There

In his teens John Eric Bartholomew was conscripted to work as a coal-miner; within a twelve-month his health had deteriorated from A1 to C3. The comedian's later heart trouble and comparatively early death can perhaps be traced to this over-stressful period in early adulthood.

See LARRY ADLER, MORECAMBE & WISE

MORECAMBE & WISE (fl1948-84)
Fools Rush In; You're Only Young Once

Although they had worked together as early as 1940 it wasn't until 1948 that these two gentlemen formed a permanent partnership – in March of that year at the Palace, Walthamstow, the young comics were billed, inaccurately, as Morecambe & Wisdom *Just Two Guys.*

As a double act the team was unique in that the straight man (ERNIE WISE) was the klutz while the comic (ERIC MORECAMBE) was the keener-witted of the two. We worked with the pair when at the peak of their popularity and were interested to observe how Mr Morecambe personally directed the comedy most meticulously, with Mr Wise nodding benignly in the background.

It is surprising to discover that early in their long association their rôles were reversed, with the comic burden sustained by Mr Wise and Mr Morecambe as the feed.

Fools Rush In was also the subscript of Lew Lane and of another double act called Stern & Bryant (fl1950s-60s).

See LARRY ADLER, WINDMILL THEATRE

MORETON, IVOR & KAYE, DAVE (fl1930-50s)
Tiger Ragamuffins

This bill-matter refers to a popular song entitled *Tiger Rag* which we may assume formed part of these piano duettists' act. The pair made numerous recordings with Columbia – mostly light medleys – and were noted for their natty attire, as stylish and immaculate as their playing. Mr Moreton shuffled off this mortal coil in 1984, and his partner followed suit fifteen years later at the age of 90.

MORETON, ROBERT (1922-57)
...and his Bumper Fun Book

Mr Moreton was an actor who found his métier as a comic during wartime service in RAF Gang Shows and in *Stars in Battledress.* His jokes were expressed in a lugubrious and ponderous style which was novel and highly appropriate for the role of the tutor in the long-running BBC radio series *Educating Archie* (see PETER BROUGH & ARCHIE ANDREWS).

Though his career was flourishing, the artiste in a fit of depression gassed himself in his room in Chelsea Cloisters, thus taking the same tragic path to suicide as Archie Andrews' second tutor, TONY HANCOCK. Another eerie similarity was that amongst both comedians' possessions were found miniature Archie Andrews dolls.

See STAINLESS STEPHEN

MORGAN, GLADYS (1898-1983)
Wales' Queen of Comedy; With her Laugh and Company

This lady was renowned for her cackling Celtic laugh; when we saw Miss Morgan *sans* family at the Ardwick Green Hippodrome c1960 her eccentric ramblings made at least one member of the audience deeply uneasy.

See STAN STENNETT

MORGAN, TOMMY (1898-1958)
Mr Glasgow

A decade or so after this entry's demise his title was being borne by Glen Daly, although Gracie Clark (1904-95) and her husband Colin Murray (1900-89) were *Mr & Mrs Glasgow* from 1926 until the 1980s. 'Scotch', it is often averred, is something you drink and is not applicable to Scots or Scottish persons. In counter to this foolish argument may we draw attention to Peel & Curtis (see ISSY BONN), Scotch Kelly (see JIMMY CLITHEROE), and to the last line of the chorus of *I Love a Lassie* which runs *Mary, Ma Scotch Blue Bell* and was written by none other than HARRY LAUDER himself? We rest our case.

MORRELL, EDDIE (b1905)
A Cavalcade of Junk

Such bill-matter must have had critics sharpening their pencils; safer if less challenging was that displayed for ten years by this entry with Jack(?) Melville (b1899) as Morrell & Melville *Two Sons of Fun.*

See FRED FORDHAM; also ALEC HALLS for identical bill-matter.

MORRIS & COWLEY (fl1923-50s)
Dear Old Pals; The Life of the Party; Top Gear Comedians

Harry (1895-1972) and Frank (d August 11th 1985) Birkenhead emerged from the family act in 1918 as The Vesta Brothers, changing to Morris & Cowley five years later.

We are fortunate enough to possess a videotape on which the brothers sing a comic song, one also dancing and the other playing a ukulele. The comedy is simple but strong, and as they march rapidly off-screen on the final bar we always want to shout 'Bravo!'

Another *Life of the Party* was JACK HAIG.

MOTHER OF...

Lucy Beaumont (1873-1937)
... Hollywood

Louisa Brown (c1825-1901)
...the Circus Profession
US honorific only

Esther Rachel Kaminska (1862-1930)
...the Yiddish Theatre
Also billed as *The Jewish Duse*, after Eleonora Duse (1859-1924). Lillian Foster (c1886-1949) was *The American Duse.*

See also: DOLLY HARMER

MOZART, GEORGE (1864-1947)
In New Types of Every Day Life

In the United States this small but hugely talented multi-instrumentalist was billed as *London's Greatest Comedian – the Only Englishman with a Sense of Humor*. The only Englishman with a sense of humour! Damn cheek – the Yanks can't even spell the word.

See DR CROCK

MURDOCK, MACKENZIE (fl1900)
The Modern Paganini

Niccolo Paganini (1782-1840) was a violinist of stupefying virtuosity; later lesser fiddlers claiming apostolic succession from the demonic prodigy were Amby Power (fl c1900-10s) *The Irish Paganini*, Alfred Rodes (b1905) (and his Eighteen Tziganes) *L'Enfant Paganini*, La Petite Sylvia (Sophie Ogilvie?) who in the 1860s-70s was being touted as *The Baby Paganini*, and CARL HERMANN UNTHAN.

MURRAY, CHIC (& MAIDIE) (fl1945-68)
Just Daft; The Long and the Short of It; The Tall Droll with the Small Doll

Chic (Charles) Murray (1919-85) was well over 6ft tall, and his diminutive wife Maidie Scott (b1922) would stand directly in front of him as he delivered the slowest, driest humour imaginable.

Miss Scott was herself billed in 1935 as *The Discovery of the Year* and after that as *A Treat for the Eye and the Ear*. This lady should not be confused with the Maidie Scott who died on July 28th 1966 and was billed as *Eve's Progress – A Song Scena in Four Cameos* or *Just a Comedienne*.

NB: REVNELL & WEST were also *The Long and the Short of It*.

MURRAY & MOONEY (fl1909-14, 1920-c45)
Even Their Relations Think They're Funny

There is a story, doubtless apocryphal, that Val Parnell saw this entry at a number three hall and booked them into one of his London halls as a joke. To his surprise they brought the roof in and the following week they were playing the Palladium.

However dubious the story there is a parable in it, for while Murray and Mooney's act – the interrupted recitation – creaked, they ponged it over with enormous gusto. It has been said that Harry Murray (1891-1968) and Harry Goodchild (1889-1972) were the first to use the line

'Kindly leave the stage.' After splitting up the latter worked until 1948 with a new partner as Harry Mooney with Victor King (1892-1964) *Mooney as Ever.*

MURRAY, RUBY (1935-96)
The Heartbeat Girl

In 1955 Ruby Florence Campbell Murray, a simple Belfast girl, had five recordings in the top 20 at the same time, a feat still unsurpassed and only equalled by Elvis Presley and Madonna. The artiste's bill-matter derives from her second release, her third being the wistful *Softly Softly*, a gentle ballad in 3/4 which suited her accent, her vulnerability, her naïveté and lack of vocal range. This entry's voice and personality were inoffensive to the point of humdrum, and it is difficult to believe that Frank Sinatra was being anything other than politely ironic when he declared Miss Murray to be 'a hell of a great singer'.

The lady's career prospered vastly until the 1960s when tax arrears, febrility, and addictions to alcohol and Valium (plus an illicit romance with the Ulster comic Frank Carson which did little for her home life) led to a rapid descent into psychiatric disorders and obscurity. It is heartening to record that before her last illness, Miss Murray, an artiste ever-bewildered and perhaps ever-overwhelmed by the magnitude and speed of her early fame, had regained a degree of control over her life, and that her ex-husband and two children were with her when she died.

MUSAIRE (1894-1984)
The Harry Lauder of the Canadian Tanks;
Music from the Air

Joseph Forrest Whiteley was born in Leeds but brought up in the Dominion of Canada, serving throughout the 1914-18 War in the Tank Corps, hence his first billing. The second refers to this entry's expertise on an early electronic instrument known as the Thérémin after its inventor Professor Léon Thérémin (1896-1993).

In 1932 Mr Whiteley gave up his day job with a piano manufacturer to become Musaire, the world's first professional Théréminist. Due to public indifference towards this auditory innovation the player was obliged to diversify, becoming a 'compère-comedian featuring his own topical and character songs in dialect, ending with a "slick-change"'.

See p.14, HARRY LAUDER

MUSHIE (fl1940s-50s)
The Forest Bred Lion & Miss Ellen

Ellen Eliza Lillian Harvey (b1917) wrote in 1950 that 'her greatest thrill was when she was presented to TRH Duke and Duchess of Gloucester on July 1st 1939 after her performance with nine cheetahs. When war came in 1939 she at once went into a war factory (Rotol Airscrews, Cheltenham) where she remained for three years, after which she was released to work in music halls with Mushie the Lion which she has done ever since. Claims to be the only trainer in the world who allows a lion to eat meat from the face while lying flat on the floor'.

See Foreword

MY FANCY (1878-1933)
The Finest Sand Dancer in the World; Marvellous Buck Dancer; Winter, Spring and Summer

Mae Rose Baker – dancer, trapezist, acrobat, illusionist – assumed the identity My Fancy for her début at the Oxford Music Hall on March 25th 1895; prior to this date the artiste had been known by her family name, and we regret that we can offer no enlightenment as to the significance of the change.

The American artiste's dancing would seem not to have been of the artsy-tartsy MAUD ALLAN-Isadora Duncan free expressive variety but something altogether more rhythmic and snappy. The word 'sand' in this entry's bill-matter suggests soft-shoe dancing; 'buck' suggests tap-dancing. That old softie W Macqueen-Pope wrote 'My Fancy was very attractive in Little Lord Fauntleroy costume and an expert in the lost art of the sand dance.'

N

NAPIER, HECTOR (c1890-1965)
The Boneless Wonder; The Human Spider

This Australian acrobat's daughter Joan Valantyne Napier (b1920) took over his act and bill-matter; Miss Napier also toured the Mother Country from 1948 with Ted Weeks as Ed Vyne & Valantyne *Noveloddities*, a contorting and balancing turn. Miss Valantyne's 1986 autobiography *Act as Known* gives a rambling but not uninteresting picture of Variety life in both Britain and the Antipodes from the 1900s through to 1960, though the authoress is still ragingly resentful at not being engaged for the London Palladium.

See VALENTINE for other *Boneless Wonders*; additional arachnid artistes are THE DEHL TRIO and Zaleski (fl 1910s) *The Golden Spider*.

NAPOLEON (1856-68)
The Wizard Dog

Napoleon was presented by G Van Hare (b1815), another of whose animal artistes was Hassan *The Gorilla Chief.* Whether the custom of naming dogs after Napoleon Buonaparte (1769-1821), the most feared, admired and charismatic commander of his day, was a compliment to the canines or an insult to the little Corporal is open to debate.

See ANIMAL & BIRD ACTS and HARRY BALL; for other Napoleons see GEORGE BARNARDO EAGLE.

NASH, 'Jolly' JOHN (1830-1901)
The Merry Son of Momus of Side-Splitting Notoriety

According to the highly experienced Palace Theatre and Drury Lane musical director Herman Finck, this entry's 'only form of jollity was to come on stage laughing and to sing laughing songs. He would laugh and laugh – far more than the audience did. Then he would suddenly begin a sentimental cornet solo; and that was where *I* began to laugh'. The artiste performed for the Prince of Wales at private parties so often that he allowed himself the familiarity of slapping HRH on the back, and that was the end of 'Jolly' Nash as a society entertainer.

Another Momus was J W LISKARD; also see ARTHUR LLOYD.

NAUGHTON & GOLD (fl1908-61)
Craziest of them All; Head & Feet; Napoleons of Fun

When Charles John Naughton (1887-1976) and James McGonigal (1886-1967) took part in the original *Crazy Week* – later *Crazy Gang* – shows at the London Palladium they had already been partners for twenty-three years and were to stay together for another thirty. A famous routine that the two Glaswegians took all round the world was a 'British working-man burlesque' called *Turn it Round the Other Way.*

When we saw the Crazy Gang in 1959 at the Victoria Palace the on-stage pranks at one point reduced Charlie Naughton to tears of helpless mirth; how heart-warming to discover that those six old men were as exuberantly anarchic as ever.

For other Napoleons see GEORGE BARNARDO EAGLE.

NAVETTE, NELLIE (d August 3rd 1938)
The English Genée

This artiste's bill-matter refers to the exquisite Danish-born ballerina Dame Adeline Genée (1878-1970); its appropriateness is questionable since Miss Navette was a popular pantomime Principal Boy and was frequently seen at the London Pavilion in the 1890s singing, for instance, *English Lady Cricketers* and *De Risin' Ob De Moon.*

NERVO & KNOX (fl1919-62)
Cashiered from their Bank; Fantastic Frolics

Jugglers and tumblers Jimmy Nervo (1897-1975), who was illiterate, and Teddy Knox (1896-1974) teamed up in 1919; their most celebrated routine was the slow-motion wrestling match, a miracle of physical control. It was this pair's own madcap touring revue *Young Bloods of Variety* in which the acts interrupted each other that sowed the seed of the *Crazy Gang* shows; Nervo & Knox were always the highest paid of the team earning at the end £1,800 a week each plus a percentage of the profits.

See CHINKO, FRED KARNO, CLARICE MAYNE

NESBIT, EVELYN (1884/5-1967)
The Girl in the Red Velvet Swing

On June 25th 1906 Miss Nesbit's husband shot to death her ex-lover, Stanford White, in the Roof Garden Theatre at Madison Square Garden. A sordid affair was rendered super-sensational by the victim's eminence as an architect – the building in which he was slain was, by the most piquant of ironies, of his own design.

It emerged that Mr White had submitted his inamorata to practices of a Continental nature, one of which involved a Red Velvet Swing upon which the then 15-year-old was obliged to oscillate in a state of *déshabillé*. In 1913 Miss Nesbit was prevailed upon to return to her vaudeville origins; for $4,000 a week the artiste sang on a Red Velvet Swing, to the great edification of the people.

NIXON, THE GREAT (b1888)
Miracles in Mentalism

Victor William Nixon made his professional début at the Frere Hall Theatre in Karachi and his first London appearance at the Crouch End Hippodrome. The artiste was also, at varying times, manager and lessee of the Opera House Calcutta, the Shintomiza Theatre Tokyo, and the Electric Cinema Bagshot.

See MAGICIANS, THE ZANCIGS

NONI & HORACE
The Clown to whom the Queen Gave a Flower; We are Going to Have a Concert

Noni (1891-1963) was a multi-lingual musical clown, regularly and with aching predictability hailed by the Press as the successor to Grock (see KING OF...); Horace was Noni's son. Their first billing derives from an incident at the 1928 *Royal Variety Performance* when Queen Mary gave Noni a flower from her bouquet, joking that she felt sorry for him.

Variety artistes have always shown extravagant regard for titles and blue-bloods, for even today Royal recognition suggests professional excellence, worthiness of character and social respectability. Or it should do.

See MUSHIE

NORMA, BEBE (1925-74)

Dancing Wizard of the Xylophone; 100% Personality Girl; The Personality Dancing Xylophonist

Miss Norma combined her talents in order to present the diverting spectacle of simultaneous tap-dancing and xylophony. Another similarly gifted artiste was Vesta (Audrey Austin b1917) of Vesta & Ashton who described herself as 'dancing xylophoniste', though whether she could emulate Miss Norma's dual feat is not clear.

See REGGIE REDCLIFFE

NORTON, HARRY (c1889-1956)

The Human Aquarium; The Human Hydrant; The Human Tank

Mr Norton, *a.k.a.* MacNorton, exhibited the singular ability to swallow and regurgitate live fish, the piscine performers seemingly untroubled by their immersion in this entry's gastric juices. Frogs also featured but we would prefer not to go into detail save to note that amphibian artistes in the United States come under the protection of the American Sociey for the Prevention of Cruelty to Animals who had that part of the act banned. As *The Human Hydrant* Mr Norton swallowed copious drafts of liquid and spurted it out tastefully and most artistically.

In 1896 at the Royal Aquarium, Westminster, Chevalier Clicquot despite being only 5ft 5ins tall swallowed a sword bayonet 21ins in length. The Chevalier also ingested a watch which a volunteer could hear ticking within. *Variety Stage* reported that in this artiste's seventeen years as a swallower 'he has had many accidents; although they are not so frequent now as when practised originally'.

See Hadji Ali (MISCELLANEOUS), SYDNEY BARNES, THE MYSTERIOUS WERTH

O

OAKLEY, ANNIE (1860-1926)
Little Sure Shot; The Peerless Lady Wing-Shot

Phoebe Anne Oakley Moses famously outshot Frank E Butler at a competition in Cincinnati. Mr Butler seems not to have taken umbrage (unlike his character in Irving Berlin's 1946 musical comedy *Annie Get Your Gun*) for they married and he became her assistant and manager.

This entry's sharpshooting abilties were quite remarkable; at thirty paces she could hit the thin end of a playing card, a dime thrown in the air, and the end of a cigarette in her husband's mouth. In Europe Miss Oakley shot a cigarette from the hand of the German Crown Prince, later Kaiser Wilhelm II. Had the performer's aim gone lethally awry on that occasion the first half of the 20th-century might have been a lot less bloody.

See CLEMENTINE

OCEANA (1858-94)
Beautiful Empress of the Slack Wire; Child of the Air

This enchantress owes her charming name to the circumstance of having been born at sea, into the Cooke circus family – we are not convinced by claims that the artiste's father was Signor ETHARDO. Of this entry a French observer carped in 1890: 'The sudden discredit into which rope-dancing has fallen during the last few years dates from the appearance of Oceana. The young woman, anxious to adopt a novelty which would exhibit her beauty without too much exertion, chose a *wire*, which, hanging slacker than the cord, enabled her, with a little oscillation, to assume the attitude of reclining in a hammock, the voluptuous poses of *Sarah la Baigneuse*.'

O'FARRELL, TALBOT (1878-1952)
The Greatest Irish Entertainer of all Time

Before parading such modest bill-matter English-born Will Parrot was on the Halls as Jock McIver *Scottish Comedian and Vocalist*. As a Scot the singer enjoyed but limited success; only on switching to an Hibernian character and repertoire did his popularity blossom.

The artiste disdained the customary knee-breeches, shamrock-'n'-shillelagh type of stage Paddy, appearing instead in beautifully cut, slightly dandyish apparel. Suddenly 'Talbot O'Farrell' was a star. The voice and the personality were the same but the image had changed, and image is all.

O'GORMAN, DAVE & JOE (fl1906-55)

Kicking the Gang Around; Laughter in the Roar; Racketeer Funmen

Dave (1891-1964) and Joe (1890-1974) were the sons of comedian Joe O'Gorman of TENNYSON & O'GORMAN. Until c1932 they worked as The O'Gorman Brothers *Who Sing, Talk and Dance* but on a trip to the US were advised to assume separate identities in case one should suddenly become a star. More fatuous advice it would be hard to imagine. On the plus side, the brothers' trip to the States did encourage them to up-date their jokes a tidge.

Laughter in the Roar was also the bill-matter of The Falcons (fl1950s) and of Harry Coady (1906-71).

O'GRADY & GRAY (fl c1950)

Foolin' & Stoolin'

If Rosie O'Grady and Terry Gray fooled and stooled what did they do for an encore?

OHMY, KING (1854-1931)

The Glittering Star of the Air; The Winged Man

Joseph Smith was gymnast, acrobat, trick-rider, clown and pioneer bungee jumper, which latter accomplishment provided him with his stage name. As the dare-devil pretended to slip from the roof of the circus, plunging head down to within a few inches of the ground, the horrified audience would invariably ejaculate 'Oh, my!'

We note here the soubriquet of one Mme Caroline (fl c1875) *Queen of the Corde Elastique*, which suggests a Gallic bungee jumper.

OLIVER, VIC (1898-1964)

Mr Show Business; The Continental Wizard; London's Favourite American Comedian; The Piano-Playing Baron

Mr Oliver was an Austrian ex-cavalry officer who possessed a louche charm and a degree of musicality – he conducted, played drums, piano and violin, and had been briefly a pupil of Mahler – which earned him a living as an entertainer. In 1931, after several chequered years in American vaudeville this entry arrived at the London Palladium with his first wife. His second was Sarah Churchill, a stage-struck and striking-looking young woman not over-hampered with talent whose father was Winston Churchill, the well-known author and MP.

The only occasion upon which we saw Mr Oliver was at the Brighton Hippodrome; he told some breath-takingly vile jokes and then sat down to accompany a soprano in the Bach-Gounod *Ave Maria.*

We have been told on excellent authority that the leading lady in Mr Oliver's company at this time was under his protection. Due to age and infirmity, however, the impresario-star was no longer able adequately to meet his obligations; it was incumbent upon the leading juvenile male, therefore, to slake the young lady's appetites while *Mr Show Business* watched.

See JULIE ANDREWS

OLIVER, WILL (1852-1916)

The Skeleton Comic

We must assume that this artiste was freakily thin – *cf* THE GREAT CARLTON and TED LUNE – a condition which never appears to us nearly so comical as being freakily fat though neither condition is really much fun.

In 1833 there died at the age of 48 and the weight of 60lb one Calvin Edson who called himself, inevitably, *The Living Skeleton*, a designation also proclaimed by Isaac W Sprague (b1841) who weighed 5lb less. Or so he said.

OLSEN & JOHNSON (fl1915-c60)

Comic Nuts; Kings of Cacophany, Unconventionality and Conviviality

It took John 'Ole' Olsen (1892-1963) and Harold 'Chic' Johnson (1891-1962) just seven years to rise from piano-violin duo in a Chicago café to the 1922 *Ziegfeld Follies,* by which time musicality had been subverted by lunatic, slapstick comedy.

Neither of these artistes was the straight man; both were comics with a penchant for inconsequential, old-style hokum exemplified at its most extravagant in *Hellzapoppin,* an every-man-for-himself free-for-all inspired by the antics of the London *Crazy Gang* shows and billed as 'a screamlined revue designed for laughing'.

ORDE, BERYL (1911-66)

Britain's Foremost Impressioniste; The World's Youngest Impressioniste

In the course of our researches we have come across a number of dubious femininisms – accordionist*e,* contortionist*e,* aerialist*e,* pianist*e,* ventriloquist*e,* violinist*e,* vocalist*e,* xylophonist*e* – but this entry is the only impressionist*e* we have met.

In the 1920s Tina Paynola, though her career must have been co-terminous with Miss Orde's, was calling herself *The Only Lady Mimic,* an indication of the rarity of impersonatrices at this time. From 1943-8 there flourished Helga Stone *Never The Same Girl Twice,* while from the 1940s into the 1950s Joan Quinlan was calling herself *A Hundred Women in One,* bill-matter which suggests the lady did not do men.

See list of MIMICS in glossary.

ORTON, ARTHUR (1834-98)

The Tichborne Claimant

In the late 1860s this entry claimed to be the missing baronet Sir Richard Tichborne; charged with perjury the Claimant went on the Halls to raise money for his defence, but 'Bullocky Orton', who weighed 28 stone, lost the case and was sentenced to 14 years' penal servitude.

As a toddler a certain Harry Relph had been very plump; customers at his father's public house would refer to him as Little Tichborne, and it was as YOUNG TICHBORNE, later LITTLE TICH, that Master Relph went on the Halls. Memories of The Claimant faded as Little Tich's reputation grew – unlike his height which never topped 4ft 6ins – and so it came about that the grossly oversized Arthur Orton became the author of a word meaning undersized. Ironic, the reader will allow.

O'SHEA, TESSIE (1914-95)

All the Fun and Sweetness Rolled into One; The Girl with the Irresistible Humour; Just Bubbling Over; Two-Ton Tessie

If not quite two tons in weight this comedienne-songstress was still a larger artiste than most, which made her curtain-call cartwheels all the more unexpected. Miss O'Shea backed up her patter and songs with, respectively, a cackling laugh and a banjulele, an instrument easier to play than listen to.

In 1963 the Cardiff artiste's boisterous all-conquering performance in (Sir) Noël Coward's *The Girl who came to Supper* made her the toast of Broadway and a welcome figure thereafter in vaudeville houses billed as *London's Own*.

See RONNÉ CONN

OTERO, LA BELLE (1868-1965)

Caroline Puentovalga, a shapely and tempestuous singer and dancer from Cadiz, became the most notorious *grande cocotte* of her day, leading an life of unremittingly lurid melodrama and adventurous excess. Gentlemen known to have enjoyed the *vedette's* favours include the Grand Duke Nicholas of Russia, Kaiser Wilhelm II of Germany, King Alfonso XIII of Spain and, inevitably, our very own Prince of Wales. Nor were the arts neglected with painting represented by Aristide Bruant and literature by Gabriele D'Annunzio.

Bernard Shaw was so smitten that after seeing her at the Empire in October 1892 he enthused 'this Otero is really a great artiste,' though Mr Shaw's seat in the auditorium is as close as the great intellectual would have wished to approach so flagrantly and gamily sensual a female, unlike those gentlemen – there were rumoured to be at least three – who, denied access to Mlle Otero's boudoir, lost no time in taking their own lives, prompting the American press to dub her *The Suicides' Siren*.

P

PALMER, GASTON (1887-69)
All the Spoons in All the Glasses

One source gives this entry's mother as the athlete, contortionist and strongwoman Athleta (see JOAN RHODES); the humorist-juggler himself stated that his mother was Adele Rancy, bareback rider of the Circus Rancy. Were these ladies the same? We think not.

Mr Palmer's climactic trick was a worrying business of balancing a lengthening tower of trays and glasses on his head into the topmost tier of which would be thrown, simultaneously, six spoons – *All the Spoons in All the Glasses.*

The juggler claimed the ability to work his act in English, French, Swedish, Italian and German. We were always relieved when this entry had concluded his exhibition in whatever language.

See p.13

PARKER, Colonel (1909-97)
...and his Amazing Dancing Chickens

It is not easy to persuade chickens to dance, though it is a lot easier if you put a hot-plate under their feet. This act was a carnival side-show which pleased Deep South rubes well enough to keep the gallinaceous promoter in mint julep and cornpone. Andreas Cornelis Van Kujik *k.a.* Tom Parker was a Dutch illegal immigrant who, like his feathered charges, scratched a living as best he could.

In Shreveport Louisiana in 1955 the Nederlander, now wheeling and dealing in the country music business, saw a Dancing Chicken which was to make him the richest and most famous Louisiana Colonel ever. This was 20-year-old Elvis Presley, and Mr Parker had him signed and sealed to a contract which had the greatest rock-and-roll singer of them all capering on a hot-plate for the rest of his sadly short career. Not until 1981 did a Memphis court declare Colonel Parker's contracts unconscionable and unenforceable. At last the electric current was switched off and the hot-plate allowed to cool. But by then it was too late. The King had been dead for four years.

See ANIMAL & BIRD ACTS

PASTOR, TONY (c1832-1908)
Clown Prince of Song

The American press dubbed Mr Pastor *The Father of Vaudeville* though this was a title he misliked, vaudeville being associated with the class of unedifying entertainment so valiantly eschewed by this entry in his own managerial enterprises. As a boy the entertainer worked in blackface for P T BARNUM's Museum Shows; as an adult he was short and stout, inexhaustibly energetic and with a claimed repertoire of over 2,000 songs. We have examined a collection of the singer's Irish songs – all of distinctly suspect provenance – and, frankly, cannot recommend any of them.

Mr Pastor is remembered in Britain for his scouting visits to engage talent. It should be noted that in his own establishments the entrepreneur not only sang but also assumed the office of Chairman, thus making him the only known gavel-wielder on the other side of the herring-pond.

See OLIVIER BASSELIN; G H ELLIOTT for other black-face artistes and also FATHER OF....

PEARSON, BOB & ALF
My Brother and I

Robert (1907-86) and Alfred (b1910) Pearson owed their careers to George Black (1890-1945), feared and fearsome managing director of GTC (General Theatres Corporation) which included the old Moss Empires circuit, for it was he who organised their settings, lighting, choice of material and general presentation, and gave them three years' bookings.

We remember the brothers well – Bob at the piano, both singing excellent two-part arrangements of popular songs and ballads – and a smarter, brighter, more polished duo we have yet to witness.

This team's bill-matter was partially poached by Alan Kane (1913-96), the very popular recording and broadcasting artiste who worked an occasional double act with his sister Gloria as *My Sister and I.*

See THE TWO LESLIES

PEERS, DONALD (1908-73)

The (Laughing) Cavalier of Song; England's Greatest Chorus Singer; Radio's Cavalier of Song

Originally *k.a.* Smiling Donald Peers *and his Ukulele* this artiste was bewilderingly popular in the 1940s and 1950s. As a performer Mr Peers gave us only modified rapture; we found his singing voice scratchy and toneless and his manner over-weeningly schmlatzy, a deeply resistible combination. When we learned that the artiste owed his start to a singing competition organised by FRED KARNO we were not surprised.

See FLORRIE FORDE for similar bill-matter; also GEORGE FORMBY jnr for fellow-ukuleleists.

PENNINGTON, W H (1832-1923)

Gladstone's Pet Tragedian

W E Gladstone (1809-98) was four times Prime Minister of Great Britain; the tragedian whom the Grand Old Man admired most, as was widely known, was the mighty lessee of the Lyceum Theatre (Sir) Henry Irving (1837-1905). We cannot think therefore that Mr Pennington's bill-matter was anything other than humorous.

PEPPER, Dr JOHN HENRY (1821-1900)

Metempsychosis – The Artist's Dream

Dr Pepper was the developer and demonstrator of Pepper's Ghost, an ingenious arrangement of lights, sheet glass and a mirror by which an artiste underneath the stage would appear, mute but spectrally transparent, on the stage. The colossal success of the device caused a tidal wave of similar inventions to break over Britain's stages, and for a while in the early 1860s the GBP couldn't get enough of them – King's Ghost, Silvester's Ghost, Graham's Ghost, W Cox's Ghost, and Alec Palmer's Ghost being just a selection.

Was Pepper's Ghost the origin of the phrase 'It's all done by mirrors'?

PETERS, ALOIS (1898-1943)

The Man with the Iron Neck

The Man who Hangs Himself inadvertently did just that during a performance in America.

Other ferrous artistes were Siegmund Breitbart (1883-1925) *The Iron King*, Ian Colquhoun (fl1890s-1920s?) *The Iron-Voiced Baritone*, and Professor Kelly (1851-79) *The Man with the Iron Jaw*. Proctorie (fl1900s) puffed himself as *The Great American Iron King and Continental Prison Breaker*, while the only *Iron Queen* of which we have knowledge is Zulima (1850-1903).

In the 1940s-50s there flourished Alan Alan *The Man You Cannot Hang*. We don't know what happened to him. Perhaps somebody called his bluff.

The unfortunate Alois Peters also presented a *Human Fly* act; for others see Mlle ALMA. For persons of unusual strength see JOAN RHODES and EUGENE SANDOW.

PICKFORD, MARY (1893-1979)
The Biograph Girl; America's Sweetheart

Toronto-born Miss Pickford may only have been 5ft in height but on screen the actress stood tall. This entry was born Gladys Smith, a good wholesome name which we would have thought ideal for an international goddess of the silver screen.

Another *Biograph Girl*, forgotten now, was Florence Lawrence (1890-1938) who also billed herself as *The Girl with a Thousand Faces* (see LON CHANEY).

PIPIFAX & PANLO
Humpsti Bumpsti

These artistes' bill-matter is a generic term for comedy knockabout acrobatics; Edwin Rece and Henry Hansen enjoyed the distinction of opening the very first *Royal Music Hall Performance* at the Palace Theatre on Monday, July 1st 1912.

This formal recognition of the once despised Halls was as important to Variety as Irving's knighthood had been to the Theatre seventeen years before, and there was much grovelling appreciation of King George V's and Queen Mary's condescending to attend. *The Era*, hyperventilating with excitement, reported that the King 'evidently looked upon his night at the Palace in the light of a lover of true Bohemianism, and his attitude towards the show was a sheer delight to watch. The Royal party stayed to the end, and His Majesty bowed from the box in acknowledgement of the ringing cheers which rose from every part of the house at the conclusion of the National Anthem.'

PLEON, ALEC (b1911)
Funny Face; Just Crazy

Mr Pleon described himself as 'comedian and yodeller', but we have decided to include him all the same.

See Harry Wulson (KING OF...)

PLUMMER, SID (1901-67)
The Xyli-Fool

That the artiste was a comedy xylophonist is arrestingly and succinctly conveyed in his bill-matter. We regard this construction as a model of its kind.

Mr Plummer played pantomime Dame on many occasions, including Sarah the Cook in *Dick Whittington*. What's the betting that the Emperor of Morocco's Palace sported a xylophone?

POLAIRE, LA (1879-1939)
The Ugliest Woman in the World

Mlle Emilie Marie Bouchaud's physiognomy was by no means as uncomely as her bill-matter most unkindly suggests. In fact in the US the French actress-*chanteuse* was considered cute rather than ugly, her famous 15¾ins waist causing great *angst* in fashionable East Coast salons. This entry was an intense, vibrant performer devoted to her art; when La Polaire sang it was said that she 'shook like an infuriated wasp'.

POTTER, GILLIE (1887-1975)
The Squire of Hogsnorton

Hugh William Peel, the son of a Wesleyan minister, was a failed Oxford undergraduate whose stage get-up was that of an effete pedagogue, with spectacles, a wide-brimmed straw boater, blazer and light flannel trousers, and flourishing an umbrella. The comedian's mock-genteel chronicling of the village of Hogsnorton was subtle, literary and oblique to the point of being esoteric, which while eminently suitable for broadcasting also, more surprisingly, enjoyed an enthusiastic hearing on the Halls. Gillie (the 'g' is hard as in gherkin) Potter was an acknowledged expert on heraldry, which somehow doesn't surprise us.

See CLAPHAM & DWYER, WINDMILL THEATRE

POWELL, SANDY (& CO) (1900-82)
The Master Magician; The World's Worst Ventriloquist

As a child Yorkshire-born Albert Arthur Powell was billed as *The Ideal Scotch Comedian*, also – just as fictitiously – as *The Singing Pit Lad*. After youthful stints with HARRY TATE and FRED KARNO this bespectacled little comedian with a big personality and a kindly nature established himself on the Halls in character sketches with such titles as *The Guardsman, The Lost Policeman* and *The Test Match*. An outstandingly popular broadcaster Mr Powell claimed to have introduced the first radio catch-phrase: 'Can you hear me, Mother?' and to have appeared in the first televised revue; he certainly sold over seven million records and starred in eight feature films.

The famous incompetent ventriloquist routine in which Mr Powell was assisted by his third wife Kay White (c1903-96) was an absolute joy, though the performer loved to tell of over-hearing a disgruntled patron in a working-men's club say 'Well, I hope his second spot's better than that ventriloquist act!'

See MAGICIANS, VENTRILOQUISTS

POWER, NELLIE (1855-87)
The Most Talented Juvenile Vocalist and Comédienne in the World

The artiste was said to be the first to change her costume entirely for male impersonation numbers, as opposed to the customary practice of donning an accessory such as a cap or jacket. Poor Nellie died destitute when she was only 32; her agent, GEORGE W WARE, got up a collection to pay for her funeral. The total raised was nearly £9 short and the undertaker sued Mr Ware for the difference. The undertaker lost.

'Very Merry Nellie', as popular with colleagues as with audiences, is remembered as the original singer of *The Boy In The Gallery* (written by Mr Ware), a number famously pirated by the teen-aged MARIE

LLOYD. Thirteen years earlier Miss Power had achieved a measure of fame with a ladies' version of *Up in a Balloon* (see GEORGE LEYBOURNE), a song often said to have been inspired by the Siege of Paris. Not so; the song was written two years earlier in 1868 to mark Britain's first Aeronautical Exhibition, held at the Crystal Palace.

See ST GEORGE HUSSEY. Also see ELLA RETFORD

PRESTIGE, YVONNE
The Pocket Prima Donna

This entry was 4ft 4ins tall and possessed of a dominating personality and a remarkably fine soprano voice. Miss Prestige was also possessed of a husband, Billy Moore (b1926), but her affections were alienated by WINDY BLOW, a balloon-modeller and lightning cartoonist. Such a heady mix of talents quite captivated the diminutive minx for with him she eloped and was Mrs Billy Moore no longer.

See JIMMY CLITHEROE

PRINCE, ARTHUR (1881-1948)
...and his Sailor Boy Jim; The Court Magician and Ventriloquist; Naval Occasions; The World's Greatest Ventriloquist; Variety's Peter Pan

Mr Prince dressed as naval officer with his dummy Jim as a cheeky AB whose impertinences were much relished by audiences bred to deference. In 1926 Jim became the first object to be televised by John Logie Baird, and two years later the first object to be televised trans-Atlantically. Mr Prince's amazing feat of drinking a glass of water while Jim sang was achieved by having an assistant doing the singing off-stage. Not cricket, we feel.

Another naval ventriloquist was Lieut (Walter) Cole (fl1860s-90s) *The Greatest Ventriloquist in the World*, though it was commonly believed that unlike Mr Prince and two other ventriloquial naval officers, Lieut Albini and Lieut TRAVIS, Mr Cole had actually held Her Majesty's commission.

See MAGICIANS, VENTRILOQUISTS

PUJOL, JOSEPH (1857-1945)

The Only Man to Pay No Author's Royalties;
Le Pétomane

It was while bathing in the sea as a young man that this entry discovered a facility for inhaling and exhaling via his sphincter. Years of practice developed an anal embouchure capable of a remarkably diverse repertoire – popular melodies, candle extinguishing, cigarette smoking and unusual impersonations, one of which – a bride on her wedding night – provoked hilarity of a quite unprecedented coarseness.

In his prime *Le Pétomane* (which translates as *The F**t Fancier*) attracted huge audiences; his fees were the largest ever paid at the Moulin Rouge and the explosions of Parisian mirth could be heard from a considerable distance.

At the time of writing one Paul Oldfield, professionally *k.a.* Mr Methane, is laying claim to be the British Boreas. We have only seen this gentleman on television and found him quite lacking in charm, personality or presentational abilities. *Le Pétomane* would be ashamed to see his art so debased.

See list of MIMICS in glossary.

Q

QUEEN OF...

Peggy 'Piano' Desmond
See WINIFRED ATWELL

Ena Bertoldi (1877-1906)
...*Equipoise*

Beryl Bryden (c1920s)
...*the Washboard*

Mme Caroline
See KING OHMY

Victoria Sanger Freeman (1895-1991)
...*the Elephants*
Great-grandniece of Lord GEORGE SANGER

Juanita Hansen (1896-1961)
...*Thrills*

Janice Hart
See SOPHIE TUCKER

The Beautiful Jessica (1864-1908)
The Only and Original Queen of the Slack Wire
See CAICEDO, TENNYSON & O'GORMAN

Gypsy Rose Lee (1914-70)
...*Burlesque*
Hubert's Museum on New York's 42nd Street advertised the appearance of Gypsy Rose Flea.
See PHYLLIS DIXEY, Fannie Leslie *infra*, Iris Sadler *infra*, FLORENCE ST JOHN

QUEEN OF... (continued):

Mary Lee (fl1940s?-60s)
...Monologues

Lillian Leitzel (1893-1931)
...Circus

Fannie Leslie (1858-1935)
...Burlesque
See Gypsy Rose Lee *supra*, Iris Sadler *infra*, FLORENCE ST JOHN

Lurline (début 1878)
...the Waters
Née Sallie Smith; also 'expert banjoist and club manipulator'

Marjorie Manners (1926-97)
...Song

Mme Marzella
See ANIMAL & BIRD ACTS

Dame Nellie Melba (1861-1931)
...Song
So-called by Oscar Wilde

Lily Morris
See HYLDA BAKER

Adelina Patti (1843-1919)
...Song
NB: Bessie Lee (1873-1904) *The Coloured Patti*; also Mlle Nikita
(JIMMY CLITHEROE).

Iris Sadler (1909-91)
...Burlesque; Naughty but Nice
See Gypsy Rose Lee, Fannie Leslie, FLORENCE ST JOHN

QUEEN OF... (continued):

Blossom Seeley (1891-1974)
...Syncopation

May Sherrard
See HYLDA BAKER

Joyce Shock (fl1940s-50s)
Britain's Future Queen of Song

Mlle Talma
See MAGICIANS

Ada Webb (b1845?)
...the Crystal Tank

Kitty Wells (b1919)
...Country Music
But Tammy Wynette (1942-98) claimed to be *The First Lady of Country Music*

Mlle Willa (fl1870s-80s)
...Clubs

Mlle Zara
See MAGICIANS

Zulima
See ALOIS PETERS

See also entries for: ANNIE ADAMS, ATLAS & VULCANA, WINIFRED ATWELL, BETTY AUKLAND, HYLDA BAKER, BESSIE BELLWOOD, CLEMENTINE, MAGGIE CLINE, PHYLLIS DIXEY, GRACIE FIELDS, JENNY HILL, MARIE LLOYD, LILLIAN LORRAINE, GLADYS MORGAN, FLORENCE ST JOHN, SUZETTE TARRI, SOPHIE TUCKER, VESTA VICTORIA, NELLIE WALLACE, ESTHER WILLIAMS

R

RAGLAN, TONI (fl1920s-40s)

As Cracked as his Jam Jars; At his Mighty Whirlitzer Jam Jars; Maestro of the Jam Jars

'Whirlitzer' is a humorous corruption of Wurlitzer, a make of cinema organ which rose from under the fore-stage in order to entertain prior to the main feature, its beaming Jehu a *diabolus ex machina* whose appearance invariably occasioned, at least when we were present, vociferous catcalls.

RANDLE, FRANK (1902-57)

The Old Hiker

Arthur Hughes' capers were scarcely less rumbustical off-stage than on, for the great comedian was an unruly Puck, a wilful and ferocious imbiber who in his cups could turn in a twinkling from slap-on-the-back bonhomie to malevolence and violence – after a disagreement over a bar bill at the Hulme Hippodrome in 1956 this entry's dressing-room was comprehensively trashed.

The Old Hiker was an uproarious character study, drawn with broad but not unperceptive brush-strokes, as were *Grandpa's Birthday* and *Any More for Sailing*. According to his son, Arthur Delaney, his father had all his teeth removed when he was 29 the better to delineate his elderly characterisations.

In private life a remote and sometimes irrational man the artiste lived only for performing and basking in the adulation of his admirers, who, in the north of England at least, were legion. It was no surprise when the stormy-petrel of Variety died at the age of only 55.

RASTELLIS, THE (fl1920s-60s)

The World's Most Famous Clowns

This entry – Oreste (b1900), his wife, their son and two colleagues – was a comedy trampoline act. The troupe also worked as the musical clowns Chocolate & Co. which in the late 1940s was the funniest act we had ever seen; we positively screamed with delight at their antics, causing less enraptured persons in the vicinity to turn and stare quite hard.

The great juggler Enrico Rastelli (1896-1931) was Oreste's cousin.

See DR CROCK

RATCLIFF, THOMAS P (1874-1952)

The Man in the White Suit

For many years Mr Ratcliff conducted the traditional singsong before the FA Cup Final at Wembley Stadium; the white suit was to make him more visible. After his death the crowd was conducted by Arthur Caiger until it became clear that the custom had outlived its time.

RAY, JOHNNIE (1927-90)

The Prince of Wails

An invention of the Press rather than actual billing, but routinely quoted of an American crooner whose trade-marks were a deaf aid and a tendency to blub.

RAY, PHIL (1872-1918)

The Abbreviating Comedian; Peculiar Abbreviator

This entry was one of those late-Victorian comedians whose nightmarish appearance recalls not so much a place of entertainment as a charnel house, but as (Sir) Max Beerbohm wrote: 'Music Hall cheered up the lower orders because it showed them a life uglier and more sordid than their own.' Mr Ray's face was painted white with his mouth a blob of red; his speciality to tell jokes with many of the words abbreviated, e.g:

> I weren't feeling right so I went down to Bright,
> To spend a few mins by the sea.
> On Victoria plat I patiently sat,
> With my little portmant on my knee.
> Then in from the junc came the 3.30 punc,
> As they shunted it in to the staysh;
> Said the guard 'Make a start – room for one, this compart.'
> I said 'Thanks for the kind informaysh.' etc., etc.

RAY, TED (1906-77)
Fiddling and Fooling

It was not until the summer of 1930 that Charles Olden from Wigan, originally Hugh Neek *The Unique Entertainer* and then Nedlo *The Gypsy Violinist*, finally found a stage identity with which he felt comfortable. As Ted Ray the comedian oozed confident geniality; other assets were a bright distinctive speaking voice and an energetic delivery which proved ideal for broadcasting. This entry's bill-matter tells us just what we need to know – that Ted Ray plays the violin and tells jokes. The compactness, elegance and metre of these three simple words combine in haiku-like flawlessness.

Similar but not so crisp was Nick Nissen's (b1907) *Fiddling Fooling Funster*.

See p.13, WILKIE BARD, JIMMY WHEELER

RAYMOND, PAUL (b1925)
Man of Mystery

The mystery about this entry is how Geoffrey Anthony Quinn rose from a third-rate mentalism act to become one of the wealthiest men in the country. Tacky strip-shows and pornography had a lot to do with it, of course. We were once asked by this entry to take part in a production of *Pyjama Tops* which he was presenting that summer in Blackpool. Having been in the play a couple of times in repertory we knew it as a reliable old French farce, but Mr Raymond's version which we saw at the Whitehall had tacked on a great deal of gratuitous nudity and insultingly crude dialogue. The audience became restless, embarrassed and bored, and we decided that Blackpool was not for us.

See MAGICIANS, THE ZANCIGS

READ, AL (1909-87)
Right, Monkey!

For his first engagement, to avoid embarrassing his family, this entry was billed at the Grand Theatre Bolton as Al Reid, *Jest for Fun*. Born into a meat-packing family, the comedian used to say he was 'from a long line of sausages'. It was as an after-dinner speaker that Mr Read developed his slice-of-life stories; the performer's professional career came about by accident, and though it took him to Top of the Bill at the Adelphi and the 1954 *Royal Variety Performance* the raconteur remained a meat-packer at heart.

REDCLIFFE, REGGIE (b1918)
The Dancing Xylophonist

The limited appeal of the xylophone was recognised by this performer who invented something called a xylo rhumba-phone. Mr Redcliffe then introduced ultra-violet lighting, he danced, he quick-changed costumes and finally, still heroically trying to keep their attention, did the whole act on ice.

See BEBE NORMA

REDFERN, SAM (1851-1915)
The Black Emperor; The Black Jester; The Black Philosopher; Black Boss of the Benighted Bohemians; The Facetious Negroist

This comic singer, who habitually wore an enveloping white coat and long boots, could, according to one report, 'have worked his act equally well without the aid of burnt cork'.

'What?' we hear him cry, 'and waste all that bill-matter?'

For other philosophers see BIG BILL CAMPBELL; For other black-face artistes see G H ELLIOTT.

REEVE, ADA (1874-1966)
The Juvenile Wonder; The World's Most Popular Comedienne

In the late 1950s a provincial lad eager to find his feet in the Metropolis lived between engagements at the Interval Club, a down-at-heel hostel for indigent theatricals in Dean St, Soho. It had opened in 1925 nominally as a Roman Catholic Club but by the 1950s was struggling financially and even the Hottentot Venus* would have been welcome. Here in the shabby first-floor lounge elderly pros would heave up the long, curving Georgian staircase each afternoon for tea and society, one of whom, leaning heavily on a stick, was an old lady with strange wide-apart eyes and her face liberally over-powdered. This was Ada

39. LA MILO

40. EVELYN NESBIT

41. LA BELLE OTERO

42. EUGENE SANDOW

*One of the high-spots of his act – blowing out a
candle from a distance of one foot.*

43. JOSEPH PUJOL
Le Pétomane

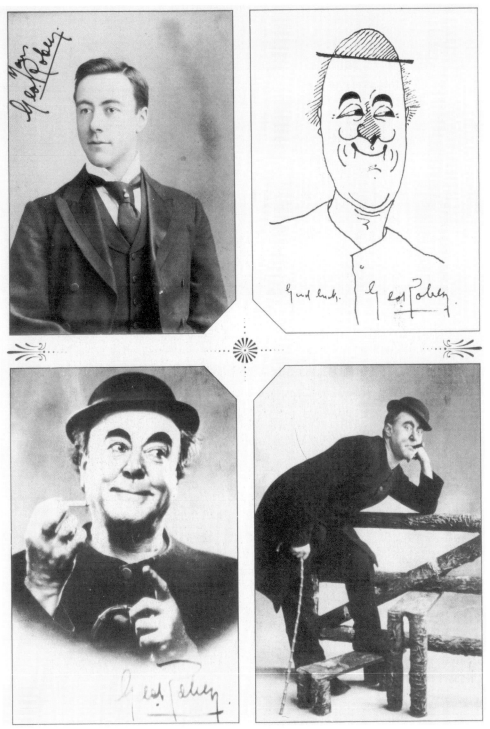

44. GEORGE ROBEY

45. DAISY SQUELCH

46. WILSON, KEPPEL & BETTY

47. ELSIE & DORIS WATERS

48. NEW THEATRE, OXFORD 1944

49. BRANSBY WILLIAMS

50. GEORGE WILLIAMS

51. ZAZEL

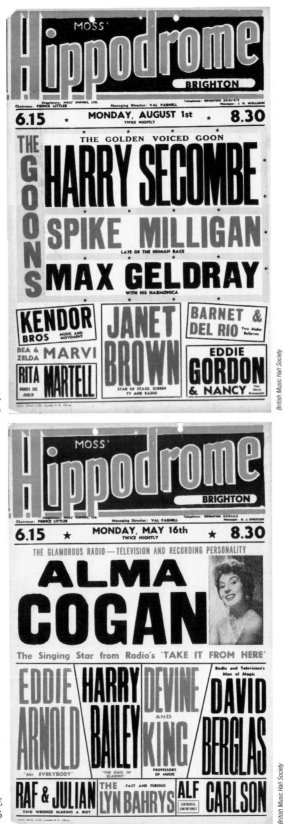

52. HIPPODROME
BRIGHTON, 1955

53. HIPPODROME
BRIGHTON, 1955

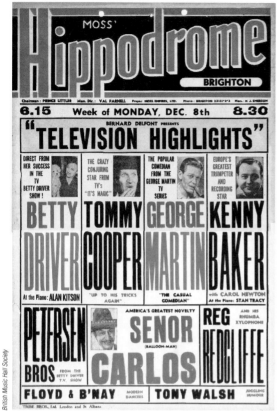

54. HIPPODROME BRIGHTON, 1958

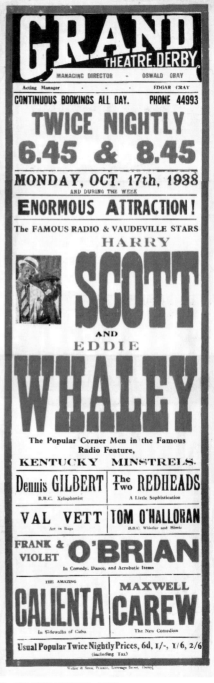

55. GRAND DERBY, 1938

Reeve, toast of *fin de siècle* London and a leading soubrette of the Variety and Musical Comedy stages on both sides of the Atlantic. We did not at the time appreciate the venerable artiste's distinction, and wish we could have again the opportunity of speaking to her of her glittering past. Miss Reeve died full of years, honour and respect and with £549 in the bank.

A monograph on the Interval Club and its legendarily eccentric secretary, Molly Balvaird Hewett, is deposited in the library of the Theatre Museum, Covent Garden.

* See SAARTJE BAARTMAN

REID, BERYL (1918-96)
'Marlene' & 'Monica'

Miss Reid's bill-matter reflects the two characters by which this difficult, wilful but brilliant comedienne-actress came to fame. The first to be aired was Monica the coy schoolgirl in BBC radio's *Henry Hall's Guest Night*. For two years Miss Reid also played her in *Educating Archie* (see PETER BROUGH & ARCHIE ANDREWS) before consolidating her reputation by introducing Marlene, an adenoidal Birmingham teenager. Playing supporting roles to a dummy must have appealed to a caustic sense of humour from which few were exempt. In 1965 this entry enjoyed colossal *succès d'estime* in *The Killing of Sister George* both on stage and screen; the role of Kath in *Entertaining Mr Sloane* was a further triumph for her powerful and oddly sinister personality. The artiste had come a long way since rats ate her knickers in the Palace, Attercliffe, though her last years, blighted by osteoporosis, were spent in a haze of wine fumes and cats' pee.

See STAINLESS STEPHEN

REINDEER, EDDIE (d October 12th 1983)
The Wise Crackpot

This was the comedian's usual bill-matter but there were the occasional peculiar alternatives like *The Jersey Jereexpeequa* (?). In the late 1960s we nearly engaged Mr Reindeer; in the event the booking came to nothing but we did elicit the comedian's weekly rate of £70, a figure acceptable at that time for an established middle-ranking comic.

RETFORD, ELLA (1886-1962)
The Breezy Comedienne; Your Old Favourite

Many female Variety artistes, from JENNY HILL and NELLIE
POWER onward, have referred to themselves as comediennes, but
how was the word perceived when it first appeared on British posters
c1870? A 'comédienne' was not necessarily a funny woman, still less a
female grotesque of the NELLIE WALLACE type; the word was
understood to describe a singer whose repertoire was light, cheeky,
saucy, and, as Miss Retford herself put it in her bill-matter, breezy.

See ANNIE ADAMS

REVNELL & WEST (fl1920s-c50)
The Cockney Kids; The Long and the Short of It;
The Two Oddments

Ethel Revnell (1895-1978) and Gracie West (1893-1989) were that *rara
avis* of Variety: the female comedy double. What a comical sight these
ladies made, to be sure, with their 'little girl' costumes and Miss Revnell
towering a head and a half taller than her partner. The pair were robust,
grimacing, low comediennes of whose effectiveness there should be
no doubt – at the *Royal Variety Performance* of 1937 they had the Palladium
in uproar, and the distinguished comedian Lupino Lane wrote of this
entry: 'Woe betide any comedian who has to follow them in any
programme without an interval between' (see THE LUPINOS).

NB: CHIC MURRAY & MAIDIE were also *The Long and the
Short of It*.

See Foreword. Also see HOUSTON & STEWART, ELSIE & DORIS WATERS.

RHODES, JOAN (fl1949-60s)
The Mighty Mannequin

This entry's bill-matter was in no wise hyperbolic. We saw *The Mighty
Mannequin* in action on many occasions, and still we wonder how the
lady could be so strong while retaining her trimness. No bulging biceps
or bull-neck for this most feminine and svelte of performers as she bent
her un-straightenable iron bars and tore through her telephone directories.
Miss Rhodes informs us that at her peak the number of such volumes
ripped up by the artiste *per annum* was in excess of one thousand.

Two more muscular maidens were Victorina (fl1880s-90s) *The Strongest Lady on Earth* and Athleta (1867-1927) *The Champion Lady Heavy Weight Lifter of the World* and *The Strongest Woman in the World* (see GASTON PALMER).

See also ANNIE MAY ABBOTT, ALOIS PETERS, EUGENE SANDOW

RHYDER, SLIM (fl1930s-50s?)
The Elongated Chump; Komedy Kapers; Oh! Shut Up

This entry was very tall and very thin but his dignity as he rode his bicycle round and round the stage performing the most comical and unexpected of tricks remained intact. The artiste's encore was somehow to ride across the stage on a bicycle no more than a few inches high. A clever and popular act, usually known by the first billing.

See BICYCLE ACTS

RICE, T D (1808-60)
The Daddy of Minstrelsy

It was the furore which greeted this American's performance of *Jump Jim Crow*, first seen in England on July 9th 1836, which established the caricature of the Deep South black as a singin', dancin', happy-go-lucky, simple-minded figure of fun, besides paving the way for the Minstrel troupes which were so strangely popular in Britain for the next two reigns. Mr Rice also brought another innovation to these shores, for which see BIRDIE BRIGHTLING.

Two of the many who rode on Mr Rice's coat-tails were John Dunn (1812-75) *The English Jim Crow* and E W MACKNEY.

See BERT ERROL and Nellie Richards (MAY HENDERSON), G H ELLIOTT.

RICKABY, J W (1870-1929)
The Big Dry Comedian

William Hargreaves, writer-composer of this entry's 1913 success *PC 49*, supplied him with another hit later that year: *Silk Hat Tony Or They Built Piccadilly For Me*. Of this song the Music Hall chronicler S Theodore Felstead wrote: 'Off hand, I am inclined to regard it as the best comic ditty I ever heard.' Having seen this *magnum opus* performed, and indeed having sung it ourself, we can but think that Mr Felstead should have got out more.

Mr Rickaby's brother, also a comic singer on the Halls, was Ted Waite *The Spasmodic Comedian.*

See ELLA SHIELDS

RISLEY, Professor (1814-74)
Classical Gymnasia and Aerial Dancing

A Risley act is one in which largish objects or smallish persons (originally children) are juggled with the feet, the antipodist lying in a padded frame called a trinka. Foot juggling had been seen at Astley's in the 1770s but it was this entry who developed and popularised the speciality which now bears his name.

There is no truth in the story that this American acrobat-wrestler-marksman killed himself after the death of a child in performance; the Professor's actual fate was scarcely less tragic however, for he lost all his money and died in a lunatic asylum.

See THE FIVE WHITELEYS. Also see CLEMENTINE, JUGGLERS.

RITCHIE, BILLIE (1878-1921)
The Different Drunk; The Original Drunk

On whom did CHARLES CHAPLIN base his Little Fellow, the most widely known and imitated comic character of all time? The younger comedian, or so Mr Ritchie claimed, was depressed at his inability to find a film character and so this entry handed over his own tramp outfit including the big boots, bowler hat and bamboo cane – and even suggested the small moustache. If this is true it constitutes the single most generous act in the history of entertainment.

Mr Ritchie's own film career was undistinguished; the Glaswegian comic died of injuries inflicted by an ostrich.

See JOHNNY COOPER

ROBERTS, ARTHUR (1852-1933)
The Girl who Lost her Honeymoon

This bill-matter was the title of one of the many musical sketches with which the spectacularly funny comedian convulsed Music Hall audiences. Others had such titles as *Some Girls Do, Some Girls Don't* and *The Woman Who Was*, which give the impression, correctly, that much of this performer's material was near the knuckle – a phrase he claimed to have invented.

Mr Roberts' extemporising powers were legendary; when the artiste went into rehearsal he didn't want a script, just a blank sheet of paper and a bottle of champagne. Another Roberts coinage sums up his life and career: spoof.

See JAMES FAWN, SKETCH ARTISTES

ROBERTS, KEN (1917-95)
The Effervescent Comedian

Mr Roberts was the most charming and the most genuine of men, better suited perhaps to sketch-work than stand-up for which his material had decidedly seen better days. As the *pater* said to us thoughtfully after seeing this entry perform a patter act at the Bexhill De La Warr Pavilion, 'Nice voice...'

See Bert Clifford (CLAPHAM & DWYER)

ROBEY, Sir GEORGE (1869-1954)
The Prime Minister of Mirth

George Robey was one of the very greatest comedians of his day; bluff, beefy, fruity, vulgar, boisterous and earthily English. Within weeks of his professional début (billed as *The Coming Man*) at the Royal Aquarium the young comic was a Metropolitan star; by the late 1890s Mr Robey was *The Prime Minister of Mirth*, bill-matter he was to use for the rest of his career except for a brief period at the London Coliseum when he was *The Touchstone of Our Time*. World War I had just broken out and it may be that the proprietor of the Coliseum, (Sir) Oswald Stoll, felt that to take the office of Prime Minister in vain at a time of national crisis could be seen as offensive and disloyal. Nor would he have wished to damage his chances of a K. Some forty years later Mr Robey himself became Sir George, though by then he was too ga-ga to know what all the fuss was about.

We wish to scotch once and for all the nonsense about this entry being a Cambridge graduate. It is simply not true; Mr Robey went to no university or polytechnic or college of any kind; he was not an engineer or professionally qualified in any way. Having said what he was not, let us say what he was: an opinionated, pompous, egotistical windbag. And a great comic.

See p.14, BARBETTE, VIVIAN FOSTER

ROBINA, FLORRIE (1867-1953)
Our English Rose

As was common practice this 'sparkling soubrette' took her bill-matter from one of her hit songs *The English Rose*. The artiste's sister Fanny Robina (1861-1927) was a male impersonator of note.

RODGERS, JIMMIE (1897-1933)
The Singing Brakeman

Mr Rodgers was obliged to relinquish his eponymous railway employment due to tuberculosis; in the remaining seven years of his life the singer-guitarist built up an imperishable legacy of recordings. The artiste's reputation spread world-wide and his popularity as a folk chronicler of American life was immense, with over twenty million records sold – and that during the Depression. Shame about the yodelling.

ROGERS, TED
Now Hear This

We have worked with this comedian once or twice and are happy to confirm the universally held opinion that you couldn't meet a nicer fellow. In 1996 Mr Rogers fulfilled the ambition of a lifetime by mounting his tribute to the great American entertainer Danny Kaye (1913-87) under the title *Danny and Me*, which caused a drag artiste named Danny La Rue to telephone an acquaintance of ours and complain tetchily 'What's this show Ted Rogers is putting on about me and him? I don't know anything about it.' In Mr La Rue's cosmos there can only be one Danny.

ROGERS, WILL (1879-1935)
The World's Number One Wisecracker; Poet Lariat

Mr Rogers was a gum-chewing Oklahoman rope-spinner and lariat-thrower of uncanny accuracy who, much to his own surprise, discovered a flair for comedy of the topical, slice-of-life variety. The artiste's reputation for profundity made his humour a reflection of the American psyche, and his death in an air crash a cause of national mourning.

See CAL McCORD

ROLLS, WILLIE (1874-1924)

He Does?

In 1922 this artiste billed himself as *Famous English Roller Skater* which may lack sparkle but does have the merit of being clearly and straightforwardly informative. And it doesn't try to be *funny!*

ROLO & LADY (fl1920s)

The Ape and the Maid

We do not know precisely what form this act took but if it is anything like a Girl 'n' Gorilla act we saw in Acapulco in 1967 it is unlikely to have played the Number Ones.

 The act did play the Palace Wellingborough, however, for it is recorded that on December 28th 1927 Rolo hurtled from his trapeze into the stalls, both killing himself and breaking a punter's leg.

RONALDE, RONNIE (b1922)

Radio's 'Voice of Variety'; The Voice of the Whistler

After an unaccountably successful Variety and recording career the siffleur-singer retired to run an hotel in Guernsey, removing in the mid-1980s to New Zealand to run a dairy farm. Having experienced this entry's whistling in the confines of an auditorium we are of the opinion that 12,000 miles is not too far to be distanced from this particular puckerer.

See SIFFLEURS & SIFFLEUSES

RONDART (b1929)

Champion Dart Blower

Rondart's very special speciality has not, to our knowledge, been attempted by any other artiste. Ronald Tomlinson's art may have been limited, but By Jiminy!, it was his own.

ROSE, CLARKSON (1890-1968)

The Modern Comedy Merchant; Royal Comic Songster

For an entertainer noted for his wit this entry's bill-matter is disappointingly unimaginative, but then his description for the Australian tour of his long-running show *Twinkle* as *A Revusical Gay-As-You-Please Show of Nimbleness and Nonsense – for Laughing Purposes Only* makes one thankful he kept his own personal subscripts simple. Mr Rose's wife and stage partner was Olive Fox (1891-1964) *Woman – Wit and Wisdom.*

ROVI (1920-96)

The Welsh Wizard

The first Welsh magician to be made an Honorary Ovate by the National Eisteddfod also became a member of the Bardic Circle, was President of the British Ring of the International Brotherhood of Magicians 1984-5 and honorary Life President of the North Wales Magic Circle. Did *The Welsh Wizard* find time to do any tricks?

See MAGICIANS

ROY, DEREK (1922-81)

Ah, Yes!; The Doctor of Mirth; An Evening with Old Favourites; The Fun Doctor

As genial resident comedian on BBC radio's *Variety Bandbox* (alternating week and week about with FRANKIE HOWERD) this entry was *a.k.a.* Doctor Roy *The Melody Boy.* Mr Roy was a particular favourite of our younger days and remains unquestionably the finest Buttons of our experience.

The ebullient performer dropped out of favour in the 1960s, perhaps due to an inability to come to terms with television, though it has been suggested to us that Mr Roy's marked propensity of getting up people's noses did not help.

RUBIE, Princess (d January 24th 1931)

The Magnetic Lady; a.k.a.The Great Rubie *La Femme Mesmer, The Only Lady Society Electrician and Hypnotist in the World*

Franz Anton Mesmer (1734-1815) was the pioneer of therapeutic hypnotism, though as this entry's husband was that arch-mountebank

WALFORD BODIE – whose hand is evident in his wife's salmagundy of a billing – we can be sure that precious little therapy was practised.

See PETER CASSON, GEORGE BARNARDO EAGLE

RUSSELL, BILLY (1893-1971)
On Behalf of the Working Classes; The Son of Toil

Adam George Brown began his career as a juvenile in a sketch called, we regret to report, *The Hot Member*. Various modes of entertaining were attempted by this entry, sometimes solo, sometimes not, at one time appearing as Baroni *the Ambidextrous Cartoonist*.

It was while serving with the South Staffs in the Great War that Mr Russell began to flesh out his celebrated navvy Old Bill, the character which supported him for the next forty years, and whose appearance was based on the Bruce Bairnsfeather cartoon character. Effortlessly making the switch to the Drama when Variety finally fell off the twig, the old comedian died literally on the job, for he suffered a fatal syncope in a television studio.

See p.14, JAMES UNSWORTH

RUSSELL, FRED (1862-1957)
The World's Greatest Ventriloquial Humorist

This much-respected artiste was also referred to affectionately as *The Father of the Profession* both for his venerableness and for his tireless work over many years on behalf of the Variety Artistes' Federation – of which he was a founder member – and for the Grand Order of Water Rats.

One of Mr Russell's five sons was Russ Carr (see VENTRILOQUISTS), another the renowned impresario Val Parnell (1894-1972) by whom we were engaged for his very last show at the London Palladium before devoting himself to television interests.

It was customary around the turn of the century for ventriloquists to appear with a multiplicity of dummies; this distinguished performer pioneered the single doll act (Coster Joe), a *methode* widely copied since. We can see why – a single dummy is cheaper to run and far easier to work.

See FATHER OF..., Lieut TRAVIS, VENTRILOQUISTS

S

ST JOHN, FLORENCE (1854-1912)

Queen of Burlesque; The Queen of Comic Opera; The Queen of Opera-Bouffe

At the age of 14 years and 7 months this Tavistock-born entry was married, unusually early even for those times, to an officer in the Royal Navy. The bridegroom was soon carried off by consumption and, having of necessity to earn a crust, the widow took to the opera stage. After some years of provincial languishing Mrs St John finally conquered the Metropolis as Germaine in Planquette's *Les Cloches de Corneville*, a rôle which established her in lasting public favour.

This entry was a handsome and fascinating singer exactly suited to her time and *milieu* and whose name alone was almost always sufficient to guarantee a show's success, even surviving the scandal of an affair with her married leading man, the Gallic charmer M. Marius (1850-96). In due course Mrs St John became the second Mme Marius, and not too long afterwards the second ex-Mme Marius. The *diva* was generous, impulsive and erratic, a star who blazed in an era rich in positive personalities.

Three other Queens of Burlesque whose details are listed under QUEEN OF... were Gypsy Rose Lee, Fannie Leslie and Iris Sadler.

SALAMBOS, THE (fl1900s)

An advertisement in *The Era* of April 19th 1902 runs as follows: 'If we had a little money, if we had a few more contracts, if we had no Agents to pay, if we had no railway journeys to make, if we could avoid the tips innumerable, we might feel content.' The disconsolate artistes were a mind-reading act, one of whom (the wife?) was named Olivette.

There was also an American fire-eating act called The Salambos – Earl Salambo (1876-1923) with his wife and daughter. The latter was Elre Cecilia Salambo *Child Historian* and *Walking Encyclopaedia*, bill-matter which seems to indicate that both families were the same, though we cannot say for certain.

See CHARLES S BERNARD, IVAN IVANITZ CHABERT, DATAS, THE ZANCIGS

SANDERS, SCOTT (1888-1956)

The Old Hawker; The Old Philosopher; Pottering Along; Rolling Round the World

For other philosophers see BIG BILL CAMPBELL (especially Eddie Lawrence). *Re* the first bill-matter: we know of no other hawking artistes, though we've known some with a nasty cough.

SANDOW, EUGENE (1867-1925)

The Monarch of Muscle; The Most Powerful Man on Earth; The Strongest Man in the World

The Prussian athlete established his pre-eminence as a strong man by seeing off all comers including the famed Samson (Alexander Zass d1962) *The Russian Strong Man.* Herr Sandow was also exceptionally personable with a blond moustache which tickled the ladies' fancies on both sides of the Pond besides possessing a magnificent physique which was exploited to puff products as diverse as cocoa and, oddly, corsets. Sad to relate *The Modern Hercules and The Perfect Man* (as Florenz Ziegfeld billed him in Chicago) died from over-exertion trying to lift his motor-car from a ditch.

If Leo Whitton (1856-99) was *The Canadian Colossus*, Georges Hackenschmidt (1877-1968) was *The Russian Lion* and from 1900-8 professional *Champion Wrestler of the World*. After retirement Mr Hackenschmidt went all mystical and wrote, amongst other impenetrable works, *Man and Cosmic Antagonism to Mind and Spirit.*

See CHARLES ATLAS, KING OF..., ALOIS PETERS, JOAN RHODES

SANGER, 'Lord' GEORGE (1825-1911)

The Wizard of the West

At the age of 15 this entry started on life's journey selling lettered rock; by 21 he had progressed to a conjuring booth and showing 'trained' canaries and mice, and two years later the young entrepreneur was exhibiting a pipe-smoking oyster. Such were the humble origins of one of Britain's greatest circus proprietors, even if his peerage was self-awarded.

Mrs Sanger (c1832-99) née Ellen Chapman was none other than Pauline de Vere *Lion Queen* and *The Lady of the Lions*, the first woman to put her head in a lion's mouth (see ELLEN BRIGHT). At the age of 63 Miss de Vere was still appearing as Britannia in the street procession as well as performing a 'serpentine dance' in the lions' den.

When Lord George died at the age of 85 it was reported that he had been battered to death by a deranged ex-employee. The truth was rather different: the circus king had befriended a young man and then accused him, quite unjustly, of stealing money. There was a scuffle in which the old man fell back in his chair but otherwise was not hurt. A few hours later, having gone to bed, he died, as much from shock as anything else, and the young man killed himself in remorse. There was a further complication in that the young man was romantically involved with the old man's grand-daughter, so it was all a messy and ridiculous end to a full and rewarding life.

See GEORGE BARNARDO EAGLE for other territorial Wizards. Also see Victoria Sanger Freeman (QUEEN OF...)

SEATON, JACK (b1929)

SAVEEN, ALBERT (1914-94)

This Southwark artiste developed his ventriloquial art while recuperating in hospital from injuries sustained on active service in World War II. His dummy Daisy May became so celebrated that she was the first of her timber to be awarded a radio series, she was listed in the London telephone directory, had her own bank account, and was even billed above her own operator, i.e. Daisy May *with Saveen*. All this attention must, we feel, have severely put out of its wooden joint the nose of Mr Saveen's other principal character, Andy the Spiv.

See VENTRILOQUISTS

SCOTT & WHALEY (fl1909-47)
Business is Business; Kolored Kings of Komedy

Harry Scott (1879-1947) and Edward Peter (1886-1961) started their careers in America with the Kentucky Minstrels and similar troupes; as a double act this entry entered vaudeville as Pussy Foot & Cuthbert but wiser counsels prevailed. Arriving on our shores in 1909 for an eight-week engagement the two black comedians found a ready welcome both on and off stage and never went home. See illustration 55.

Eddie Whaley retired to Brighton where he played a good deal of golf. On one occasion, having narrowly lost a game, he blamed his defeat on the school-boy caddy who, he claimed, had given him the wrong club. Dear reader, we were that caddy.

SCOTT, MALCOLM (1872-1929)
The Impromptu Comedian; The Woman who Knows

Mr Scott was a most unusual female impersonator whose obscure and esoteric material was often way over the heads of the *hoi polloi*, though the GBP loved him even if they didn't always understand him. According to Sir Louis Fergusson the comedian 'invariably wound up his turn with his back to the audience and the lower half of his right leg revolving like a Catherine Wheel', which must have made an odd sight if the artiste were appearing as Catherine Parr, Boadicea, Nell Gwyn, or any of his other famed characters.

The son of a London solicitor and thus that rarity on the Halls, a genuine member of the professional classes, this entry must have been something of an embarrassment to his elder brother Admiral Sir Percy Scott RN. While strolling along the beach at Brighton, Mr Scott is said to have remarked to a fisherman mending his nets, 'I've got a brother in your line.'

See BARBETTE, CLAPHAM & DWYER

SEATON, JACK (b1929)
Did I Say Something Funny?; The Relaxed Comedian

As a boy this entry's bill-matter was *A Bit of a Lad!* Mr Seaton was introduced to the world of entertainment at his school, a seminary which stood – and still stands – in Great Windmill Street directly opposite the WINDMILL THEATRE. Master Seaton and his school-mates discovered that by standing on the desks it was possible to see into the ladies' dressing-rooms across the way. Such early exposure to exposure could only have been character-building.

For thirteen years, from 1984 to 1997, Mr Seaton was chairman of the British Music Hall Society, an excellent body of enthusiasts on whose behalf the comedian worked indefatigably.

See WILKIE BARD

SECOMBE, Sir HARRY (b1921)
The Golden Voiced Goon

After the cessation of hostilities, having cut his teeth as an entertainer while in uniform, the then Mr Secombe followed a well-trodden path to the WINDMILL, though this entry's subsequent Variety career was by no means plain sailing – his shaving routine did not incur unanimous approval and at the Grand, Bolton, in 1947 he was famously paid off after the first performance. But the comedian's clarity of diction, good-hearted incorrigibility and fine tenor made him a radio favourite; in 1951 *The Goon Show* (originally *Crazy People*) was to propel him willy-nilly into stardom and legend.

As recorded in the Introduction we first had the privilege of working with this distinguished artiste at the London Palladium for the 1959/60 pantomime *Humpty Dumpty*, an engagement which permitted us to experience at first hand Sir Harry's kindness, generosity and concern for his fellow-artistes – traits not by any means always found in the Number 1 dressing-room.

See Foreword, p.11, p.15, PAT FEENEY, BETTY JUMEL, SPIKE MILLIGAN, PETER SELLERS, STAN STENNETT

SELLERS, PETER (1925-80)
Speaking for the Stars

By chance this entry follows that of fellow-Goon Sir HARRY SECOMBE. Like TONY HANCOCK Mr Sellers reached the WINDMILL by way of RAF Gang Shows, after which his initial foray into show business was as a drummer-comedian, flatly billed as *Drumming Man*. It was BBC producer Roy Speer who provided the artiste with his big break after a telephone conversation with celebrities Kenneth Horne and Richard Murdoch turned out to be a conversation with the unknown 'character impressionist comedian'.

Mr Sellers was not unknown for long; from drummer to impressionist to radio comic to film star this entry became one of the few Britons to make a significant reputation in Hollywood, before his unique talents were snuffed out by a psychotic temperament and heart failure.

See SPIKE MILLIGAN, Mrs SHUFFLEWICK; also list of MIMICS in glossary.

SENYAH, Mme (1841-1910)

Champion Teeth Performer of the World; Empress of the Air and Flying Meteor; Witch of the Air

Senyah is the reverse of Haynes, the family from which this trapezist and rope-dancer sprang. Sometimes an extra 'e' was added – Senyeah – for class. A *Teeth Performer* or *Dental Artiste* is one who swings by the pearlies from a great height or from whose mouth others are suspended. When enough was enough the *Witch of the Air* descended to *terra firma* and thenceforth ran a dog act.

See Jack 'Dental' Riskit (BARBETTE)

SHAKESPEARE, BILLY (b1916)

A Midsummer Night's Scream; Much Ado About Nothing

The bill-matter devised by comedian Billy Shakespeare (his family name) proudly reflects two of his illustrious namesake's most popular plays. Note *Scream* instead of *Dream* – how the Swan of Avon would have chuckled at that!

See DE HAVEN & PAGE

SHATTUCK, TRULY (1876-1954)

The California Nightingale

It is, we know, cheap to make fun of a person's name, but as we wondered on p.14 why by all that's holy should Clarice Etrulia de Bucharde have selected for her stage alias a first name of such coy affectation and a second of such consonantal ugliness.

Even worse was the name of the lady we had to introduce many years ago in a West London hostelry overlooking Wormwood Scrubs: 'Ladies and gentleman, your own, your *very* own, Miss Lydia Crotch!'

For other Nightingales see JENNY LIND

SHIELDS, ELLA (1879-1952)

The Ideal of Ideals

Miss Shields originally came to Britain from Baltimore as a 'coon-shouter'. It was in 1910 that this entry first took up male impersonation, and in 1914 the writer-composer William Hargreaves (1880-1941) offered her the song with which her name will forever be associated *Burlington Bertie from Bow*. Mr Hargreaves also happened to be Miss Shields' husband, but by 1923 he had failed to repeat that signal success and the performer divorced him. Show business can be so cruel.

See MAY HENDERSON, ST GEORGE HUSSEY, J W RICKABY

SHIELDS, SAMMY (1872-1933)

The (Original) Football Enthusiast; The Merry Scot; The Speakable Scot

At the age of 33 this entry abandoned security as a clerk in the Glasgow Stock Exchange and made his initial assault upon the Variety Stage. With his loud check suits, tam o'shanter hat and fund of 'mean Scotsman' stories the new comedian swiftly made his mark on both sides of the border and was booked by all the major combines and syndicates.

Mr Shields' recreations included drilling, but lest it appear that the artiste was a dentist *manqué* it should be explained that he held a commission in the West London Regiment (Westminster Battalion). We do not know what *The Speakable Scot* means.

SHORT, JACK (1896-1982)

The Man the Germans Couldn't Kill

Mr Short felt himself entitled to this bill-matter on account of losing a leg in France in 1918, and who shall say him nay? The following year the Glaswegian entertainer-accordionist met May Dalziel (d1969), an artiste whose bill-matter – *The Street Singer* – was chosen to save on wardrobe. Professionally the pair were *k.a.* Short and Dalziel *Two Drops of Scotch*; their union produced five children, all of whom became entertainers. One is Annie Ross, the internationally respected jazz songstress, and another is the doyen of North British show business, Jimmy Logan.

Mr Logan's choice of stage name was a tribute to May's sister Ella Logan, a Broadway star; as nephew Jimmy's reputation grew all the family, even his parents, gradually became Loganised. Having obliged in two pantomime seasons with the actor-comedian we can understand the devotion this fine performer inspires in the hearts of his fellow-countrymen and women.

See ARTHUR TRACY

SHUFFLEWICK, Mrs (c1927-82)

Radio's Favourite Housewife; A Drop of the Hard Shuff

Rex Jameson, this entry's alternative stage name, had followed the Gang Show-WINDMILL route of so many, including TONY HANCOCK and PETER SELLERS. 'Shuff', as the artiste's intimates called him, spent his last decade in an alcoholic daze, only able to perform sitting down but still wonderfully effective as a shabby genteel, accident-prone widow who was 'broadminded to the point of obscenity'. Only the Demon Drink stopped the comedian enjoying a full-scale national re-discovery.

Mr Jameson's manager of many years Patrick Newley informs us that his client had at one time been engaged to HYLDA BAKER, surely one of show business's most unlikely alliances.

See BARBETTE

SIFFLEURS & SIFFLEUSES:

Arthur Astill (1887-1962)
The Whistling Ploughboy

Gladys Church (b1910)
The Whistling Songstress

Irving Kaye (1902-62)
The Whistling Violinist

Doreen McKay (fl1930s-40s)
Champion Siffleuse

Fred Mason (1865-95)
The Whistling Coster
Though born in Brooklyn billed in the US on his return from Britain as *England's Greatest Whistling Comedian.*

SIFFLEURS & SIFFLEUSES (continued):

Paul Mill (1862-1916)
The Whistling Comedian

Tom Murray (1854-95)
Champion Whistler

Arthur Slater (fl1890s-1910s)
The Whistling Man in White

Erroll Stanhope
England's Lady Whistler

Rich Taylor
See VENTRILOQUISTS

Helen Trix
See HARRY FRAGSON

Herr Von Joel (1784-1865)
The German Whistler

Professor Wallace (fl1870s-80s)
The American Siffleur

Nora Williams
America's Whistling Songstress

See also: RONNIE RONALDE, EUGENE STRATTON

SIRDANI (1899-1982)
Don't Be Fright; The Radio Magician

Sidney Daniels, a South African comedy magician, affected an Italian accent for the most incongruous form of entertainment ever devised: magic on radio. All the tricks had to be explained (there was always a studio audience, if we recall aright) but so ebullient was this entry's personality that his turns were more effective than might have been thought possible.

Mr Sirdani stated that he was the first to introduce conjuring into a BBC programme in 1944, though Cyril Shields was billing himself as *The Wireless Magician* in the 1920s.

See MAGICIANS

SKETCH ARTISTES:

Sir George Alexander (1858-1918)
A Social Success

The Bogannys (fl1900-43)
Five Minutes in China Town; The Lunatic Bakers or Fun in a Bakehouse
Founded by Joe Boganny (1873-1943) with his brothers.

The Boissets (fl1870s-1900s)
The Bricklayers; The Evening Party

George Carney (1877-1947)
Almost Human; The Fool of the Force

The Famous Craggs (fl1862-?)
Gentlemen Acrobats; Laughter Land
Possibly related to Gaston of GASTON & ANDRÉE.

Joe Elvin (& Co) (1862-1935)
Fares, Please; On The Flat
From 1872-95 worked with father Joseph Keegan (1841-1901) as Keegan & (Little) Elvin *Thirty Minutes' Roars of Laughter.*

Will Evans & Co (1867-1931)
The Gay Burlesquer; Harnessing a Horse; Yachting; Laying a Carpet

The Fothergill Family (fl1890s-1910s)
Jealousy – A Screaming Absurdity

Fred Ginnett & Co
Dick Turpin's Ride to York; Rejected Remounts
Mr Ginnett (1859-1924) was a scion of the famous circus family.

Sir Cedric Hardwicke (1893-1964)
England's Greatest Character Actor
Toured sketch called *The Carrier Pigeon*.

Keegan & Elvin
See Joe Elvin *supra*

Horace Kenney (1890-1955)
Almost a Film Star; The Trial Turn;
The Stagehand's Impromptu

Neil Kenyon (1873-1946)
The Caddy; The Elder of the Kirk;
The Postmaster of Dunrobin

Lew Lake (c1874-1939)
The Rib-Nosed Baboon
Sketch featuring 150 extras. With Bob Morris (1866-1945) worked
as Nobbler & Jerry *The Bloomsbury Burglars*.

The (Original) Leopolds (fl c1870-1900s)
La Belle France; Frivolity

Ernie Lotinga (1876-1951)
Josser, KC
Married (and divorced from) HETTY KING. At one time with
the Six Brothers Luck *infra*.

SKETCH ARTISTES (continued):

Six Brothers Luck (fl1890s-1910s)
The Demon of the Cellar
Possibly a spoof on HARRY HOUDINI's *The Demon of the Cells.*
See Ernie Lotinga *supra*

The McNaughtons *a.k.a.* The Two McNaughtons
The Prompter
Fred (1869-1920) and brother Tom (1867-1923). In 1909 Tom
married ALICE LLOYD and left for the US; he was replaced
by Augustus Howard (1884-1969) *k.a.* Augustus Le Clerq and
as Gus McNaughton.
See The Poluskis *infra*

Paul Martinetti & Co (fl1875-c1910)
Robert Macaire; A Terrible Night; A Duel in the Snow;
Paris by Night; The Village Schoolmaster

Mark Melford & Co (1851-1914)
My Wife Won't Let Me; Non-Suited

Jack Melville (b1899)
The Hydro
For FRED KARNO's company.

Wal Pink & Co (c1866-1929)
The Parrot; The QC

Miss Poluski (d March 21st 1888)
Young Brilliant
See next entry

The Poluskis (fl1877-1922)
Black Eel; The Bo'sun; The Tallyman; The Tipster
Originally Will Govett (c1858-1923) and Joe (surname unknown).
When Joe left the act in 1886 Will was joined by his brother Sam

SKETCH ARTISTES (continued):

(1866-1922). Later personnel included Will's sons Will jnr (1887-1929) and George (1894-1939), also Joseph Ford (d January 12th 1931). Will jnr married ROSIE WOOD; Will's and George's sister Lottie married Gus McNaughton of The McNaughtons (see *supra*). Also see previous entry.

Sir Herbert Beerbohm Tree (1853-1917)
Macbeth (Sleeping Walking Scene); *The Man Who Was; Trilby* (abridged)

Verno & Voyce
See BICYCLE ACTS

Harry Weldon (1881-1930)
Stiffy the Goalkeeper; *The White Hope*

See also entries for: CHARLES AUSTIN, BROWN, NEWLAND & LE CLERQ, FRED EMNEY, FREDDIE FRINTON, GEORGE GRAY, GRIFFITHS BROTHERS, TOMMY HANDLEY, THE HANLON-LEES, WILL HAY, JIMMY JAMES, FRED KARNO, CHARLES LAURI, JOHN LAWSON, ALFRED LESTER, LUCAN & McSHANE, THE LUPINOS, ARTHUR ROBERTS, HARRY TATE, NITA VAN BIENE, ROBB WILTON, WEE GEORGIE WOOD

SLOMAN, CHARLES (1808-70)
The Only English Improvisatore

Mr Sloman's improvisations would today fall foul of the Trade Descriptions Act; having been asked to improvise a rhyme on, say, Disraeli the 'improvisation' might take this form:

> *I take off my hat to Disraeli,*
> *For he is a good man and true;*
> *When put to the test,*
> *He's one of the best,*
> *So here's to the red, white and blue.*

It becomes apparent that all the *Improvisatore* had to do was to change the name; we have attempted this dodge ourself and can testify to its effectiveness. But as poor Sloman ended his days in the Strand Union Workhouse we don't intend to try it too often.

See BILLY BENNETT, CYRIL FLETCHER

SMITH & DALE (fl1898-1950s)
Dr Kronkheit and his Only Living Patient

Joe (Sultzer) Smith (1884-1981) and Charlie (Marks) Dale (1881-1971) were originally with a troupe called the Avon Comedy Four, apart from which our ignorance concerning this entry is profound. But the bill-matter is irresistible, *n'est-ce pas?*

SMITH, JACK (1897-1950)
The Whispering Baritone

This American singer's low-powered style, relaxed and with oodles of *portamento*, became known as crooning from the Dutch word *kreunen* meaning to groan or lament – it is no coincidence that Bing Crosby was known as The Old Groaner. Despite enormous record sales and great popularity as a nightclub performer Mr Smith retired in 1940, possibly due to being gassed in the Great War (which may also have had something to do with the confidentiality of his delivery).

SQUELCH, DAISY (fl1910s-20s)
...and her Big Brass Six

By the outbreak of War the Blackpool cornettiste (Daisy Squelch was her real name) had expanded her Six into a *Magnificent Spectacular Musical Production in Four Scenes including Britannia's Realm*. The company, which included singer and organist Al Leon, had recently returned from the United States with a black artiste; on visiting an Army camp occupied by South African soldiers the presence of a black face on stage so enraged our colonial allies that 'this poor man had to flee the stage in fear of his life as these people were going to kill him'. We were apprised of this shameful incident by Mr Leon's daughter.

See p.14

STANELLI (1895-1961)
...and his Hornchestra

Despite the finest training at both the Royal Academy of Music and the Royal College of Music Edward Stanley de Groot could not resist the Syren-call of Variety, making his début in 1914. By 1928 the comedy-musician was well enough established to take part in that year's *Royal*

Variety Performance with a partner as Stanelli & Douglas *Fiddle Fanatics*. The Hornchestra was a rack of bulb-horns from which the maestro coaxed tunes.

This entry at one time declared himself to be *He of the Smoke-Screen Voice*, bill-matter which may have been a comment on that displayed by Norman Raynor (fl1920s-30s) *He of the Voice*. Mr Stanelli was also celebrated amongst his fellow-artistes for possessing the largest organ of generation in the Profession.

Another classically trained Variety musician was Elsie Southgate (1890-1946) *The Royal Violinist* (Lady Odin Pearse) who at the age of only 15 played under Sir Henry Wood.

See DR CROCK

STANLEY, WALLY & LESTER, EDITH (fl c1940s)
The Chance of a Laugh Time

These artistes' bill-matter is identical to that displayed by Bryan Burdon (MISCELLANEOUS).

STEAD, J H (1827-86)
The Perfect Cure

This bill-matter is the title of an 1861 song for which Mr Stead, in a close-fitting striped suit and a dunce's cap, executed a lengthy sequence of bizarre stiff-legged jumps. The performer's interpretation had a colossal vogue, wearisomely so, but Mr Stead was never able to find another song of comparable impact and disappeared from public view, only to surface many years later when he wrote to a sporting periodical requesting financial assistance. Investigation showed that Jemmy Stead had a sizeable fortune tucked away; donations were returned and the deranged *Cure* died soon after.

An artiste called Davis in the 1860s was billed as *The Cure Upside Down* presumably because he delivered the song standing on his head, a mode of performance also assumed by JOE LAWRENCE.

STENNETT, STAN (b1925)
Certified Insanely Funny

Having been demobilised the tiro comedian toured with *Stars in Battledress*, a nursery for so many post-war talents. A wider audience was reached with BBC radio's *Welsh Rarebit*, a showcase for artistes from the Principality such as GLADYS MORGAN, HARRY SECOMBE, and Ossie Morris (c1915-68) *Hush – Must Have Hush.*

In 1948 Mr Stennett joined The Harmaniacs, a comedy vocal group, but a year later the artiste reverted to a solo act under the bill-matter quoted *supra* whose wording, like that of MICHAEL BENTINE, would not be acceptable in these more sensitive and considerate days (see also James E Sullivan under ANNETTE KELLERMAN).

STEPHEN, STAINLESS (1892-1971)
The Famous B.B.C. (Semi Conscious) Comedian; The Renowned Wireless Entertainer; Semi-Colon

By pointedly exposing the workings of a joke while delivering it Arthur Clifford Baynes was what might be described as an anti-comic – BERYL REID and ROBERT MORETON used similar wiles. A Yorkshire ex-schoolmaster who broadcast as early as 1924 but did not hang up his mortar-board and gown until c1937, this entry articulated his dialogue's punctuation marks, an innovation both witty and novel, if a touch cerebral for some. Also novel though not what we would call witty was the comedian's dress – dinner jacket, bow tie, stainless steel dicky and a bowler hat with a stainless steel ribbon.

STRATTON, EUGENE (1861-1918)
The Dandy-Coloured Coon; The Idol of the Halls; The Whistling Coon

The ranking black-face performer of his day first came to these shores from the States with Haverly's Mastodons, a leading minstrel troupe. Descriptions of the artiste all bear witness to the hypnotic feather-blown lightness of his soft-shoe dancing and of his artistry, for what Mr Stratton's singing lacked in tonal quality was more than made up for in subtlety and depth of interpretation.

The Dandy-Coloured Coon was the title of one of the performer's most popular songs, though forgotten today. Still heard are *Lily of Laguna*, *Little Dolly Daydream*, and *I May Be Crazy*, all by master tunesmith Leslie Stuart. Surviving recordings by Mr Stratton of his hall-mark songs sound harsh and laboured, but as has been noted singing was not this entry's strong suit.

See SIFFLEURS & SIFFLEUSES for other whistlers; for other Coons see G H ELLIOTT, especially NELLIE CHRISTIE; for other Idols see GUS HARRIS. Also see CHRIS WORTMAN.

STUART, DONALD B (b1894)
The Longest Laugh in Variety

The Australian comedy-magician served in both World Wars, ending the second show with the rank of captain, a rare Variety commission. Mr Stuart's bill-matter referred to his height of 6ft 7ins, which, the artiste proudly stated, enabled him to 'hang his hat on a nail 9ft 6ins high during act'.

SUESSE, DANA (1909-87)
The Girl Gershwin

Despite this entry's undoubted talents as pianist and composer in the symphonic jazz idiom we would not consider that George Gershwin was ever in any danger of being labelled *The Boy Suesse.*

SUMMERS, JILL (1910-97)
The Pin-Up of British Railways

After wartime service in ENSA Miss Summers returned to Variety as a 'vocal comedienne', and it was in this period that the above-quoted bill-matter appeared. Like many another Variety artiste this entry turned herself into a very serviceable actress, being especially remembered from the television serial *Coronation Street* in which for fourteen years this most warm-hearted of performers graced the rôle of Phyllis Pearce.

SUTTON, RANDOLPH (1888-1969)
Britain's Premier Light Comedian

And indeed the entertainer was the most consummately polished and stylish light comedian of our experience. With his neat figure immaculately attired in white tie and tails and with a gleaming topper on his head, Mr Sutton sang comic songs and sentimental songs with a charm that was palpable; the artiste's voice, flexible and with its soft Bristolian burr, was both caressing and compelling.

We have written elsewhere of the performer's technique of getting his audience to join in, say, *On Mother Kelly's Doorstep.* Rather than demanding 'All together, now!' he cupped a hand to his ear in gentle invitation, and so much did we wish to please the performer that we responded with a will.

SWAFFER, HANNEN (1879-1962)

The Pope of Fleet Street

This entry was not a performer but a more than usually opinionated *Daily Herald* critic and columnist whose reputation today rests upon having his face slapped by an aggrieved actress and by failing to spot that BOBBIE KIMBER was a man in drag. But then, nor did James Agate who most definitely should have twigged.

See GRACIE FIELDS

T

TANGUAY, EVA (1878-1947)

America's Idol; Cyclonic Comedienne; Electrified Hoyden; The Evangelist of Joy; The Girl who Made Vaudeville Famous; The Human Gyroscope; Miss Tabasco; Mother Eve's Merriest Daughter

Whether Miss Tanguay was actually talented seems irrelevant beside the impact of her obliterating personality. No behaviour was too outrageous and no vice too extreme for this child of nature who lived only for her own immediate gratification and to whom scandal accreted with every excess.

The artiste's dynamism, fiery temperament and utter indifference to convention made her every performance an event; anything could happen and not infrequently did. No wonder she packed 'em in.

At the age of 53, having lost her fortune in the Wall Street crash, *The Girl who Made Vaudeville Famous* went blind, but her sight was restored after an operation paid for by SOPHIE TUCKER.

TARBUCK, JIMMY (b1939)

The Lad from Liverpool

Mr Tarbuck cracks out his jokes with such charm and pace that criticism is disarmed. This entry is also the quickest-witted comedian we have ever met. Twice during *Dick Whittington* at the Bromley New (in which we gave our King Rat) Mr Tarbuck instantly improvised a rhyming couplet to cover technical mishaps – one when the Good Fairy's flying wire stranded her in the flies. This entry, though now a senior and respected member of the British show business establishment, still maintains an image of youthful cheeky insolence, and long may he do so.

TARRI, SUZETTE (1881-1955)

Radio's Queen of Comedy; Still on the Shelf; Tarri Awhile

Miss Tarri was unquestionably popular both on the Halls and on the wireless, her large features and horsey teeth aiding the visual aspect of her comedy and her strident Cockney accent materially assisting the aural. It has to be said that the tenor of her material occasionally shaded into the improper, not entirely redeemed by the artiste's insistence on invariably closing her act by singing *Red Sails in the Sunset.*

For other Queens of Comedy see HYLDA BAKER. Also see QUEEN OF...

TATE, HARRY (& CO) (1872-1940)
Motoring

Ronald MacDonald Hutchison (not Hutchinson) took his stage name from the sugar dealers Henry Tate & Sons for whom he worked until taking the professional plunge at the age of 23. At that time the artiste was billed as *The New Mimic*, graduating to *Premier Mimic* and finally ascending the throne as *The King of Mimics.*

After the success of *Motoring* Mr Tate concentrated on sporting sketches such as *Billiards, Fishing, Flying, Gardening,* and *Golfing,* but whatever the subject the comedian always wore a huge, seemingly prehensile moustache. Harry Tate died at the age of 67 from injuries sustained during a German air raid on, of all places, Dundee. He was godfather to HUGHIE GREEN.

See GEORGE CLARKE, KING OF..., SANDY POWELL, SKETCH ARTISTES, also list of MIMICS in glossary.

TENNYSON & O'GORMAN (fl1881-1901)
Patter Propagators; The Two Irish Gentlemen

This pioneering cross-talk act was originally *k.a.* O'Gorman & Devine – Joe Tennyson (1858-1926) felt that to use his real name would be seen as disrespectful to the Poet Laureate. How wonderful to have lived in a society in which respect for a poet, or indeed for anyone, still mattered.

Joe O'Gorman (1863-1937) was father of DAVE & JOE O'GORMAN and member No 1 of the Variety Artistes' Federation; his second wife was The Beautiful Jessica (see QUEEN OF...).

TERMINI, JOE (1891-1964)
The Somnolent Melodist

Such uninviting bill-matter belied an extremely clever comedian who – a rarity amongst American artistes – wrought his humour in mime.

THOMPSON, BOBBY (1911-88)
The Little Waster

Regional bill-matter is sometimes unclear to outsiders; *The Little Waster* is a fond Geordie epithet meaning The Little Scallywag or Scapegrace.

Mr Thompson never strayed far from his home ground and in consequence, except to aficionados of comedy, is little known outside the North East. We have seen the comedian on film, performing in a club where the depth of affectionate, proprietorial delight aroused by the artiste is almost tangible. In a close-knit corner of England, proud of its heritage and its accent, Mr Thompson, like all the best dialect comics, articulated the everyday pinpricks of local life and made his auditors see themselves as in a distorting mirror – recognisable but comically awry.

THOMPSON, LYDIA (1836-1908)
...and her British Blondes

The mewling infant of American burlesque rapidly achieved adulthood with the arrival in 1868 of Miss Thompson and her dancers, buxom and strapping examples of English womanhood all. The troupe opened at Woods' Museum and Menagerie in New York to such acclaim that the artistes were able to deploy their charms throughout the United States for the next twenty years.

Whether the ladies' popularity was due to their artistry or to the unprecedentedly generous display of lower limb and other bodily parts is a matter upon which we will not adjudicate, but when the dramatic critic of the *Chicago Times* had the temerity to impugn the honour of Miss Thompson and one of her Blondes, Pauline Markham, both ladies horse-whipped the saucy scribe in the street.

Miss Markham did later fall from grace, we are sorry to report, by becoming the mistress of a Southern Governor, an indiscretion which did business no harm at all.

See Deveen (MAGICIANS) for copy-cat bill-matter.

THURSTON, HOWARD (1869-1936)
King of Cards; The Man who Mystified Herrmann

The Herrmann in this instance was not The Great (Alexander) Herrmann (1843-96), the most celebrated American magician of his day, but his nephew Leon (1867-1909), who was also a conjuror. So is

Mr Thurston guilty of deception? Let us rather regard it as what his fellow practitioners of the black arts would call mis-direction. What mystified Leon Herrmann was, it seems, a rising card trick or 'effect', the more dignified preferred term. Mr Thurston's secrets were handed down to his illusion-builder and protégé, DANTE.

Other *Kings of Cards* were CARL HERTZ and HOUDINI.

See KING OF...

TICH, LITTLE (1867-1928)
The Incomparable; The Little Lump of Fun;
The Napoleon of the Army of Fun; One Tich of Nature
makes the Whole World Grin

Harry Relph may have been short in stature but his standing as a headliner in Britain and America and on the Continent was immense. This astonishing artiste was neither a midget nor was he a dwarf – he just stopped growing at 4ft 6ins. Perhaps his father's age of 77 when Harry was born had something to do with it. When we met Tich's daughter Mary in 1990 and were shown the Relph family tree we suddenly realised we were in the presence of someone whose grandfather had been born in 1790!

The story of Harry Relph's childhood would melt a heart of stone; especially upsetting is when the 12-year-old, cast out to fend for himself, was sitting on a bench in a railway station and writing to his mother. He was alone, penniless, homeless, and as well as his freakish lack of inches had six partially webbed fingers on each hand. As he wrote the tears rolled down his cheeks into a bag of boiled sweets he had bought with his last penny, congealing the contents into one inedible lump.

What we have always wondered about this extraordinary performer is how he learnt to dance so superbly (Nijinsky called him 'a dancer of genius'), how he learned to play so many instruments, and, even stranger, how he learned to score his own band-parts.

Despite Mr Relph's shortness and malformed hands he was never short of female company, marrying three times and running a bewilderingly complex love life. One lady who had the misfortune to fall in love with him was the musical comedy star JOSÉ COLLINS. A well-built woman of formidable temperament, Miss Collins was so incensed when Tich, a married man, told her that her passion must remain unrequited she knocked him down.

Another *Incomparable* was CINQUEVALLI, also see SAMMY CURTIS and Scotch Kelly (JIMMY CLITHEROE); for other small persons JIMMY CLITHEROE; for the derivation of 'Little Tich' see ARTHUR ORTON, also next entry; for female impersonation see BARBETTE.

TICHBORNE, YOUNG (1867-1928)

The Claimant's Bootlace; Little Black Storm; The Picco Soloist; The Pocket Mackney

Sometime in the early 1880s this entry abbreviated his stage name to LITTLE TICH; *The Claimant* was ARTHUR ORTON.

See G H ELLIOTT, E W MACKNEY

TILLER GIRLS, THE

The Mystic Hussars; The Quaint Little Village of Honeysuckle Hollow

John Thomas Tiller (1854-1925) assembled his first troupe, four juveniles called Les Jolies Petites, in Manchester in 1890. Within twenty years Mr Tiller's chorus lines were renowned the civilised world over for pulchritude, hard work, and artistic excellence. That the impresario couldn't dance a step didn't stop him choreographing their *enchainments*, devising the sketches, writing the music, and designing the scenery and costumes. In recompense, one might say, for all this work and responsibility it was not unknown for the occasional Girl to offer Mr Tiller the supreme sacrifice, but there was never any scandal.

In June 1932 posters for the London Palladium stated that 'J. Sherman Fisher presents his Sixteen Girls *who Have Never Missed Their Last Train*', a clear reference to a saucy MARIE LLOYD song.

TILLEY, JOHN (1898-1935)

Mutterer

As a young man the writer and comedian Eric Barker (1912-90) worked with this entry at the WINDMILL. Mr Barker said that he 'never cared for vaudeville' finding the *genre* vulgar and its participants uncongenial. But he much admired Mr Tilley's subtlety and his meticulously considered characters such as a lecturer, an explorer or a scoutmaster. He even went so far, in his autobiography, as to describe John Tilley as 'a great comedian'.

TILLEY, VESTA (1864-1952)
The London Idol

As a child Matilda Alice Powles, daughter of HARRY BALL, was billed as The Great Little Tilley *The Pocket Vesta* after the new wax-stemmed matches, themselves named after the Roman goddess of hearth and household; later bill-matter for the youthful performer was *The Pocket Sims Reeves* (see HENRY COLLARD and PERCY HENRY for similar).

Vesta Tilley was universally acknowledged as the greatest male impersonator of them all. Of her Sir James Fergusson wrote 'within its self-imposed limits, her art was faultless'. It was *Punch* who first named this entry *The London Idol* in 1890, though in the United States the critic Alan Hale dubbed Miss Tilley *The Irving of the Halls* (which may have been as much a dig at the eminent actor Henry Irving as praise for the popular singer).

Miss Tilley retired at the peak of her popularity at the age of only 56; recordings show that her voice was shot. Her farewell at the Coliseum was a celebratedly lachrymose occasion, presided over by the great and gracious Ellen Terry herself. Immensely proper and coldly charitable, Miss Tilley married Walter de Frece, a Variety manager who by 1920 had become Colonel Sir Walter de Frece MP and so grand that he was known in the Profession as Sir Altered de Frece.

See p.14, ST GEORGE HUSSEY; also FRED BARNES, JENNY HILL. For other Idols see GUS HARRIS.

TIM, TINY (1922-96)
The Human Canary

Herbert Kaury was surely the most talentless phenomenon ever to disgrace the Royal Albert Hall. In his late forties, beak-nosed, awkward, grinning inanely, the American visitor appeared carrying, if memory serves, a Sainsbury's plastic bag from which he took a ukulele to accompany himself in popular songs, all of which, like his sole hit *Tip Toe through the Tulips*, were delivered in a quavering falsetto voice. One might have been forgiven for thinking the entire excruciating performance to be a hoax, but it would appear that the performer was sincere, if two quavers short of a semibreve.

TINSLEY, TOM (1853-1910)
The Young John Bull

Mr Tinsley abandoned the boards to become a prominent chairman and manager for the Gatti Brothers, Swiss caterers who amongst other enterprises ran Music Halls under Charing Cross station (Gatti's-under-the-Arches) and in Westminster Bridge Road (Gatti's-in-the-Road).

A drawing by Joseph Pennell shows Mr Tinsley at the chairman's table in the former, but it was at the latter venue that this functionary earned his footnote in Music Hall history by giving HARRY LAUDER that all-important first London booking.

See JOE COLVERD, VICTORIA MONKS, Verno & Voyce (BICYCLE ACTS)

TORR, SAM (1846-99)
To Be There

Mr Torr's bill-matter is the title of the song with which the Minor Lion made his reputation and whose lyrics burlesqued that estimable body The Salvation Army, then newly formed (1878). Sensitivity was never this entry's forte for he was also responsible for organising the syndicate which in 1884 first put JOSEPH MERRICK *The Elephant Man* on public display.

Another of Mr Torr's repertoire was *On the back of Daddy-O!* in which an ingeniously devised costume gave the impression that the artiste was being carried piggyback by his elderly father. In 1904 Mr Torr retired from the Halls, having injured himself by falling off stage whilst performing this item legless.

TRACY, ARTHUR (1899/1903-1977)
The Street Singer

The birth-year of this Ukrainian-born American 'bari-tenor', as he described himself, is variously given and we declare no preference. In his early days on CBS radio *The Street Singer* was anonymous, a publicity ploy later copied on the BBC by Cavan O'Connor (1899-

1996) *The Vagabond Lover*. Two British *Street Singers* were Pat O'Brian (fl1930s-40s) and May Dalziel (see JACK SHORT).

Mr Tracy's sentimental ballads – *It's My Mother's Birthday Today, In a Little Gypsy Tea Room, Trees,* and especially his signature tune *Marta (ha-Rambling Rose of the Wild ha-Wood)* – were enjoyed by innumerable admirers including notably the artiste himself, for according to the distinguished British screen actress Margaret Lockwood this entry 'would sit for hours in his dressing-room listening to his own recordings with tears in his eyes'.

See p.11

TRAVERS, HYRAM (1850-1922)
The Original 'Rorty Tom'; The Pearly King

Mr Travers was a 'quaint little' master of both Cockney rhyming and back slang. *Rorty Tom* (rorty meaning dashing or lively) was the title of a song introduced not by this entry at all but by Harry Rickards (1841-1911), a fellow performer from whom Mr Travers had purchased the rights.

The Cockney custom of decorating clothes with pearl buttons dates from the 1880s; it is possible that Mr Travers was the first to give Music Hall expression to this novel aspect of London life. Or was that Mr Rickards again?

See WALTER LABURNUM

TRAVIS, Lieut FRANK (1854-1931)
The Society Ventriloquist

With the hidden aid of an intricate assortment of levers, pedals and pneumatic pipes Lieut Travis could work as many as thirteen dummies, the prestige of a ventriloquist being at that time in direct ratio to the number of figures on display.

The artiste's wife was Madeleine Rosa (d September 19th 1907) *The World's First Lady Ventriloquist*. After retiring in 1905 Lieut Travis took on a protégée: Bessie Astor *The Only Girl Ventriloquist*. That these two ladies' bill-matter conflicts is very apparent; we like to think that Miss Astor's mentor refrained from any serious tutelage until after his wife's lamented expiry.

See ARTHUR PRINCE, FRED RUSSELL, VENTRILOQUISTS

TRENET, CHARLES (b1913)

Le Fou Chantant

This byname we have seen translated as *The Singing Madman*, though we would not agree that this quite catches M. Trenet's especial flavour. The *chanteur* has written over 600 songs including *Boum* and *La Mer*, the latter being used at one time by Japanese radio as its signature tune. Such are the ramifications of fame and talent.

TREWEY, FELICIEN (1848-1920)

Twenty-Five Heads under One Hat

Of this entry it was written 'Trewey was a mimic, juggler, facialist, card manipulator, musician, shadowgraphist, dancer, painter, and chapeaugrapher. He performed a type of balancing that led to the coinage of a new word, "Trewyism".' Unfortunately the neologism did not survive and its meaning is lost.

What has survived is *chapeaugraphy*, for we witnessed within the last twelvemonth a young man who performed the life of Napoleon, battles and all, with the aid only of a ring of felt. He was fairly entertaining.

See THEO BAMBERG, JUGGLERS, GEORGE F MOORE

TRINDER, TOMMY (1909-89)

Loads of Nonsense; You Lucky People!

A lanky, lantern-jawed, fast-talking comedian who originally reversed his surname as Red Nirt *Eccentric Dancing and Comicalities*. Mr Trinder's later jokes were better, and the artiste most assuredly possessed that forceful personableness which is the mark of all the best stand-up comedians.

On one occasion in the late 1960s, having introduced this entry to the audience, we heard him deliver the following joke: 'The wife was moaning on about her work never being done. She was ironing at the time so I said, "Well, you needn't iron that bra for a start – you've got nothing to put in it." She said, "I iron your underpants, don't I...?"'

Over thirty years later a late-night 'alternative' television show featured a sketch in which a wife at the ironing board was complaining about her chores. When her husband in the armchair began to say

'Well, you needn't iron that bra for a start...' and the young right-on audience screeched with mirth we suddenly felt very old.

See WILKIE BARD, CASEY'S COURT, TOMMY HANDLEY

TRIPP, JACK (b1922)

Plymouth's Fred Astaire

There was only one Fred Astaire and we venture to suggest that there is only one Jack Tripp. The screen immortal, had he ever seen Mr Tripp on stage, would have had no cause to complain that his name was in any way being demeaned. This entry started his notable career in concert party with the famous *Fol de Rols*; in wartime Mr Tripp was one of the *Stars in Battledress*, and after the cessation of hostilites he understudied SID FIELD.

We have only ever seen this consummate artiste as Dame in pantomime, in which rôle the comedian has for some years surely been unsurpassed for style, coy charm, and, as his bill-matter suggests, twinkling toes.

TUCKER, SOPHIE (1884-1966)

The Last of the Red-Hot Mommas; The Mary Garden of Syncopation; The Queen of Jazz

Miss Tucker began her vaudeville career in black-face as *The World Renowned Coon Shouter*, an aberration which was short-lived. In her slim youth Miss Tucker was not exactly beautiful but the artiste had a compelling way with a song, and her claim to have originated jazz singing on stage is not without justification.

Known for her exuberant fruitiness as much as her plangent tones, this entry when in London fell foul of the prissy Sir Oswald Stoll who objected to the tone of some of her material. 'You shouldn't be running a Music Hall,' expostulated the singer, 'you should be a bishop!'

Mary Garden (1874-1967) was a vivid operatic soprano who though born in Scotland spent most of her career in the USA. Another *Queen of Jazz* was Janice Hart (fl1920s-40s) who was also billed as *The Golden Brown Personality*.

See G H ELLIOTT, QUEEN OF..., Francis Renault (BARBETTE), EVA TANGUAY

TURNER, JOAN (b1922)

The Girl with a Thousand Voices; The Wacky Warbler

We always felt that this bubbly, effervescent performer never was quite able to focus her talents; Miss Turner boasted an excellent lyric soprano, her comedy was strong, and her impressions good. But somehow this entry always disappointed us, letting herself down with poor material and too much reliance on the same well-tried repertoire of funny faces and funny voices.

See PAUL J BARNES; also list of MIMICS in glossary.

TURNER, CLARENCE 'Tubby' (1882-1952)

Hif Hit's Ho Kay with You Hit's Ho Kay with Me

Mr Turner was famous for his deck-chair routine, in which the artiste attempts to put it up. After falling over it, through it and under it and getting in the most awful tangle the performer throws the intractable object away in disgust, whereupon it lands perfectly opened out. We have seen this feat performed by that great Scotch comic and actor Rikki Fulton; also, in simplified form on the silver screen, by NORMAN WISDOM.

U

UNSWORTH, JAMES (1821-75)
Stump Orator

Prior to developing his burlesque public speaking (a line of business which he is said to have originated and whose last practitioner was BILLY RUSSELL) this entry was billed as *Female Impersonator and Negro Comedian.*

Mr Unsworth's discourses were enlivened by topical allusions – here, for instance, are the orator's *bien pensées* on Charles Darwin's theories of evolution: '...and yet they tell us man is more like a monkey every day. Now what is a monkey? Is it a fish? No. Is it a fowl? No. Is it a good red herring? It is not. A monkey is an inhabitant of woods and forests. Have we not seen some splendid specimens of this kind of ape? (*whacks table with umbrella.*) Am I right, or any other man?'

For other female impersonators see BARBETTE; for black-face acts see G H ELLIOTT.

UNTHAN, CARL HERMANN (1848-1929)
The Pedal Paganini

Herr Unthan was an armless artiste who played the violin with his feet, hence the otherwise puzzling bill-matter; the Prussian also mastered the piano and cornet. In the Great War this entry visited hospitals to give advice and succour to amputees, and the musician's autobiography shows him to have been a shrewd and resourceful man for whom very little was not possible.

Others who successfully exploited the same grave disadvantage were Elroy (b1889) who called himself *The Armless Wonder* as did Charles Tripp (1855-1939) a generation earlier, Tommy Jacobsen (b1921) *The Armless Pianist*, and The Lutz Brothers who formed the only double armless act we have knowledge of. Elroy we once saw perform: he drew lightning cartoons and demonstrated sharp-shooting with his feet, a quite remarkably dextrous display.

For other *soi-disant* Paganinis see MACKENZIE MURDOCK; for legless artistes see PEG-LEG BATES.

UTTERIDGE, WILLIAM (c1875-1948)
The Act Beautiful

That the act was indeed ravishing we do not doubt, but what was it?

V

VALENTINE (d March 7th 1907)
The Boneless Wonder

It is possible that this particular *Boneless Wonder* is the one recalled by no less eminent a personage than (Sir) Winston Churchill who, in the House of Commons on January 28th 1931, witheringly attacked Ramsay Macdonald, then Prime Minister, in a speech whose peroration ran as follows: 'I remember, when I was a child, being taken to the celebrated Barnum's Circus, which contained an exhibition of freaks and monstrosities, but the exhibit...which I most desired to see was the one described as "The Boneless Wonder". My parents judged that that spectacle would be too revolting and demoralising for my youthful eyes, and I have waited 50 years to see the boneless wonder sitting on the Treasury Bench.'

This Valentine should not be confused with Cardini (see MAGICIANS).

Other human invertebrates were The Padley Brothers (fl1880s-1920s) *Boneless Wonders*, Frankey (fl c1850) *The Boneless Youth*, H B Marinelli (1864-1924) *The Boneless Wonder*, HECTOR NAPIER, and Sells & Young (Emilie S Sells b1867 and her husband Fritz Young) *The Boneless Lady/The Human Corkscrew/The Snake Woman.*

Other contortionists were THE BENEDETTI BROTHERS, DAN LENO and Minnie Spray (fl c1900) *The Human Enigma, The World's Wonder, Contortionist, Bender, High Kicker and Legmania Artiste.*

See P T BARNUM

VAN ALBERT, JAN (b1897)
The Tallest Man in the World

Claiming a greatly exaggerated height of 9ft 3½ins this entry regularly toured with a midget called Seppetoni, whose sister Minna – also a midget – he married. Don't ask.

For other tall persons see Captain GEORGE AUGER.

VAN AMBURGH, ISAAC A (1800-65)
Brute Tamer from Pompeii

The internationally renowned circus artiste was, despite his overwrought bill-matter, from Peekshill, New York; his uncanny power over wild animals fascinated Queen Victoria who saw his performance no fewer than seven times. Mr Amburgh was a very strong man, but we suspect that his lions and tigers and leopards and panthers were impressed not so much by his muscularity as by his pronounced squint.

See ANIMAL & BIRD ACTS

VAN BIENE, NITA (fl1920s)
The Girl with the Cello

Miss Van Biene's cellist father Auguste Van Biene (1850-1913) for many years presented on the Halls a sentimental sketch at the end of which the old musician died, his beloved instrument clutched in his hand. The conclusion of one performance was more than usually convincing, for Mr Van Biene had given his all for his art by passing on in public.

See RONNÉ CONN, SKETCH ARTISTES

VAN DYK, KATYA (b c1905)
The Tallest Woman in the World

Originally this altitudinous artiste toured with her sister Charlotte (who stood 5½ins shorter at 7ft 11ins) as The Van Droysen Sisters; their bill-matter was *The Two Biggest Women in the World* which was probably true.

See Captain GEORGE AUGER

VANCE, ALFRED (1839-88)
The Versatile! The Inimitable!

The Great Vance made his name c1870 with *The Chickaleary Cove*, a Cockney song whose lyrics defy exegesis. Although Mr Vance guyed the swaggering swells of the Row and the Strand this *Lion Comique* was also noted for the finesse of his characterisations.

In a dramatic monologue at the Sun Music Hall, Knightsbridge, on Boxing Day 1888, counsel was waiting tensely for the jury's verdict. 'Not guilty!' said the foreman whereupon, to thunderous applause, the victorious barrister sank to the floor in a swoon. The Great Vance was dead.

Jessie Stanley's bill-matter *The Original Female Vance* implies that there were others, but if so they have eluded our researches.

See GEORGE LEYBOURNE

VARNEY, REG (b1916)

As a teenager Mr Varney's bill-matter was *Music and Madness*, for despite a total lack of musical training this entry played accordion and novelty piano, the novelty being that he played it blindfolded. In the 1990s satellite repeats of his television series *On the Buses* brought the artiste a new and appreciative audience and an unexpected but welcome enhancement of his bank account.

We once read in a newspaper that only in Britain in the 1960s could an artiste like Reg Varney have become a star. Discuss.

See BENNY HILL

VARNEY & BUTT (fl1920S-40s)

'Absurdities' by Bert Lee; 'Silly Sagacities' by Bert Lee & R P Weston

Rarely were writers of comedy material afforded recognition in bill-matter, but such was the reputation of Bert Lee (1880-1947) and his long-time collaborator R P Weston (1878-1936) that Messrs Varney and Butt obviously felt their names would enhance the act's distinction.

VAUGHAN, NORMAN (b1923)

Aspirin to Fame; The Furtive Funster

When we first worked with *The Furtive Funster*, at the Bristol Hippodrome, he was tormented by personal crises which were serious enough to require therapy. We next encountered the comedian at the Devonshire Park Theatre, Eastbourne, by which time his daemons had been exorcised and the problems resolved.

Mr Vaughan was an attractive and lively but twitchy performer who did not sustain his initial rise to fame. But this entry made – and kept – a great deal of money which is why he now lives in Portugal playing golf.

See p.15, WINDMILL THEATRE

VENTRILOQUISTS:

Adkin (fl1910s)
The Motoring Ventriloquist
Appeared in a real motor-car accompanied by his doll Sammy.

VENTRILOQUISTS (continued):

Lieut Albini
See ARTHUR PRINCE

Harry Benet (fl1950s-60s)
The Ventertainer
Possibly related to Harry Benet (1877-1948), agent and producer.

Russ Carr (1889-1973)
The Military Ventriloquist
Son of FRED RUSSELL

Johnson Clark (1886-1956)
The Sportsman Ventriloquist; a.k.a. Vernando
Also worked a scena entitled *Hodge at the Cross Roads.*

W H Clemart (1865-1915)
On the Benches; On the Sands
Founder member and Chairman of the Variety Artistes'
Federation.

Lieut Cole
See ARTHUR PRINCE

John W Cooper (fl late 19th cent)
The Black Napoleon of Ventriloquism;
The Polite Ventriloquist

The Great Coram (1883-1937)
In Ventriloquial Scena; The Military Ventriloquist
With 'Jerry' first ventriloquist to perform on radio. Father of
Billy Whitaker (see MISCELLANEOUS).

Sidney Dolman (fl c1880)
The Talking Hand

Tom Edwards (1879-1933)
The Huntsman Ventriloquist; The Modern Valentine Vox
See VALENTINE VOX

VENTRILOQUISTS (continued):

Gillin (1868-1942)
The Vent with Laughter Intent

Terry Hall
*The English Ventriloquist with Micky Flynn the Irish
    Dummy; ...with Lenny the Lion*

John Howard (b1910)
The Debonair One

G W Jester (fl1860s-70s)
The Man with the Talking Hand

Basil King (fl1920s)
The Police Inspector Ventriloquist

Nelson Lloyd (fl1940s-50s)
Watch his Lips
See Fred Lovelle *infra*

Fred Lovelle (fl1940s-50s)
Me and My Shadow; Watch his Lips
See Nelson Lloyd *supra*

Jenny McAndrew (fl1930s)
The Schoolgirl Ventriloquist

Clement Minns (b1893)
*The Magical Ventriloquist;
The World's Youngest Ventriloquist*
See MAGICIANS

Fred Neiman (1860-1910)
*...with his (Original) Ventriloquial Minstrels;
The Youngest Ventriloquist in the World*

VENTRILOQUISTS (continued):

Charles Prelle (fl c1910)
...with his Ventriloquial Dogs
See ANIMAL & BIRD ACTS

Madeleine Rosa
See Lieut TRAVIS

Canfield Smith (b1906)
...with the almost human Snodgrass

Rich Taylor (d November 14th 1956)
The Only Whistling Ventriloquist
See SIFFLEURS & SIFFLEUSES

Vento (1832-99)
The Squire of Haslemere

Edward Victor (1884-1964)
Hand-Made Humour

Señor Wences (1896-1999)
The World's Finest Ventriloquial Entertainer

Sydney Wilson (b1903)
The Singing Ventriloquist

Arthur Worsley (b1920)
It's In The Bag; The World's Youngest Ventriloquist
See THE THREE LOOSE SCREWS

See also entries for: PETER BROUGH & ARCHIE ANDREWS, LYDIA DREAMS, BOBBIE KIMBER, SANDY POWELL, ARTHUR PRINCE, FRED RUSSELL, SAVEEN, Lieut TRAVIS, VALENTINE VOX, HARRY WORTH

VICTORIA, VESTA (1873-1951)

Queen of Domestic Comedy; A Vesta that will Strike Anywhere

Miss Victoria's father was the Upside-Down comic singer JOE LAWRENCE, so it is not surprising that his daughter started on the Halls as Baby Victoria, progressed to Little Victoria and finally emerged as Vesta Victoria *The Nan of the Music Halls* after her first successful song *Good-for-Nothing Nan* (from a character in J B Buckstone's play *Good for Nothing*).

The artiste, plump, toothy and energetic (*cf* MARIE LLOYD), was as popular in the United States – where she toured regularly for over thirty years – as in her native Britain, and is particularly remembered for such songs of misfortune as *Waiting At The Church, Poor John, Now I Have To Call Him Father* and, greatest of all, *Daddy Wouldn't Buy Me A Bow-Wow*.

In 1906 an aristocrat offered Miss Victoria £25,000 to give up her career and marry him: the lady refused. Perhaps she should have taken the money and the title, for her subsequent matrimonial misadventures left her with neither.

For other Queens of Comedy see HYLDA BAKER. Also see JOE LAWRENCE and QUEEN OF... For derivation of the name Vesta see VESTA TILLEY.

VOLANTS, THE FIVE (fl1947-60s)
Whirlwind Tumblers

The Volants – the number varied – were founded by the wonderful Johnny Hutch (b1913), a small, wiry acrobat who was still actively performing until well into his seventies and is now much in demand by film and theatrical companies as a tumbling consultant.

It was in *Aladdin* at the London Palladium that we first encountered the Johnny Hutch and the Half-Wits, a fast and furious spring-board/vaulting-horse act which never failed to have the house in shrieking paroxysms and in which the veteran acrobat appeared as a little old lady.

Three of the Half-Wits were young French lads; to hear their *patron* address them in Geordie-accented circus French was a joy.

VOX, VALENTINE
The Wizard of the West

This entry's stage name derives from Henry Cockton's 1840 novel *The Life and Adventures of Valentine Vox, the Ventriloquist.* 'Vox' is, as every schoolboy used to know, the Latin for voice, and we have discovered three other Valentine Voxes (Voces?): one who in 1864 published *The Cabinet of Irish and Yankee Wit and Humour* (1864), another who was an

American ventriloquist and died in 1943 at the age of 49, and the third who in 1981 wrote *I Can See Your Lips Moving: The History and Art of Ventriloquism.*

Another *Wizard of the West* was 'Lord' GEORGE SANGER while GEORGE BARNARDO EAGLE claimed to be *The Wizard of the South* and JOHN HENRY ANDERSON to be *Wizard of the North.* Nobody, it would appear, wished to be *Wizard of the East.*

See MAGICIANS, VENTRILOQUISTS (especially Tom Edwards)

W

WALL, MAX (1908-90)

The Boy with the Educated/Obedient Feet; Irresponsible; Laughing Legs

Maxwell George Lorimer, a Brixton boy, was the son of Jack Lorimer (1883-1920) *The Hielan' Laddie* and godson of MARIE LLOYD. A fine eccentric dancer, singer, guitarist, pianist and comic, Mr Wall wrecked his career in the mid-1950s by leaving his wife and their five children. After a second failed marriage the multi-talented performer's eventual rehabilitation was boosted by the theatrical intelligentsia who acclaimed his grotesque concert pianist Professor Wallofski as one of Music Hall's greatest creations – 'I've become a cult,' he'd leer.

Mr Wall's resonant speaking voice and cadaverous face also aided a late flowering as a dramatic actor, again reducing the critical establishment prostrate with wonderment. But despite leaving £193,004 the old comedian died lonely and embittered.

See WILKIE BARD

WALLACE, NELLIE (1870-1948)

The Essence of Eccentricity; Queen of Comedy; The Quintessence of Quaintness; She Makes the House Rock with Laughter

Miss Wallace was one of the very few female grotesques to find favour on the Halls. We are of the opinion that though the GBP had no objection to female comics it has never cared for women who put their femininity at risk. This entry was so lovable that despite her skinny frame, jumble-sale attire, snackle-teeth and large beak of a nose Britain – and America – found her irresistibly funny. Most of the performer's material treated of her regrettable lack of male companionship, and because we knew Miss Wallace was in private life a happily married woman (and a mother) we felt free to laugh all the more.

For other Queens of Comedy see HYLDA BAKER. Also see GEORGE BEAUCHAMP, GRACIE FIELDS, QUEEN OF..., ELLA RETFORD.

WALLETT, WILLIAM FREDERICK (1807?/1813?-92)
The Queen's Jester; Shakespearean Jester

A well set-up and handsome man who wore traditional jester's dress but with the addition of a large mid-19th-century moustache, this entry made an unique reputation as a declaimer from all the best poets, including the Bard of Avon, not in the theatre or on the Halls but *in the circus ring!* In this unpromising arena Mr Wallett also gave popular representations of classical statuary and sang comic songs. Not, we presume, at the same time.

Another *Shakespearian Jester* was H B Williams (fl c1875).

WALTER, J H (fl1880s-90s)
The Celebrated Serpent Man

Beset by gambling debts this contortionist sold his skeleton (in advance) to a surgeon for one thousand guineas, having forever after to tour a coffin containing embalming instructions and the medico's address.

WARE, GEORGE W (1829-95)
The Great Wonder of the Day

In *The Era* of September 27th 1863 Mr Ware 'again cautions a great many singers who are singing his unpublished songs, written by him for himself and his wife, and which have been clandestinely stolen from them'. Generally speaking the performer-tunesmith's lyrics were better than his prose and he took to advertising himself as *The Old Reliable*, able to provide a 'guaranteed' song success for any artiste on any subject.

After retiring from the boards this entry combined songwriting with running an artistes' agency, his clients including MARIE LLOYD and NELLIE POWER. It was for Miss Power's funeral costs that he was dunned, unsuccessfully of course.

WARNER, JACK (1896-1981)
Blue Pencil

Mr Warner made his name in the BBC war-time radio variety show *Garrison Theatre*, and it was on a poster for a stage version at the London

Palladium that we spotted this bill-matter. It referred to censored or blue-pencilled letters which the actor-comedian would read out from his imaginary soldier-brother Sid. In that show Mr Warner also introduced the catch-phrase 'Mind my Bike', though we have no cognisance of its use as bill-matter.

A generation later the performer was to become part of the British way of life with his portrayal of the stolid, dependable copper on the beat in the long-running television series *Dixon of Dock Green*. Each episode began at the door of the police-station with Mr Warner as PC Dixon saluting and saying 'Evening, all' direct to camera. Visiting Tokyo in 1967 we were bemused to see Constable Dixon appear on the television set in our hotel room. He raised his hand, saluted, and opened his mouth. But instead of the comforting tones of Britain's favourite policeman we heard the eerie wail of a Japanese dubber.

This entry's sisters were ELSIE & DORIS WATERS.

WATERS, ELSIE & DORIS (fl1923-70s)
Gert & Daisy

Elsie Waters (c1895-1990) and her sister Doris (c1904-78) owed their careers to chance, for their hugely popular double act in which the artistes chatted inconsequentially about 'Gert's' fiancé Wally, 'Daisy's' husband Bert and the small change of working-class Cockney life originated as a last minute fill-in for a record. The casual, realistic style of the sisters' delivery was particularly suited to radio and they became greatly beloved of the nation, evoking an affection which never waned and whose morale-boosting importance during World War II was recognised in 1946 by their appointment as OBE.

The Misses Waters never married, and two attempts in the 1980s to mount stage versions of their career foundered due to the surviving Elsie's refusal to permit any mention of their brother, JACK WARNER, or of the sisters' alleged long-standing sharing of the same gentleman's favours.

See BILLIE HOUSTON, REVNELL & WEST. Also see JACK WARNER.

WELTON, MAX (fl1930s)
'Brays' are Bonny

This entry and his bill-matter travesty the opening of the beautiful folk-song *Annie Laurie*: 'Maxwellton braes are bonnie...' If Mr Welton was a Scot he should have been ashamed of himself.

WERTH, THE MYSTERIOUS (fl late 19th cent.)

Banana Skin and Stone Manipulator

Even our most vivid of imaginations has been unable to envisage an act which combines banana skins and stones. In the middle of the 17th-century Signor Francis Battalia announced himself as a *Stone Eater* or *Lithophagus*, bill-matter which, while lapidarily indigestible, is at least intelligible.

See SIDNEY BARNES, HARRY NORTON

WHEELER, JIMMY (1910-73)

Ay! Ay! That's Yer Lot!

Ernest Remnant's bill-matter was the catch-phrase with which he invariably ended his act. Having dabbled in ballroom dancing, film acting and band-leading, this entry joined his father on the Halls in 1929 as Wheeler & Wilson *The Sailor & The Porter*. After war service in the RAF Mr Wheeler rejoined his father, finally going solo in 1949.

We have always said, and we say it again here, that next to MAX MILLER Jimmy Wheeler was the funniest thing on two legs. Like TED RAY he played the fiddle and told jokes, but Mr Wheeler was much riper and ruder. Not long before he died we saw this entry at the Greenwich Theatre; he had not worked for two years due to illness and so was perhaps a little rusty. A reference to an ancient political scandal got the bird, but by the end of his forty-five-minute turn the house rose and cheered, and rightly so.

See WILKIE BARD

WHELAN, ALBERT (1875-1961)

Australian Entertainer

Failing to strike it rich in the Coolgardie goldfields of Western Australia Albert Waxman kept body and soul together by entertaining the prospectors, a class of person tending to the uncouth. A West End audience must have been a push-over, though Mr Whelan's first booking at the Coliseum would have tried the patience of a saint. With an over-booked programme (Sir) Oswald Stoll allowed him a mere eight minutes, only giving the performer time to saunter on whistling *Die lustige Brüde*, slowly remove his top hat, coat, scarf and gloves, replace them and saunter off. But such was the Antipodean's style and elegance that audiences were intrigued and after a month the dictatorial manager relented, allotting his *Australian Entertainer* a full eighteen minutes.

The entrance and exit never varied, and when we saw this entry half a century later, the year after he had lost a leg, *The Jolly Brothers* still brought him on and took him off – in fact, Mr Whelan is said to have originated the whole concept of the 'signature tune'.

See BILLY BENNETT

WHITE, STAN (& ANN) (fl1940s-50s)
Apart from the Obvious

Apt use of an unhackneyed phrase as bill-matter meets with our hearty approval, and we wish we knew more of the team which we have also seen billed as Stan 'Poker Face' White & Ann *Musical Madness*.

See DR CROCK

WHITELEYS, THE FIVE (fl1899-? and 1924-36)
Eastern Antics –The Super Acro-Risley Musical Pot-Pourri

This multi-faceted family proliferated to a bewildering degree, with divers combinations of relations and in-laws performing under divers titles, e.g. Henri Alexander (1872-1951) *Antipodean Marvel*, Leonora Whiteley (b1909) *The Musicality Girl*, brothers Ben (b1901) and Harold (b1903) who with the former's son Derek (b1920) worked from 1936-60s as Tom, Dick & Harry (fl1936-60s) *Three Boys who are Here, There and Everywhere* and *Three Sea Doggy Lads*, Hal & Laurel (fl1950s-60s) *The Tumbling Funsters*, Peta & Paula (fl1941) *Two Little Maids from Moscow* and White & Simone (fl1940s) *Comedy in Cameo*.

See THE DELEVANTIS, ZAZEL; also see Professor RISLEY for explanation of a Risley act.

WILLIAMS, BILLY (1878-1915)
The Australian Tom Woottwell; The Man in the Velvet Suit

The Melbourne artiste made his London début in 1900; abandoning the clown-like costume and make-up of most comic singers of the day Mr Williams appeared in straight make-up and a well-cut velvet suit. The performer recorded prolifically, cutting over 500 discs in his short career – his best-known number *When Father Papered The Parlour* came out on more than thirty different labels.

At that time all Music Hall songs had a musical bridge between the end of the chorus and the start of the next verse known as the symphony, during which the artiste would cavort about the stage, perhaps dancing or exchanging pleasantries with the audience. On his recordings this entry all too frequently covered the symphonies with a pawky chuckle, an infuriating practice which many other artistes, including HARRY LAUDER, copied.

Tom Woottwell (1865-1941) *The India Rubber Man* and *The Loose-Legged Comedian* was a popular comic singer and eccentric dancer none of whose songs has lasted. We can categorically state that we have spelled this artiste's name correctly because we have read an article by Mr Woottwell himself on his unusual patronymic.

WILLIAMS, BRANSBY (1870-1961)

Actor Mimic; Characters from Dickens; The Hamlet of the Halls; Negro Comedian, Character Impersonator and Lightning Cartoonist

Mr Williams was a histrion of the old school, ransacking the works of Charles Dickens (1812-70) for his *Characters*. It has been pointed out that there are so many eccentrics in Dickens because the novelist grew up at a time when much of the population was half-crazed with malnutrition. Be that as it may, this entry was not in truth much of an actor but he was a fine-looking man, confident and forceful, and because he brought Shakespeare into the Halls he was regarded with awe by his colleagues.

It must be said that while Mr Williams was respected for bringing Culture to the Halls his forays into the legitimate theatre were not conspicuously successful – one only has to listen to the performer's recording of *The Green Eye Of The Little Yellow God* to understand why.

Around the 1900s Arabella Allen was parading herself as *The Dickens Girl*; for another Dickensian see OWEN McGIVENEY. For other black-face artistes see G H ELLIOTT.

For other impressionists see list of MIMICS in glossary.

WILLIAMS, GEORGE (1910-95)

I'm Not Well; Quaint Comedian; Radio & TV's Out-Patient

Mr Williams, the most gentle-natured of men whom we knew well and admired greatly, specialised in 'ill' jokes, e.g. 'I was just leaving the cemetery after the funeral and the grave-digger said "You're not going, are you? We're stock-taking...".' We often booked the quiet, diffident comic in his latter years and rarely knew him fail, though some audiences were initially disconcerted by his frail frame, crumpled costumes and chalk-white make-up.

In Mr Williams' unpublished autobiography no reference is made to the event which devastated his career. In 1953 after his pantomime season at the Kemble Theatre, Hereford, the artiste was sent to prison for eighteen months for homosexual offences involving National Servicemen from the nearby Bryanston Army Camp.

See GEORGE BEAUCHAMP, REG DIXON

WILLIS, DAVE (1895-1973)
The Joy Germ

In the 1930s the Glaswegian comic was giving a burlesque impersonation of Adolf Hitler. Such disrespect to the Führer prompted a complaint from Berlin to the Foreign Office, and Lord Inverclyde was sent to advise Mr Willis to desist from offending a 'friendly' power. To his lasting regret the artiste complied with the Government's request, yet another instance of the craven posture adopted by Chamberlonian appeasers.

Mr Willis' son Denny Willis (1920-95) we encountered in *Aladdin* at the Connaught Theatre, Worthing; a Scotch comic on the Sussex coast might not have seemed the ideal booking but as Dame Mr Willis was quite irresistible. 'What d'ye expect for seven quid?' expostulated Widow Twankey to one matinée house which was cruelly deriding her attempts to be dramatic. 'Meryl *Strrreeep?!*'

See ELSIE BOWER, Claud 'Medals' Williams (MAGICIANS)

WILSON, KEPPEL & BETTY (c1928-63)
Cleopatra's Nightmare

This most celebrated of all speciality acts – two spectrally thin men in Egyptian costume dancing lasciviously round a shapely maiden – originated in Des Moines, Iowa, where Betty Knox joined the Liverpudlian Jack Wilson (1894-1970) and Joe Keppel (1895-1977), a Cork man, in the late 1920s. In May 1941 Miss Knox was succeeded by her daughter Patsy (b1924), after whom there were several Bettys, the last being Jeanne MacKinnon (b1932) who informs us that Betty Knox died in Dusseldorf in the late 1950s.

In the early days of their partnership as 'Wooden Shoe hoofers' in big and small-time American vaudeville Wilson & Keppel played 'everything from a medicine show to curtain raiser in Jewish drama'.

See p.13

WILTON, ROBB (1881-1957)
The Confidential Comedian/Comic; The Day War Broke Out; Still Muddling

Mr Wilton originally abandoned a career in engineering to become an actor, in pursuit of which ambition the future comic spent three and a half years in stock companies. On the Halls the performer was often billed by the title of one of the many sketches for which he was so popular – *The Fire Station, The Magistrate, The Police Station*, etc., etc. – and in which the artiste was assisted by his wife Florence Palmer (d1956). *The Day War Broke Out* were the opening words of Mr Wilton's classic series of monologues informing the nation of his doings in the Home Guard ('I'm the only one the overcoat'll fit...'); *Still Muddling* referred to his character *Mr Muddlecombe, JP*.

In Australia in 1925 this entry was billed as *The Funniest Comedian of All Time* – see WILKIE BARD, TOM BURKE and DAN LENO for similarly daunting advance billing.

Also see REG DIXON, TONY HANCOCK, SKETCH ARTISTES

WINDMILL THEATRE (1931-64)
We Never Closed

Under the management of Vivian Van Damm (1889-1960) the Windmill was the only West End theatre to remain open throughout the London blitzkrieg of 1940-2, hence the bill-matter. The house was perhaps even more celebrated for its unclad young ladies. These pert young misses – Mr Van Damm was very keen on pert – first appeared disrobed in 1937 and were strictly injuncted by the Lord Chamberlain not in any wise to move whilst displaying their charms; opera glasses and binoculars were prohibited and be-mackintoshed male patrons would gradually move closer to the stage during the six daily performances.

Just some of the many fledgling performers given a boost to their careers there were: AFRIQUE, David Berglas (MAGICIANS),

TOMMY COOPER, Howard De Courcy (MAGICIANS), DICK EMERY, ARTHUR ENGLISH, Erikson (MAGICIANS), TONY HANCOCK, TOM MENNARD, MORECAMBE & WISE, David Nixon (MAGICIANS), GILLIE POTTER, HARRY SECOMBE, PETER SELLERS, Mrs SHUFFLEWICK, Harold Taylor (MAGICIANS), JOHN TILLEY, NORMAN VAUGHAN, John Wade (MAGICIANS), and HARRY WORTH. Unsuccessful auditionees were CHARLIE DRAKE and BENNY HILL.

PERCY EDWARDS seems an unlikely Windmill performer but he only appeared there in its fully clothed days in 1932.

Also see PHYLLIS DIXEY, JACK SEATON.

WINTERS, MIKE & BERNIE (c1948-78)
Just Nuts

Mike (b1929) Weinstein, classically-trained as a clarinettist, was the somewhat charmless straight man to his zany brother Bernie (1932-91). We first saw this team at the Glasgow Pavilion when Mike, enraged at Bernie's noisy fooling on his drum-kit, said 'You're nothing but an idiot!' 'I know but I'm happy,' replied Bernie, a response which, such was the sympathy aroused by the comic, was received with great laughter and applause.

We also saw Bernie after he had split from Mike and taken a new partner, a St Bernard dog called Schnorbitz. The show was a pantomime at the Grand Leeds; we were so dismayed by two such lazy, self-indulgent performances that at the interval we fled.

See ANIMAL & BIRD ACTS, THE THREE LOOSE SCREWS

WISDOM, NORMAN (b1920)
Abnormally Foolish; The Successful Failure

It was the Army which gave Mr Wisdom a thorough musical training and the physical disciplines which were to stand him in such good stead as a physical comic. This entry's gump character emerged while stooging for David Nixon (MAGICIANS) during a summer season in Scarborough; the decent, lovable, resilient if accident-prone little man formed the basis of the comedian's entire subsequent career and proved astonishingly successful on the silver screen.

The political innocuousness of Mr Wisdom's films made him a particular favourite of the repressive ruling *junta* in Albania, and in 1995 the comedian toured that tortured country as a guest of the

Ministry of Culture and was given the freedom of Tirana, something very few Albanians had ever enjoyed under the insanely tyrannical Enver Hoxha.

We worked with this artiste only once in a sketch in a television game show when he gravely displeased the director by over-running. However, such is Mr Wisdom's legend and longevity that, as we speak, the performer is in danger of becoming mythologised as the Grand Old Man of British Comedy.

See SID FIELD, FRED FORDHAM, CLARENCE 'Tubby' TURNER

WISE, ERNIE (1925-99)

England's Mickey Rooney; The Jack Buchanan of Tomorrow

When Mickey Rooney (b1922) was a teen-aged American film star Jack Buchanan (1891-1957) was a sophisticated luminary of the British musical comedy theatre. Neither of these celebrities is remotely discernible in the performer who attained huge popularity as the shorter half of MORECAMBE & WISE; it has to be admitted that after the taller half's demise Mr Wise's career did not flourish. We suggest in all charity that this entry's true gift was to make his partner appear even funnier.

WONG, ANNA MAY (1907-61)

The World's Most Beautiful Chinese Girl

The enigmatic film star's name translates as Frosted Yellow Willow. We can now reveal that in 1933 Miss Wong's height was 5ft 4ins and her weight 8st 8lbs and that her elder sister, Ying Wong, was her business manager.

From 1934 British Variety audiences could relish the charms and skills of Eva May Wong *China's Sweetest Personality (Girl)* who was a plate-spinner, acrobat and contortionist of distinction; whether Anna May Wong was similarly gifted we think to have been unlikely.

WOOD, DAISY (1877-1964)

Lancashire's Own Principal Boy

This entry was a sister of none other than the great MARIE LLOYD herself and therefore a Cockney born and bred. The bill-matter indicates

Lancastrian affection rather than any literal claim on the artiste's origins. Miss Wood's husband was Will Poluski jnr (see SKETCH ARTISTES).

WOOD, WEE GEORGIE (1895-1979)

Black Hand George (His Black Hand);
Boy Impressionist; Mrs Robinson and her Son;
The Nursery at Bedtime; The Peter Pan of the Music
Halls; The Uncrowned King of Music Hall

Peter Pan was the boy who never grew up; like JIMMY CLITHEROE, Wee Georgie Wood was a midget who worked all his professional life in the guise of a child, appearing in sketches comic and sentimental. Touchy, opinionated and cantankerous, Mr Wood for many years contributed a weekly column of semi-literate, suspension-dotted ramblings to *The Stage* which we found unreadable.

See DOLLY HARMER, SKETCH ARTISTES

WORTH, HARRY (1918-89)

Figure of Speech; In Ventriloquial Scena

Mr Worth made his reputation not as a ventriloquist but as an actor in his television series *Here's Harry*, playing a man who was well-meaning, polite, cosily eccentric and with a self-deprecating half-laugh.

And how well the performer's abstractedness suited him in *Harvey*. Though far too old for the rôle of Elwood P Dowd and with not the slightest attempt at an American accent Mr Worth, with immense charm and a childlike belief in the goodness of what everyone else knows to be a wicked world, gave a display of sheer likeableness we have rarely seen equalled and perhaps never surpassed.

See SID FIELD, VENTRILOQUISTS, WINDMILL THEATRE

WORTMAN, CHRIS (1901-89)

It's All Madam!; Songs, Steps and Style;
A Man of Many Parts; Original Negro Studies

When *The Jazz Singer* was released in Britain the Garrick Cinema in Hereford did not possess any sound apparatus; Mr Wortman was employed to stand at the side of the screen and sing synchronously with a silent AL JOLSON. *It's All Madam* was this entry's bill-matter for his Dame-type drag act which included fourteen Russian elevations.

In 1949 the character comedian and dancer was touring with a show called *Stars We'll Remember* in which Mr Wortman impersonated EUGENE STRATTON, the black-face star who had died thirty years before. But then as we speak artistes are still impersonating Mr Jolson, and he handed in his dinner-pail a lot longer ago than that.

See G H ELLIOTT

WRIGHT, BERT (& ZENA) (fl1929-50s)

The Agile Ancient

Originally a solo performer Bert (b1903) was joined by Zena in 1934, a partnership which, as so often happened then and still does today, led two years later to Holy Wedlock. A poster for the Empress, Brixton, that year comically misprints their bill-matter as *The Agile Agent.*

WRIGHT, TONY (1926-86)

Mr Beefcake

Beefcake was the male equivalent of cheesecake, words which reached our shores from the United States in the 1930s and indicated sexual allure. Mr Wright was a star of British films, though that meant very little in the big cinematic world outside these islands. The actor was a broad-shouldered, louchely good-looking blond without the class of his contemporaries such as Derek Bond, Donald Sinden, Stewart Granger, Kenneth More, or even Anthony Steel.

The last time we saw this entry was sad, for *Mr Beefcake*, then an alcoholic in his late fifties, was wearing a gold lamé dinner jacket for his job as meeter-and-greeter at an Old Time Music Hall over a pub in Putney.

Y

YARWOOD, MIKE (b1941)
Making a First Impression

This entry had a huge vogue in the 1960 and 1970s, primed by his uncannily accurate impersonation of Harold Wilson, then Prime Minister. We recall also one of Mr Yarwood's less familiar but also striking impressions – that of Vic Feather, general secretary of the Trades Union Congress.

The artiste had the misfortune to suffer a catastrophic mid-life crisis, when a combination of alcohol and loss of confidence cost him his wife and his reputation. Attempts to rekindle the performer's career have all come to naught, not assisted by an appearance on a Christmas television show in which Mr Yarwood gave the worst MAX MILLER impersonation we have ever seen.

See list of MIMCS in glossary.

YOUNG, SELINA (fl1850s-62)
Female Blondin and Heroine of the Thames

On June 29th 1862 this intrepid lady peeved in *The Era* that 'various parties travelling the Provinces have taken her name,' which may be a reference to Mme GENEIVE who was also billed as *The Female Blondin* (and whose Christian name was also Selina).

On October 18th 1863 Miss Young gave notice that she was opening a beer-house in Provost Street off City Road, London, because of 'the unfortunate accident which befell her at Highbury Barn whilst pursuing her avocation as a rope dancer'.

Under the name of Pauline Violante this entry was billed as *Heroine of the Crystal Palace*, an erection sited in Hyde Park to house the Great Exhibition of 1851. It was re-built (1852-4) in South London as a concert hall and entertainment venue and utterly destroyed by fire in 1936.

See BLONDIN

Z

ZAEO (1863-1906)
An Athenian Idyll; Filambulist and Gymnastics; The Marvel of the World

The aerialist was celebrated for the daring of her costumes no less than her feats. On her return to the Royal Aquarium in 1890 after a world tour Miss Zaeo's décolleté was displayed on posters with an emphasis which outraged the sonorously named Central Vigilance Society for the Repression of Immorality. The posters were withdrawn but the attendant publicity whipped up a frenzy of cash-paying interest. *Filambulist* is not listed in the *Oxford English Dictionary (1989 edition)* but we may assume that the word meant one who performs on a filament or vertical rope. In private life Zaeo was Adelaide, Mrs Harry W Wieland, and the mother of Clara Wieland *The Engish Vanoni*, after Marie Vanoni, the French Canadian *vedette* who had a great hit at the Alhambra in 1888.

ZANCIGS, THE
Two Minds with but a Single Thought

The bill-matter of Julius Zancig (1857-1929) and his hunch-backed wife Agnes (d1916) has passed into common parlance – a jocular variation may be seen in the entry for RONALD FRANKAU. The mind-reading act, with Agnes identifying objects handed to Julius by members of the audience, was brought to its highest peak of attainment with these artistes, and so ingenious was the code used (plus an uncredited third member of the act who, planted in the audience, assisted in the relay of information) that many, including Sir Arthur Conan Doyle, were convinced of their psychic powers. Truly, there is one born every minute.

After Mrs Zancig died her widower tried other stage partners but with limited success. Eventually he sold his act to HOUDINI and retired to California selling crystal balls at $5 and $10 a time.

See JOHN HENRY ANDERSON, The Amazing Fogel (MAGICIANS), Al Koran (MAGICIANS), Malotz (MAGICIANS), Micro (JIMMY CLITHEROE), THE GREAT NIXON, Rayanne & Partner (MAGICIANS), PAUL RAYMOND, THE SALAMBOS, Van Der Koors (MISCELLANEOUS), Zahla (MAGICIANS), Zara (MAGICIANS), The Bewildering Zodiacs (MAGICIANS).

ZAZEL (1862-1922)
The Human Cannon Ball

It was at the Royal Aquarium on April 2nd 1877 that the 14-year-old Miss Rosa M Richter (later Mrs George O Starr), gymnast and wire-walker, became the first to perform this stunt. The cannon was then as now spring-loaded, the flash and bang being merely for effect.

After many hundreds of firings Miss Zazel missed the safety net and broke her back, spending the rest of her life in a steel-corset. The performer's trainer was G A Farini, adoptive father of another fearless young aerialist EL NINO FARINI.

Zazel is sometimes confused, though not by us, with Katherine Hefferman (1862-1922), an American vaudevillian who worked with a partner as Zazell & Vernon.

Two other early ballisticians were Professor John Holtum (b1845) *King of the Cannon Ball* and Mme (Laurine) Gregory (1852-1940) *The Cannon Queen* whose daughter Leonora (1875-1969) married Henry Whiteley of THE FIVE WHITELEYS.

See THE DELEVANTIS

Glossarial Classification

Names in capital letters indicate substantive entries

ACROBATS

THREE ABERDONIANS, BILLY COTTON, The Famous Craggs (SKETCH ARTISTES), THE DELEVANTIS, DRUM & MAJOR, Signor ETHARDO, GASTON & ANDRÉE, GRIFFITHS BROTHERS, THE HANLON-LEES, RICHARD HEARNE, CHARLES JOANNYS, FRED KARNO, Marie Marzella (ANIMAL & BIRD ACTS), MY FANCY, HECTOR NAPIER, KING OHMY, Pantzer Brothers (M. CANDLER), La Piere (PEG-LEG BATES), PIPIFAX & PANLO, Professor RISLEY, THE FIVE VOLANTS, Warren Latona & Sparks (MISCELLANEOUS), Eva May Wong (ANNA MAY WONG)

ACTORS and ACTRESSES

IRA ALDRIDGE, ETHEL BARRYMORE (includes Lionel Barrymore, Katherine Cornell, and Helen Hayes), JOHN BARRYMORE, Lucy Beaumont (MOTHER OF...), Master BETTY, CLARA BOW, SAM COWELL, JEAN HARLOW, Esther Rachel Kaminska (MOTHER OF...), ADAH MENKEN, MARY PICKFORD, TONY WRIGHT

AERIALISTS

BARBETTE, Eli Bowen (PEG-LEG BATES), BONAR COLLEANO, EL NINO FARINI, Mlle Lu-Lu (EL NINO FARINI), Jack 'Dental' Riskit (BARBETTE), Professor RISLEY, ZAEO

ANIMAL & BIRD TRAINERS

See ANIMAL & BIRD ACTS

ANIMAL & BIRD IMPERSONATORS

Chassino (THEO BAMBERG), PERCY EDWARDS, M. GOUFFÉ, GRIFFITHS BROTHERS, RICHARD HAYDN, CHARLES LAURI, Bernard 'Skeets' Martin (PERCY EDWARDS), Hervio Nano (Mlle ALMA), Olmar (KING OF...), ROLO & LADY

ASCENSIONISTS – see SPIRAL ASCENSIONISTS and TIGHTROPE WALKERS

BALLOONOLOGISTS

LARRY BARNES, WINDY BLOW

BLACK-FACE ARTISTES
See G H ELLIOTT

BONELESS WONDERS
HECTOR NAPIER, VALENTINE (includes six similar)

BUNGEE JUMPERS
KING OHMY, Mme Caroline (KING OHMY)

CATAPULTIST
EL NINO FARINI

CHAPEAUGRAPHISTS
Will Cummin (MISCELLANEOUS), FELICIEN TREWEY

CHILD IMITATOR
HARRY HEMSLEY

CHILD PRODIGIES
JULIE ANDREWS, Master BETTY, NORMAN CARROL, SAM COWELL, EL NINO FARINI, William Robert Grossmith (Master BETTY), PERCY HENRY, DAN LENO, NELLIE POWER, ADA REEVE, Joseph Santley (Master BETTY)

CLOWNS
CHARLIE CAIROLI, LYDIA DREAMS, DRUM & MAJOR, Grock (KING OF...), CHARLES JOANNYS, BILLY MERSON, NONI & HORACE, KING OHMY, TONY PASTOR, THE RASTELLIS, Dan Rice (KING OF...), Little Tony (JIMMY CLITHEROE), Billy Whitaker & Mimi Law (MISCELLANEOUS)

COMICS
BEN ALBERT, FRED ALBERT, DAVE ALLEN, FRED ALLEN, MOREY AMSTERDAM, DON ARROL, ARTEMUS, ARTHUR ASKEY, CHARLES AUSTIN, MAX BACON, HARRY BAILEY, HYLDA BAKER, HARRY BALL, FREDDIE BAMBERGER & PAM, BARCLAY & PERKINS, WILKIE BARD, FRED BARNES, NORA BAYES, GEORGE BEAUCHAMP, BESSIE BELLWOOD, BILLY BENNETT, JACK BENNY, MICHAEL BENTINE, HAROLD BERENS, MILTON BERLE, GEORGE & BERT BERNARD, JOE BLACK, GEORGE BOLTON, ISSY BONN, VICTOR BORGE, BREWSTER & LOTINGA, LENNY BRUCE, MAX BYGRAVES, DOUGLAS BYNG, NORMAN CALEY, WYN CALVIN, HERBERT CAMPBELL, CANTOR &

LEE, NORMAN CARROL, EMMA CARUS, BILLY CARYLL & HILDA MUNDY, CASEY'S COURT, ROY CASTLE, HARRY CHAMPION, CHARLIE CHESTER, CLAPHAM & DWYER, GEORGE CLARKE, ANDREW 'DICE' CLAY, JIMMY CLITHEROE, COLLINSON & DEAN, JOE COOK, TOMMY COOPER, LEON CORTEZ, DR CROCK, LESLIE CROWTHER, BRIAN CRYER, PAMELA CUNDELL, BILLY DAINTY, BILLY DANVERS, JEANNE De CASALIS, De HAVEN & PAGE, THE DEHL TRIO, DESMOND & MARKS, REG DIXON, KEN DODD, CHARLIE DRAKE, MARIE DRESSLER, T E DUNVILLE, JIMMY DURANTE, JACKSON EARLE, GUS ELEN, GEORGE ELRICK, DICK EMERY, FRED EMNEY, ARTHUR ENGLISH, NORMAN EVANS, JAMES FAWN, SID FIELD, GRACIE FIELDS, WC FIELDS, FLANAGAN & ALLEN, GEORGE FORMBY snr, FRED FORDHAM, BRUCE FORSYTH, FORSYTHE SEAMON & FARRELL, VIVIAN FOSTER, TOM FOY, W F FRAME, RONALD FRANKAU, FREDDIE FRINTON, CHARLES GODFREY, HARRY GORDON, DUNCAN GRAY, LARRY GRAYSON, HACKFORD & DOYLE, JACK HAIG, ALEC HALLS, TONY HANCOCK, TOMMY HANDLEY, GUS HARRIS, WILL HAY, HAYMAN & FRANKLIN, ARTHUR HAYNES, HARRY HEMSLEY, DICK HENDERSON, DICKIE HENDERSON, EDDIE HENDERSON, BENNY HILL, ERNEST HOGAN, SYDNEY HOWARD, FRANKIE HOWERD, ROY HUDD, TOM E HUGHES, G W HUNTER, NAT JACKLEY, DAISY JAMES, JIMMY JAMES, GEORGE JESSEL, JEWEL & WARRISS, BETTY JUMEL, FRED KARNO, DAVY KAYE, KEMBLE KEAN, BILL KERR, R G KNOWLES, HARRY KORRIS, WALTER LABURNUM, GEORGE LACY, LILLIE LANGTRY, JAY LAURIER, JOE LAWRENCE, TOM LEAMORE, JIMMY LEARMOUTH, LILY LENA, DAN LENO, THE TWO LESLIES, ALFRED LESTER, GEORGE LEYBOURNE, BEATRICE LILLIE, HARRY LISTON, ARTHUR LLOYD, MARIE LLOYD, HENRY LLOYD-PARKER, Jimmy Logan (JACK SHORT), THE THREE LOOSE SCREWS, LUCAN & McSHANE, TED LUNE, LYTTON & AUSTIN, JAMES MADISON, ERNIE MAYNE, SAM MAYO, TOM MENNARD, BILLY MERSON, MIKE-ROGUES, BERNARD MILES, MAX MILLER, SPIKE MILLIGAN, NAT MILLS & BOBBIE, ALBERT MODLEY, BOB MONKHOUSE, HAL MONTY, MORECAMBE & WISE, ROBERT MORETON, GLADYS MORGAN, TOMMY MORGAN, EDDIE MORRELL, MORRIS & COWLEY, GEORGE MOZART, CHIC MURRAY & MAIDIE, MURRAY & MOONEY, 'Jolly' JOHN NASH, NAUGHTON & GOLD, NERVO & KNOX, Max & Harry Nesbitt (MISCELLANEOUS), DAVE & JOE O'GORMAN, O'GRADY & GRAY, VIC OLIVER, WILL OLIVER, OLSEN & JOHNSON, ALEC PLEON, GILLIE POTTER, SANDY POWELL, NELLIE POWER, FRANK RANDLE, PHIL RAY, TED RAY, AL READ, SAM REDFERN, ADA REEVE, BERYL REID, EDDIE REINDEER, REVNELL & WEST, BILLIE RITCHIE, ARTHUR ROBERTS, KEN ROBERTS, GEORGE ROBEY, TED ROGERS, WILL ROGERS, CLARKSON ROSE, DEREK ROY, BILLY RUSSELL, SCOTT & WHALEY, JACK SEATON, HARRY SECOMBE, BILLY SHAKESPEARE, SAMMY SHIELDS, SMITH & DALE, WALLY STANLEY & EDITH LESTER, STAN STENNETT, STAINLESS STEPHEN, DONALD B STUART,

RANDOLPH SUTTON, EVA TANGUAY, JIMMY TARBUCK, SUZETTE TARRI, TENNYSON & O'GORMAN, BOBBY THOMPSON, LITTLE TICH, JOHN TILLEY, SAM TORR, HYRAM TRAVERS, JACK TRIPP, JOAN TURNER, CLARENCE 'Tubby' TURNER, ALFRED VANCE, REG VARNEY, VARNEY & BUTT, NORMAN VAUGHAN, VESTA VICTORIA, MAX WALL, NELLIE WALLACE, WILLIAM FREDERICK WALLETT, JACK WARNER, ELSIE & DORIS WATERS, MAX WELTON, JIMMY WHEELER, ALBERT WHELAN, GEORGE WILLIAMS, DAVE WILLIS, DENNY WILLIS, ROBB WILTON, MIKE & BERNIE WINTERS, NORMAN WISDOM, HARRY WORTH, CHRIS WORTMAN, BERT WRIGHT & ZENA

CONTORTIONISTS

Athleta (GASTON PALMER), BENNEDETTI BROTHERS, M. CANDLER, EMMELINE ETHARDO, Carla (MISCELLANEOUS), Little George (DAN LENO), Minnie Spray (VALENTINE), J H WALTER, Eva May Wong (ANNA MAY WONG), Ed Wynn & Valantine (HECTOR NAPIER)

DANCERS

THE THREE ABERDONIANS, MAUD ALLAN, JOSÉPHINE BAKER, PEG-LEG BATES, GEORGE & BERT BERNARD, JOE BLACK, CARL BRISSON, Carla (MISCELLANEOUS), Eddie Cantor (CANTOR & LEE), ROY CASTLE, HARRY CHAMPION, LOTTIE COLLINS, JOE COOK, JOHNNY COOPER, SAMMY CURTIS, BILLY DAINTY, DELFONT & TOKO, Donato (PEG-LEG BATES), G H ELLIOTT, Bob Evans (PEG-LEG BATES), BRUCE FORSYTH, FORSYTHE SEAMON & FARRELL, GANJOU BROTHERS & JUANITA, GASTON & ANDRÉE, GRAD & GOLD, LEW GRADE, JENNY HILL, PERCY HONRI, NAT JACKLEY, DAISY JAMES, ANNETTE KELLERMAN, DAN LENO, JIMMY LYNTON, E W MACKNEY, JESSIE MATTHEWS, HAL MONTY, MORRIS & COWLEY, BEBE NORMA, LA BELLE OTERO, Orville Parker (MISCELLANEOUS), The Two Petries (G H ELLIOTT), The Three Phoites (MISCELLANEOUS), Pop White & Stagger (MISCELLANEOUS), Charles Raymond (PEG-LEG BATES), REGGIE REDCLIFFE, Maurice Rocco (MARGARET COOPER), Mr Ryley & Miss Barnum (MISCELLANEOUS), Jack Stanford (MISCELLANEOUS), EUGENE STRATTON, LYDIA THOMPSON, LITTLE TICH, TILLER GIRLS, Little Tony (JIMMY CLITHEROE), FELICIEN TREWEY, TOMMY TRINDER, MAX WALL, JIMMY WHEELER, WILSON KEPPEL & BETTY, Sisters Winterton (THE DELEVANTIS), Tom Woottwell (BILLY WILLIAMS), CHRIS WORTMAN

DART-BLOWER

RONDART

DENTALISTS

Jack 'Dental' Riskit (BARBETTE), Mme SENYAH

DIABOLO MANIPULATORS – see JUGGLERS

ANNETTE KELLERMAN

ECDYSIASTS

PHYLLIS DIXEY, Fifi (MISCELLANEOUS), CARRIE FINNELL, Gypsy Rose Lee (QUEEN OF...)

ENTORTILLATIONISTS

THE HANLON-LEES

EQUILIBRISTS

CAICEDO, M. CANDLER, HECTOR NAPIER, Pantzer Brothers (M. CANDLER), Snakella & Travella (BILLY MERSON)

ESCAMOTEUR

Cazman (THEO BAMBERG)

ESCAPOLOGISTS

LARRY BARNES, HOUDINI, JIMMY LYNTON, Proctorie (ALOIS PETERS)

FEMALE IMPERSONATORS

BARBETTE (includes nine similar), DOUGLAS BYNG, LYDIA DREAMS, BERT ERROL, BOBBIE KIMBER, Danny La Rue (TED ROGERS), Eric Lloyd (VERA LYNN), Mlle Lu-Lu (EL NINO FARINI), MALCOLM SCOTT, Mrs SHUFFLEWICK, JAMES UNSWORTH,

FILAMBULISTS

ZAEO

FIRE EATERS

CHARLES S BERNARD (includes Cristoforo Buonocore, The Fire Eating Dubarrys, Mlle Le Never, The Ngfys, Eugene Rivalli, and William E Smith), IVANITZ CHABERT, THE SALAMBOS

FUNAMBULISTS – see TIGHTROPE WALKERS

GYMNASTS

PEG-LEG BATES (includes Eli Bowen, La Piere, Mons. Zampi), PAUL CINQUEVALLI, GASTON & ANDRÉE, Gertrella (MISCELLANEOUS), THE HANLON-LEES, Olmar (KING OF...), CINQUEVALLI, Snakella & Travella (BILLY MERSON), KING OHMY, Professor RISLEY, ZAEO

HORSE RIDERS

ADAH MENKEN, KING OHMY, Adele Rancy (GASTON PALMER)

HUMAN ANOMALIES

Captain GEORGE AUGER (includes nine other tall artistes), SAARTJE BAARTMAN, Professor CHEER, CHANG & ENG, JIMMY CLITHEROE (includes twelve other small artistes), HENRY COLLARD, Mme GASCOYNE, Laloo (CHANG & ENG), JOSEPH MERRICK, Millie-Christine (CHANG & ENG), YVONNE PRESTIGE, JOSEPH PUJOL, Tom Thumb (HENRY COLLARD),, WEE GEORGIE WOOD, JAN VAN ALBERT, KATYA VAN DYK

HUMAN CANNONBALLS

ZAZEL (includes John Holtum and Mme Gregory)

HUMAN FLIES

Mlle ALMA (includes six similar), DEHL TRIO, ALOIS PETERS

HUMAN GASOMETER

JUNA

HUMAN MAGNETS

ANNIE ABBOT (includes Mona Magnet and Resista)

HUMAN SALAMANDERS – see FIRE EATERS

HUMAN SPIDERS

DEHL TRIO, HECTOR NAPIER, Zaleski (HECTOR NAPIER)

HYPNOTISTS

ARTEMUS, WALFORD BODIE, THE GREAT CARLTON, PETER CASSON, Kennedy (PETER CASSON), Mlle KORINGA, CARROLL LEVIS, Paula (ANIMAL & BIRD ACTS), Princess RUBIE

IMPALERS

Mr & Miss Nemo (JUGGLERS)

IMPRESSIONISTS – see MIMICS

INSTRUMENTALISTS – see MUSICIANS

JUGGLERS – see JUGGLERS (from p140)

LADDER BALANCERS

DU CALION (includes Tom Gilbey, Ivor Gridneff, and Great Scott)

LIGHTNING CALCULATORS

THEA ALBA (includes Professor William S Hutchings and Jacques Inaudi)

LIGHTNING CARTOONISTS

LARRY BARNES, Countess Bekoffska (MISCELLANEOUS), JOE COOK, CHARLES JOANNYS, BILLY RUSSELL, CARL UNTHAN, BRANSBY WILLIAMS

LIMBLESS ARTISTES

PEG-LEG BATES (includes seven similar), CARL UNTHAN (includes Elroy, Charles Tripp, Tommy Jacobsen, and the Lutz Brothers)

LIONS COMIQUES – see VOCALISTS

GEORGE LEYBOURNE, ARTHUR LLOYD, G H MACDERMOTT, ALFRED VANCE

LIVING SKELETONS

WILL OLIVER (includes two similar)

LIVING STATUES

LA MILO (includes Edward Von Kilyany and The Olympiers)

MAGICIANS – see MAGICIANS (from p172)

MALE IMPERSONATORS

BESSIE BONEHILL, Nellie Coleman (ST GEORGE HUSSEY), ST GEORGE HUSSEY, HETTY KING, May Level (ST GEORGE HUSSEY), NELLIE POWER, Fanny Robina (FLORRIE ROBINA), ELLA SHIELDS, VESTA TILLEY

MECHANICAL MEN

AL CARTHY (includes four similar), Cire (MAGICIANS)

MEMORISERS

THEA ALBA, DATAS, Leslie Welch (DATAS), THE SALAMBOS

MENTALISTS

THEA ALBA, JOHN HENRY ANDERSON, The Amazing Fogel
(MAGICIANS), Will Hutchins (THEA ALBA), Jacques Inaudi (THEA ALBA),
Al Koran (MAGICIANS), Micro (JIMMY CLITHEROE), THE GREAT
NIXON, Rayanne & Partner (MAGICIANS), PAUL RAYMOND, THE
SALAMBOS, Van Der Koors (MAGICIANS), THE ZANCIGS, The Bewildering
Zodias (MAGICIANS)

MIMICS and FACIALISTS – see PROTEAN & QUICK CHANGE ARTISTES

AFRIQUE, PAUL J BARNES, MEL BLANC, PETER CAVANAGH, LON
CHANEY, FLORENCE DESMOND, CHARLES JOANNYS, Florence
Lawrence (LON CHANEY), George Layman (LON CHANEY), Cissie Loftus
(MARIE LOFTUS), BERYL ORDE (includes three similar), GEORGE F MOORE
(includes four similar), JOSEPH PUJOL, Victor Seaforth (PAUL J BARNES),
PETER SELLERS, FELICIEN TREWEY, JOAN TURNER, David Warfield
(GEORGE BEAUCHAMP), BRANSBY WILLIAMS, WEE GEORGIE WOOD,
MIKE YARWOOD

MONOLOGUISTS/RECITERS – see PROTEAN & QUICK CHANGE ARTISTES

BILLY BENNETT, CYRIL FLETCHER (includes Pam Ayres, Marriott Edgar,
Stanley Holloway, and Nosmo King), J MILTON HAYES, G W HUNTER,
NELLY LENNOX & KATE RALEIGH, SCOTT SANDERS, BRANSBY
WILLIAMS

MUSICIANS

LARRY ADLER (includes seven similar), CARLOS AMES, WINIFRED
ATWELL, BETTY AUKLAND, MAX BACON, Kenny Baker (EDDIE
CALVERT), HARRY BALL, Barrett & Knowles (MISCELLANEOUS),
BENEDETTI BROTHERS, IRVING BERLIN, BI-BO-BI, VICTOR BORGE,
TEDDY BROWN, EDDIE CALVERT, Murray Campbell (EDDIE CALVERT),
ROY CASTLE, SISTERS CHESTER, Chocolate & Co. (THE RASTELLIS),
G H CHIRGWIN, PEGGY COCHRANE, JOE COOK, MARGARET
COOPER, BILLY COTTON, DR CROCK (includes many similar), Peggy 'Piano'
Desmond (WINIFRED ATWELL), DU CALION, The Elliotts (BICYCLE
ACTS), MAY ERNE, EMMELINE ETHARDO, GEORGE FORMBY jnr
(includes three other ukelelists), BRUCE FORSYTH, Will H Fox (WINIFRED
ATWELL), HARRY FRAGSON, Barclay Gammon (MARGARET COOPER),
CORNEY GRAIN, HACKFORD & DOYLE, Bill Hall Trio (DR CROCK),
Henry Hall (BERYL REID), ALEC HALLS, HERSCHEL HENLERE, PERCY
HONRI, Tommy Jacobsen (CARL UNTHAN), Spike Jones (DR CROCK),
TOMMY JOVER, Charles Kunz (WINIFRED ATWELL), THE TWO
LESLIES, Roxy La Rocca (PEGGY DESMOND), Al Leon (DAISY

SQUELCH), Liberace (MARGARET COOPER), NORMAN LONG, J W LISKARD, JOE LOSS, MACARI, MURDOCH MACKENZIE (includes three similar), Mendel (WINIFRED ATWELL), CLARICE MAYNE, SAM MAYO, FELIX MENDELSSOHN, SPIKE MILLIGAN, Sid Millward (DR CROCK), Barbara Ward Morris (TED ANDREWS), IVOR MORETON & DAVY KAYE, GEORGE MOZART, MUSAIRE, BEBE NORMA, VIC OLIVER, BOB & ALF PEARSON, SID PLUMMER, TONI RAGLAN, TED RAY, REGGIE REDCLIFFE, Syd Seymour (DR CROCK), JACK SHORT, DAISY SQUELCH, STANELLI, DANA SUESSE, STAN WHITE & ANN, Al Trahan (WINIFRED ATWELL), FELICIEN TREWEY, CARL UNTHAN, REG VARNEY, Auguste Van Biene (NITA VAN BIENE), THE FIVE WHITELEYS, NORMAN WISDOM

OMNIVORES

SYDNEY BARNES, M. Mangetout (SYDNEY BARNES), THE GREAT WERTH

PAPER TEARERS

LARRY BARNES, Terri Carol (LARRY BARNES)

PLATE SPINNERS

Eva May Wong (ANNA MAY WONG)

POSTURERS – see CONTORTIONISTS

PROTEAN & QUICK CHANGE ARTISTES – see IMPRESSIONISTS and MONOLOGUISTS/RECITERS

Adelina (GEORGE F MOORE), OWEN McGIVENEY (includes Chanti, R A Roberts, Mlle Von Etta)

REGURGITATORS

Hadji Ali (MISCELLANEOUS), HARRY NORTON

RISLEY ACTS

Professor RISLEY, THE FIVE WHITELEYS

ROLLER SKATERS

Belle Avalon (DAISY JAMES), WILLIE ROLLS

ROPE DANCERS – see TIGHTROPE WALKERS

ROPE SPINNERS

TEX McLEOD, WILL ROGERS

SERIO-COMIQUES – see VOCALISTS

ANNIE ADAMS, BEATRICE LILLIE, MARIE LLOYD

SHADOWGRAPHISTS

THEO BAMBERG (includes four similar), CHARLES JOANNYS, FELICIEN TREWEY

SHARP SHOOTERS

CLEMENTINE (includes Elroy and Berthe Bordeverry), CHARLES JOANNYS, ANNIE OAKLEY, Professor RISLEY, CARL UNTHAN

SIFFLEURS – see SIFFLEURS and SIFFLEUSES (from p241)

SKETCH ARTISTES – see SKETCH ARTISTES (from p243)

SPIRAL ASCENSIONISTS see TIGHTROPE WALKERS

JOE COOK, Signor ETHARDO

STRONG MEN & WOMEN

Athleta (GASTON PALMER), ATLAS, ATLAS & VULCANA, HARRY BAILEY, Henry E Dixey (ATLAS), AHMED MADRALI, ALOIS PETERS (includes six similar), JOAN RHODES, EUGENE SANDOW (includes George Hackenschmidt, Samson, and Lex Whitton), Victorina (JOAN RHODES)

STUMP ORATORS

James Unsworth

SWIMMERS see TANK ARTISTES

SWORD SWALLOWER

Chevalier Clicquot (HARRY NORTON)

TANK ARTISTES

Blatz and Enoch (both ANNETTE KELLERMAN), ANNETTE KELLERMAN, Ada Webb (MISCELLANEOUS)

TIGHTROPE WALKERS *a.k.a.* FUNAMBULISTS, ROPE DANCERS, or WIRE WALKERS

(Funambulists who walked up inclining ropes or wires were *a.k.a.* Ascensionists – but see SPIRAL ASCENSIONISTS)

HARRY BAILEY, BARBETTE, BLONDIN (includes four similar), CAICEDO (includes five similar), Con Colleano (BONAR COLLEANO), JOE COOK, Guillermo Farini (EL NINO FARINI), Mme GENEIVE, GRIFFITHS BROTHERS, The Beautiful Jessica (QUEEN OF...), Lulu (Mrs Winifred Gilbert - EL NINO FARINI), OCEANA, Mme Rossini (Mme GENEIVE), Mme SENYAH, SELINA YOUNG, ZAZEL

TRAMPOLINISTS

Ernie Dillon (KING OF...), JUMPIN' JAX, Paulette & Renée (JUMPIN' JAX)

TRAPEZISTS

BARBETTE, CINQUEVALLI, HALA, CHARLES JOANNYS, JULES LÉOTARD, BILLY MERSON, MY FANCY (includes Azella, Alfred Corell, and Pfau), Charlie Rivel (CHARLIE CHAPLIN), ROLO & LADY, Mme SENYAH

TRICK CYCLISTS – see BICYCLE ACTS

TRICK RIDERS – see HORSE RIDERS

TUMBLERS – see ACROBATS and GYMNASTS

VENTRILOQUISTS – see VENTRILOQUISTS (from p266)

VOCALISTS – see LION COMIQUES and SERIO-COMIQUES

JULIE ANDREWS, TED ANDREWS, JOSÉPHINE BAKER, FRED BARNES, IDA BARR, T W BARRETT, NORA BAYES, BESSIE BELLWOOD, BEVERLEY SISTERS, ISSY BONN, AL BOWLLY, CARL BRISSON, TOM BURKE, LILY BURNAND, BIG BILL CAMPBELL, IRENE CAMPBELL, KATE CARNEY, ROY CASTLE, ALBERT CHEVALIER, HARRY CLAFF, MAGGIE CLINE, ALMA COGAN, HENRY COLLARD, JOSÉ COLLINS, RONNÉ CONN, FRANK COYNE, LEO DRYDEN, GEORGE ELRICK, 'Happy' FANNY FIELDS, FLORRIE FORDE, GEORGE FORMBY jnr, LOTTIE GILSON, GERTIE GITANA, ADELAIDE HALL, JESSIE HARCOURT (includes five similar), DOLLY HARMER, ELTON HAYES, JENNY HILL, ERNEST HOGAN, MICHAEL HOLLIDAY, HILDA HOOPER, HOUSTON & STEWART, ALEC HURLEY, JACK & EVELYN, AL JOLSON, HELEN KANE, PAT KIRKWOOD, GEORGE LASHWOOD, HARRY LAUDER, VICKI LESTER, JENNY LIND (includes ten similar), VICTOR LISTON, ALICE LLOYD, JOSEF LOCKE, MARIE LOFTUS, LILLIAN LORRAINE, VERA LYNN, JOHN McCORMACK, JESSIE MATTHEWS, CLARICE MAYNE, ETHEL MERMAN, RUBY MURRAY, TALBOT O'FARRELL, LE BELLE OTERO, TONY PASTOR, DONALD PEERS, LA POLAIRE, NELLIE POWER, YVONNE PRESTIGE, JOHNNIE RAY, ADA REEVE, T D RICE, FLORRIE ROBINA, RONNIE RONALDE, Annie Ross (JACK SHORT), FLORENCE ST JOHN, HARRY SECOMBE, TRULY SHATTUCK, JACK SMITH, J H STEAD, EUGENE STRATTON, JILL SUMMERS, RANDOLPH SUTTON, JOE TERMINI, TINY TIM, ARTHUR TRACY, CHARLES TRENET, SOPHIE TUCKER, GEORGE W WARE, ALBERT WHELAN, DAISY WOOD

WIRE WALKERS – see TIGHTROPE WALKERS

Index

Excluding entries in the main text.
Venues are listed under location, i.e. for Moulin Rouge see Paris: Moulin Rouge.
Titles of films and shows are included but not sketches.

Barnum's Circus, VALENTINE
Baroni, BILLY RUSSELL
Barr Brothers & Roza, THE THREE
    ABERDONIANS
Barret & Knowles, MISCELLANEOUS
Barrie, James, THE LUPINOS
Barrymore, Lionel, ETHEL BARRYMORE
Barrymore, Maurice, ETHEL
    BARRYMORE
Bartholomew, John Eric, ERIC
    MORECAMBE
Barton, Sam, BICYCLE ACTS
Bass, Harry, MISCELLANEOUS
Bassett, James, MAGICIANS
Battalia, F, THE GREAT WERTH
Baylis, Lilian, AFRIQUE
Beaumont, Lucy, MOTHER OF...
Beauty, THE GREAT LAFAYETTE
Beck, Wee Georgie, JIMMY CLITHEROE
Beecham's Pills, GEORGE BEAUCHAMP
Beerbohm, Max, DAN LENO, PHIL RAY
Bekoffska, Countess, MISCELLANEOUS
Belgians, King & Queen of the, De HAVEN
    & PAGE
Belmont, George E, p.13
Benet, Harry, VENTRILOQUISTS
Bennett & Martell, BILLY BENNETT
Benyon, The Great, MAGICIANS
Berglas, David, MAGICIANS,
    WINDMILL THEATRE, ill.53
Bergman, Ingrid, LARRY ADLER
Berlin, Irving EMMA CARUS, ANNIE
    OAKLEY
Bernard, Les, GEORGE & BERT BERNARD
Bernhardt, Sarah, MARIE LLOYD,
    MARIE LOFTUS
Bernie, Ben, JACK BENNY
Bertoldi, Ena, QUEEN OF...
Best, Willie, MISCELLANEOUS
Betra, Millie, ANIMAL & BIRD ACTS
Bexhill: De La Warr Pavilion, DICK
    EMERY, GEORGE LACY, KEN
    ROBERTS
Bey, Ali, MAGICIANS
Beyond the Fringe, SPIKE MILLIGAN
Bianchi, Mario, GRACIE FIELDS
Biddle, Mrs Ben, BLONDIN
Billy & Bob, JUMPIN' JAX
Billington, JOHNNY COOPER, THE
    GREAT HUGHES, MAGICIANS
Binnie, Jimmy, MAGICIANS
Birkenhead: Argyle, TOM FOY, DAVY
    KAYE
Birmingham: Aston Park, Mme GENEIVE
    Vauxhall, Mme GENEIVE
Bishop, Jeannie, JENNY LIND
Bithell, Fred, ANIMAL & BIRD ACTS
Black and White Minstrel Show, The, DON
    ARROL
Black, George, BILLY CARYLL & HILDA

MUNDY, BOB & ALF PEARSON
Blair, Tony, JIMMY LYNTON
Bland, James, GUS HARRIS
Blatz, ANNETTE KELLERMAN
Blight, Ellen, ELLEN BRIGHT
Bliss, Charles, Mlle ALMA
Blore, Eric, TOMMY HANDLEY
Boadicea, MALCOLM SCOTT
Bogannys, The, SKETCH ARTISTES
Boissets, The, SKETCH ARTISTES
Bolton: Grand, AL READ, HARRY
    SECOMBE
Bolony, Alf, THE THREE LOOSE SCREWS
Bond, Derek, TONY WRIGHT
Bongo, Ali, MAGICIANS
Bordeverry, Mlle Berthe, CLEMENTINE
Bosch, Hiëronymus, THE GREAT
    CARLTON
Bostock, Edward H, P T BARNUM
Boucicault, Dion, PAT FEENEY
Bowden, Ellen, THE DELEVANTIS
Bowden, John, THE DELEVANTIS
Bowen, Eli, PEG-LEG BATES
Bradford: Alhambra, JIMMY CLITHEROE
Bradley & Partner, THEO BAMBERG
Braley, George, BARCLAY & PERKINS
Brandon, Sydney, NORMAN CARROL
Braund, George, MAGICIANS
Breen, Billy, LARRY GRAYSON
Breen, Bobby, COLLINSON & DEAN
Breen, May, GEORGE FORMBY jnr
Breitbart, Siegmund, ALOIS PETERS
Brezin, Fred, MAGICIANS
Brighton:
    Hippodrome, VIC OLIVER, ills.52,
    53, 54
    Palace Pier Theatre, NAT JACKLEY
    Theatre Royal, CLEMENTINE
Bristol: Hippodrome, DESMOND &
    MARKS, NORMAN VAUGHAN
British Actors' Equity Association,
    WINDY BLOW
British Empire Exhibition 1922, TOMMY
    HANDLEY, TOMMY TRINDER
British Music Hall Society, JACK SEATON
British Medical Research Council, PETER
    CASSON
Brixton: Empress, ISSY BONN, BERT
    WRIGHT & ZENA
Bromley: New, JIMMY TARBUCK
Broodway, Van der Clyde, BARBETTE
Brooks, Foster, JOHNNY COOPER
Brooks, Reuben R, BIRDIE BRIGHTLING
Brough, Arthur, PETER BROUGH &
    ARCHIE ANDREWS
Brown, Adam George, BILLY RUSSELL
Brown, Janet, ill.52
Brown, Louisa, MOTHER OF...
Bruant, Aristide, LA BELLE OTERO
Bruce, Boy, BRUCE FORSYTH

Brummell, Beau, GEORGE LASHWOOD
Bryden, Beryl, MISCELLANEOUS,
    QUEEN OF...
Buchanan, Jack, ERNIE WISE
Buchanan, Jimmy, CHARLIE CAIROLI
Buckstone, J B, VESTA VICTORIA
Bundy, Henry, JIMMY CLITHEROE
Bunn, Alfred, JENNY LIND
Buonaparte, Napoleon, GEORGE
    BARNARDO EAGLE, GEORGE
    BARNARDO EAGLE (The Great
    Everhart), NAPOLEON, NAUGHTON
    & GOLD, FELICIEN TREWEY,
    VENTRILOQUISTS (John W Cooper)
Buonocore, Cristoforo, CHARLES S
    BERNARD
Burdon, Albert, (Bryan Burdon)
    MISCELLANEOUS
Burdon, Bryan, MISCELLANEOUS
Busoni, Ferruccio, MAUD ALLAN
Butler, Frank, ANNIE OAKLEY
Byron, Lord, ADAH ISAACS MENKEN

Caiger, Arthur, THOMAS P RATCLIFF
Caine, Bridget, Mme GASCOYNE
Calcutta:
    SHEK BEN ALI
    Opera House, THE GREAT NIXON
Calienta, ill.55
Calienta & Lolita, ill.48
Cambridge University, GEORGE ROBEY
Campbell, Murray, EDDIE CALVERT
Campbell & Wise, MAGICIANS (Vic Wise)
Cannon & Ball, THE THREE LOOSE
    SCREWS
Cardiff: New, WYN CALVIN, NAT
    JACKLEY, GEORGE LACY
Cardini, MAGICIANS, VALENTINE
Carew, James, BILLY BENNETT
Carew, Maxwell, ill.55
Carla, MISCELLANEOUS
Carlos, Señor, ill.54
Carlotte, Mlle, BLONDIN
Carlson, Alf, ill.53
Carmo, The Great, MAGICIANS
Carney, George, SKETCH ARTISTES
Carol, Terri, LARRY BARNES
Caroline, Mme, KING OHMY, QUEEN
    OF...
Carp, Professor Edwin, RICHARD HAYDN
Carr, Fred, MISCELLANEOUS
Carr, Russ, FRED RUSSELL,
    VENTRILOQUISTS
Carroll, Mildred, GEORGE FORMBY jnr
Carson, Frank, HUGHIE GREEN, RUBY
    MURRAY
Carson Sisters, MISCELLANEOUS
Carter, The Great (Charles J), MAGICIANS
Carter, Jack, MISCELLANEOUS
Caruso, Enrico, BETTY AUKLAND

Cash, Morny, TED LUNE
Cassidy, Jack, JACKSON EARLE
Cave, J Arnold, BIRDIE BRIGHTLING
Cazman the Great, THEO BAMBERG
Cellsus, MAGICIANS
Central Pool of Artists, 'Cheerful'
    CHARLIE CHESTER
Central Vigilance Society, ZAEO
Chalklin, Richard Alfred, LEON CORTEZ
Chamberlain, Neville, DAVE WILLIS
Chanti, OWEN McGIVENEY
Chapman, Ellen, 'Lord' GEORGE SANGER
Chase, Mary, SID FIELD
Chassimo, THEO BAMBERG
Chesney, Ronald, LARRY ADLER
Chester, Erne, MAY ERNE
Chicago Times, LYDIA THOMPSON
Chichester: Festival Theatre, FLANAGAN
    & ALLEN
Chocolate & Co., DR CROCK, THE
    RASTELLIS
Chopin, Frédéric, LESLIE CROWTHER
Chorley: Grand, HARRY LAUDER
Chrysanthemum, PAT KIRKWOOD
Church, Gladys, SIFFLEURS &
    SIFFLEUSES
Churchill, Sarah, VIC OLIVER
Churchill, Winston, GEORGE FORMBY jnr,
    VIC OLIVER, VALENTINE
Cinderella, ISSY BONN, FRED EMNEY,
    DEREK ROY
Cingalee, The Great, MAGICIANS
Cire, AL CARTHY, MAGICIANS
Ciselatus, MISCELLANEOUS
Claff, Harry jnr, HARRY CLAFF
Clark, Charles, BROWN, NEWLAND &
    LE CLERQ
Clark, Eddie, MISCELLANEOUS
Clark, Johnson, VENTRILOQUISTS
Clark & Murray, TOMMY MORGAN
Clark & Ritchie, BICYCLE ACTS
Clarke Brothers, DAVY KAYE
Clarke & Clements, GEORGE CLARKE
Clarke, Leoni, ANIMAL & BIRD ACTS
Claud, The Great, MAGICIANS (Claud
    Williams)
Clayton, Lou, JIMMY DURANTE
Clemart, W H, VENTRILOQUISTS
Clicquot, Chevalier, HARRY NORTON
Clifford, Bert, CLAPHAM & DWYER
Clifford, Jack, MISCELLANEOUS
Clifford, Leon, KARDOMA, MAGICIANS
Clifton, Herbert, BARBETTE
Clifton, Kate, ST GEORGE HUSSEY
Clive, Colin, JEANNE De CASALIS
Clivette, THEO BAMBERG
Cloches de Corneville, Les, FLORENCE ST
    JOHN
Clofullia, Josephine, MISCELLANEOUS

Club for Acts & Actors, PAMELA CUNDELL
Coady, Harry, DAVE & JOE O'GORMAN
Coborn, Charles, W F FRAME
Cochran, Charles B, FREDDIE BAMBERGER & PAM, SID FIELD
Cocteau, Jean, BARBETTE
Cockton, Henry, VALENTINE VOX
Cole, Lieut, ARTHUR PRINCE, VENTRILOQUISTS
Cole, Charles, WINDY BLOW
Coleman, Mrs, DAISY JAMES, MISCELLANEOUS
Coleman, Nellie, ST GEORGE HUSSEY
Colleano, Con, BONAR COLLEANO
Collins, Stephen, LOTTIE COLLINS
Collinson & Breen, COLLINSON & DEAN
Colquhoun, Ian, ALOIS PETERS
Concert Artistes' Association, PAMELA CUNDELL
Conray, Will, HARRY CHAMPION
Conyers, Hutton, JIMMY JAMES & CO
Cook, Bobbie, JESSIE HARCOURT
Cook, Peter, PEG-LEG BATES
Cooke circus family, OCEANA
Cooper, John W, GEORGE BARNARDO EAGLE, VENTRILOQUISTS
Cooper, Cyanide Sid, p.15
Coram, The Great, MISCELLANEOUS (Billy Whitaker & Mimi Law), VENTRILOQUISTS
Coram & Mills, THE BEVERLEY SISTERS
Corello, Alfred, BLONDIN, LÉOTARD
Cornell, Katherine, ETHEL BARRYMORE
Corney, Arthur, GUS HARRIS, MISCELLANEOUS
Coronation Street, p.16, TOM MENNARD, JILL SUMMERS
Corvan, Ned, BOBBY THOMPSON
Coventry: Coventry Theatre, FRANKIE HOWERD
Coward, Noël, TESSIE O'SHEA, RICHARD HAYDN
Cox's Ghost, W, Dr PEPPER
Coyne, Frank snr, FRANK COYNE
Coyne, Fred (1), FRANK COYNE
Coyne, Fred (2), FRANK COYNE
Crachami, Caroline, JIMMY CLITHEROE
Cragg, Arthur, GASTON & ANDRÉE
Craggs, The Famous, GASTON & ANDRÉE, SKETCH ARTISTES
Craig, Mystic, MAGICIANS
Crazy Gang, The, BILLY CARYLL & HILDA MUNDY, FLANAGAN & ALLEN, EDDIE GRAY, NAUGHTON & GOLD, OLSEN & JOHNSON
Crazy People, HARRY SECOMBE
Crazy Week, BILLY CARYLL & HILDA MUNDY, NAUGHTON & GOLD
Crick, Monte, RONALD FRANKAU

Cronow, John, GEORGE F MOORE
Crosby, Bing, MICHAEL HOLLIDAY, JACK SMITH
Crotch, Lydia, TRULY SHATTUCK
Crowe, Johnny, LARRY ADLER
Crump, William Henry, HARRY CHAMPION
Crushington, 'Lord' Adolphus, CLAPHAM & DWYER
Cryer, Barry, BRIAN CRYER
Crystal Palace, see London
Cullen, James H, MISCELLANEOUS
Cummin, Will, MISCELLANEOUS
Cutler, Myra, THE THREE KEATONS
Cuvier, Baron, SAARTJE BAARTMAN
Czarnowski, Mlle ALMA

Daily Mail, SIDNEY BARNES, MAX MILLER
Daily Express, GRACIE FIELDS
Daily Herald, HANNEN SWAFFER
Dales, The, JESSIE MATTHEWS
Daly, Glen, TOMMY MORGAN
Dalziel, May, JACK SHORT, ARTHUR TRACY
Dampier, Claude, CLAPHAM & DWYER, RONALD FRANKAU
Daniels, Sidney, SIRDANI
Daniels, Trevor, PAUL DANIELS
D'Annunzio, Gabriele, LA BELLE OTERO
Danny & Me, TED ROGERS
Dante (1869-99), DANTE,
Darby, Edward Charles, AHMED MADRALI
Darwin, Charles, JAMES UNSWORTH
Davis, J H STEAD
Dead of Night, PETER BROUGH & ARCHIE ANDREWS
Dean, Ella, JESSIE HARCOURT
De Bessell, M. A, MISCELLANEOUS
De Bucharde, Clarice Etrulia, p.14, TRULY SHATTUCK
De Courcy, Howard, MAGICIANS, WINDMILL THEATRE
De Dio, Mlle, MISCELLANEOUS
De Frece, Walter, VESTA TILLEY
De Groot, Edward Stanley, STANELLI
Delaney, Arthur, FRANK RANDLE
Delavanti Troupe, DELEVANTIS, THE
Delevines, Three/Five, DELEVANTIS, THE
Delfont Boys, DELFONT & TOKO, HAL MONTY
Dell, Freddie, DEHL TRIO
Dell, Gladys, DEHL TRIO
Delvaine, Dot, JIMMY CLITHEROE
Demain, Jack, MAGICIANS
Dene, Dorrie, p.14, MISCELLANEOUS
Denville Hall, ADELAIDE HALL
Derby: Grand, ill.55

Desmond, Peggy 'Piano', WINIFRED
ATWELL, QUEEN OF...
Desmonde, Jerry, SID FIELD, NAT
JACKLEY
Deveen, MAGICIANS, LYDIA
THOMPSON
De Vere, Pauline, ANIMAL & BIRD ACTS,
ELLEN BRIGHT, GEORGE SANGER
Devine & King, ill.53
Devine, Laurie, MISCELLANEOUS
Devoe, Joe, JUGGLERS
Dewars, The, BARCLAY & PERKINS
Dick Van Dyke Show, MOREY
AMSTERDAM
Dick Whittington, BRUCE FORSYTH, SID
PLUMMER, JIMMY TARBUCK
Dickens, Charles, W C FIELDS, CYRIL
FLETCHER, HENRY LLOYD-
PARKER, OWEN McGIVENEY,
BRANSBY WILLIAMS
Dillon, Bernard, ills. 37, 38
Dillon, Ernie, JUMPIN' JAX
Disraeli, Benjamin, G H MACDERMOTT
Dixey, Henry E, CHARLES ATLAS
Dixon of Dock Green, JACK WARNER
Dolcini, Clementini, CLEMENTINE
Dolman, Sidney, VENTRILOQUISTS
Donegan, Lonnie, KING OF...
Donn, Alex & Nicols, Nick MILTON BERLE
Donovan, Terry, BRIAN CRYER
Doonan, George, JACK HAIG
Dore, Demaris, MISCELLANEOUS
Dormer, Dainty Doris, DAISY JAMES
Dors, Diana, p.14
Dove, Roy, JUGGLERS
Dowler, Arthur, THE GREAT HUGHES,
MAGICIANS
Downs, T Nelson, KING OF...,
MAGICIANS
Doyle, Arthur Conan, HOUDINI, THE
ZANCIGS
Doyle, Bunny, MISCELLANEOUS, ill.48
Doyle, Patsy, MISCELLANEOUS
Drew, Georgina, ETHEL BARRYMORE
Driver, Betty, ill.54
Drury Lane Theatre Royal, see London
Dubarrys, The Fire-Eating, CHARLES S
BERNARD
Dudley: Hippodrome, BOB BEMAND'S
COMEDY PIGEONS
Dumas, Alexandre père, ADAH ISAACS
MENKEN
Duncan, Isadora, MY FANCY
Dunlop, Bobby, THE GREAT CARLTON
Dunn, John, T D RICE
Dunz, Christianna D, Captain GEORGE
AUGER
Duse, Eleonore, MOTHER OF...(Esther
Rachel Kaminska)
Dutch Mill, MACARI

Dyer, Bob, BIG BILL CAMPBELL
Dymott, Renée, MISCELLANEOUS

Earl, Roy, MAGICIANS
Easley, Bert, JOHNNY COOPER,
MAGICIANS
East Lynne, HENRY LLOYD-PARKER
Eastbourne: Devonshire Park, NORMAN
VAUGHAN
Edgar, Marriott, CYRIL FLETCHER
Edinburgh: Empire, THE GREAT
LAFAYETTE
Edmondson, Jimmy, MISCELLANEOUS
Edson, Calvin, WILL OLIVER
Educating Archie, JULIE ANDREWS,
PETER BROUGH & ARCHIE
ANDREWS, TONY HANCOCK,
ROBERT MORETON, BERYL REID
Edward VII, King, ill.10
Edward VIII, King, De HAVEN & PAGE
Edwardes, Jack, CHARLIE DRAKE
Edwards, Cliff, GEORGE FORMBY jnr
Edwards, Lou, GEORGE JESSEL
Edwards, Maudie, MISCELLANEOUS
Edwards, Sydney, GEORGE
BEAUCHAMP
Edwards, Tom, VALENTINE VOX,
VENTRILOQUISTS
Egbert Brothers, FRED EMNEY
Eggena, Mrs, LA MILO
Eight Lancashire Lads, CHARLES CHAPLIN
Einstein, Albert, WILL HAY
Eldanis, The, PAUL DANIELS
Electra, La Belle, WALFORD BODIE
Elliott, Joan & Roche, Billie, p.14,
MISCELLANEOUS
Elliotts, The, BICYCLE ACTS
Elroy, CLEMENTINE, CARL
HERMANN UNTHAN
Elvin, Joe (& Co), SKETCH ARTISTES
Emerson & Jayne, MAGICIANS
Emery, Ann, DICK EMERY
Emmett, Frankie, RONNÉ CONN
Emney, Fred jnr, FRED EMNEY
Enoch (Man Fish), ANNETTE
KELLERMAN
ENSA, ALEC HALLS, DOLLY HARMER,
JILL SUMMERS
Entertaining Mr Sloane, BERYL REID
Era, The, ANNIE MAY ABBOTT, JENNY
HILL, LA MILO, PIPIFAX & PANLO,
THE SALAMBOS, GEORGE W
WARE, SELINA YOUNG
Era Annual, The, CHARLIE CHESTER
Erikson, MAGICIANS, WINDMILL
THEATRE
Ernest, Professor, DR CROCK
Evans, Bob, PEG-LEG BATES
Evans, John Philip, BI-BO-BI
Evans, Will (& Co), SKETCH ARTISTES

Gladstone, William Ewart, G H
  MACDERMOTT, W H PENNINGTON
Glasgow:
  Alhambra, HARRY GORDON
  Empire, DON ARROL
  Empress, ill.9
  Pavilion, MIKE & BERNIE WINTERS
Gleason, Jackie, MISCELLANEOUS
Glen, Archie, JOHNNY COOPER
Glen, Gwen, DRUM & MAJOR, DAISY
  JAMES
Glenroy, James Richmond,
  MISCELLANEOUS (James Richmond)
Gloucester, Duke & Duchess of, MUSHIE
Glyn, Elinor, CLARA BOW
Goldfaden, Abraham, ISSY BONN
Goldin, Horace, MAGICIANS
Good For Nothing, VESTA VICTORIA
Goodchild, Harry, MURRAY & MOONEY
Goodman, Benny, KING OF...
Goon Show, The, SPIKE MILLIGAN,
  HARRY SECOMBE, PETER SELLERS
Gordon & Nancy, Eddie, BICYCLE ACTS,
  LEW GRADE
Gordon, Eddie & Nancy, ill.52
Gordon, Paul, CAICEDO
Gorky, Maxim, THEA ALBA
Goulay, Gilda, RONNÉ CONN
Gould, Leslie, MISCELLANEOUS
Gounod, Charles, VIC OLIVER
Govett, Lottie, THE POLUSKIS
Govett, Sam, THE POLUSKIS
Govett, Will, THE POLUSKIS
Gow, Chang Woo, GEORGE AUGER
Grade, Leslie, LEW GRADE
Grade & Sutton, HAL MONTY
Grafton, Jimmy, p.11
Graham's Ghost, Dr PEPPER
Grand Order of Water Rats, 'Cheerful'
  CHARLIE CHESTER, FRED RUSSELL
Granger, Stewart, TONY WRIGHT
Grant, Ivy, 'Happy' FANNY FIELDS
Grant, Kitty, DRUM & MAJOR
Gravelet, Émile, BLONDIN
Gray, Rita, LEW GRADE
Great Exhibition of 1851, SELINA YOUNG
Gregory, Mme (Laurine), ZAZEL
Gridneff, Igor, DU CALION
Grock, CHARLIE CAIROLI (& CO),
  KING OF..., NONI & HORACE
Grossmith, William R, Master WILLIAM
  BETTY
GTC, BOB & ALF PEARSON
Guilbert, Yvette, MARIE LOFTUS
Gwyn, Nell, MALCOLM SCOTT
Hackenschmidt, George, EUGENE
  SANDOW
Haig, F M Earl, BOB BEMAND'S
  COMEDY PIGEONS, De HAVEN &
  PAGE

Hal & Laurel, THE FIVE WHITELEYS
Hale, Alan, VESTA TILLEY
Hale, Lionel, MAX MILLER
Hales, Robert, Captain GEORGE AUGER
Hall Trio, Bill, DR CROCK
Hall, Henry, BERYL REID
Hall, Terry, VENTRILOQUISTS
Hallett, Wilson, HARRY MAY HEMSLEY
Hamlet, JOHN BARRYMORE, VICTOR
  BORGE, BRANSBY WILLIAMS
Hammerstein, Willie, THE CHERRY
  SISTERS
Hancock's Half Hour, BILL KERR
Hand, Esmé, MISCELLANEOUS
Handy, W C, FATHER OF...
Hansen, Henry, PIPIFAX & PANLO
Hansen, Juanita, QUEEN OF...
Happidrome, HARRY KORRIS
Hardwicke, Cedric, SKETCH ARTISTES
Hargreaves, William, J W RICKABY,
  ELLA SHIELDS
Harlem, Chick, FLANAGAN & ALLEN
Harley, Lily, LEO DRYDEN
Harmaniacs, The, STAN STENNETT
Harper Brothers, CANNON & BALL
Harris, Augustus, GUS HARRIS
Harris, Freddie, MAGICIANS
Harrison, Syd & Max, THE THREE
  LOOSE SCREWS
Hart, Janice, QUEEN OF..., SOPHIE
  TUCKER
Harvey, SID FIELD, HARRY WORTH
Harvey, Ellen, MUSHIE
Hassan, NAPOLEON
Hastings, Gilbert, G H MACDERMOTT
Haverly's Mastodons, EUGENE STRATTON
Haverly's Minstrels, MAY HENDERSON
  (Nellie Richards)
Hay, Will jnr, WILL HAY
Hayes, Arthur Hull, ARTEMUS
Hayes, Catherine, JENNY LIND
Hayes & Gardner, BARBETTE
Hayes, Helen, ETHEL BARRYMORE
Hayes, Rich, MISCELLANEOUS
Haynes family, Mme SENYAH
Healy, Dan, HELEN KANE
Hear My Song, HAROLD BERENS,
  JOSEF LOCKE
Hearn, Tom, JUGGLERS
Hefferman, Kate, ZAZEL
Heliot, Claire, ELLEN BRIGHT
Hellzapoppin, OLSEN & JOHNSON
Henderson Twins, DICKIE HENDERSON
Henry Hall's Guest Night, BERYL REID
Henry, Les (Cedric Monarch), LARRY
  ADLER
Henry Tate & Sons, HARRY TATE
Henson, Leslie, J MILTON HAYES
Herbert, Terry, MAGICIANS

Hereford:
  Garrick Cinema, CHRIS WORTMAN
  Kemble Theatre, GEORGE WILLIAMS
Hermann, Professor Eugene, Mlle ALMA,
  MAGICIANS
Herrmann, Alexander, HOWARD
  THURSTON
Herrmann, Leon, HOWARD THURSTON
Hewett, Molly Balvaird, ADA REEVE
Hill, Helen, JENNY LIND
Hilton, Polly, ANIMAL & BIRD ACTS,
  ELLEN BRIGHT
Himmebrand, Abraham, TEDDY BROWN
Hines, Harry, DR CROCK
Hitler, Adolf, CHARLIE CHESTER,
  TOMMY HANDLEY, DAVE WILLIS
Hockridge, Edmund, BRIAN CRYER
Hoffa, Portland, FRED ALLEN
Hoffman, Charles, MAGICIANS
Hoffman, Max jnr, HELEN KANE
Hoffmann, Professor, MAGICIANS
Hoffmans, The Two, FREDDIE
  BAMBERGER & PAM
Holloway, Stanley, CYRIL FLETCHER
Holmes, Leslie, THE TWO LESLIES
Holtum, Prof. John, KING OF..., ZAZEL
Honri, Mary, PERCY HONRI
Honri, Peter, PERCY HONRI
Hope, Bob, SID FIELD
Hope & Keen, THE THREE LOOSE
  SCREWS
Hopkin, Mary, HUGHIE GREEN
Horne, Betty, ill.48
Horne, Kenneth, PETER SELLERS
Hottoff, Professor, MAGICIANS (Ben Said)
Houdin, Robert, FATHER OF..., HARRY
  HOUDINI, MAGICIANS
Houston Sisters, HOUSTON & STEWART
Howard, John, VENTRILOQUISTS
Howard, Paul, MAGICIANS
Howe, Laurie, GEORGE BEAUCHAMP,
  JOE BLACK, DICK EMERY
Howe, Len, MISCELLANEOUS
Howson, Pat, GEORGE FORMBY jnr
Hoxha, Enver, NORMAN WISDOM
Hugo, Captain, GEORGE AUGER
Hull: Tivoli, LUCAN & McSHANE
Hulme Hippodrome, see Manchester
Humpty Dumpty, ROY CASTLE, BETTY
  JUMEL, HARRY SECOMBE
Hunt, G W, G H MACDERMOTT
Hunt, Selina, Mme GENEIVE
Hunt, William, EL NINO FARINI
Hutch, Johnny (& the Half-Wits), THE FIVE
  VOLANTS
Hutchings, William S, THEA ALBA
Hutchison, Ronald M., HARRY TATE
Hutton, Betty, IRENE CAMPBELL

Hylton, Jack, FREDDIE BAMBERGER &
  PAM

Ibsen, Henrik, MARIE DRESSLER
Inaudi, Jacques, THEA ALBA
Inland Revenue, Commissioner of,
  MICHAEL HOLLIDAY
International Brotherhood of Magicians,
  ROVI
International Typographical Union of North
  America, ARTEMUS
Interval Club, ADA REEVE
Inverclyde, Lord, DAVE WILLIS
Inverness: Empire, HARRY LAUDER
Ionia, MAGICIANS
Irving, Henry, MARIE LOFTUS, W H
  PENNINGTON, PIPIFAX & PANLO,
  VESTA TILLEY
ITMA (It's That Man Again), GEORGE
  FORMBY jnr, TOMMY HANDLEY
Ivanitz, Ivan, CHARLES S BERNARD

Jackley, Dave, SAMMY CURTIS
Jackley, George, NAT JACKLEY
Jackson, Eddie, JIMMY DURANTE
Jackson, Joe, BICYCLE ACTS
Jackson, Joe jnr, BICYCLE ACTS
Jackson, Syd, DICKIE HENDERSON
Jackson, Walter, MISCELLANEOUS
Jacobs, Joseph, MAGICIANS
Jacobsen, Tommy, CARL HERMANN
  UNTHAN
Jack & The Beanstalk, JIMMY LYNTON
Jameson, Rex, Mrs SHUFFLEWICK
Jazz Singer, The, GEORGE JESSEL,
  CHRIS WORTMAN
Jefferson, Jackie, BRIAN CRYER
Jerome, Daisy, LILLIE LANGTRY
Jessica, The Beautiful, QUEEN OF...,
  TENNYSON & O'GORMAN
Jester, G W, VENTRILOQUISTS
Johnson, Bob, JUMPIN' JAX
Johnson, Winifred E, BIRDIE
  BRIGHTLING, R G KNOWLES
Jo-Jo, MISCELLANEOUS
Jolies Petites, Les, THE TILLER GIRLS
Jolson, Harry, JOLSON, AL
Jones, Sissieretta, MISCELLANEOUS
Jones, Spike, DR CROCK
Joplin, Scott, KING OF...
Josephs, Young, MISCELLANEOUS
Jover, Julian, TOMMY JOVER with
  NENA & RAF
June & Valette, ill.48

Kalanag, DANTE
Kaminska, Esther Rachel, MOTHER OF...
Kane, Alan, BOB & ALF PEARSON
Kane, Gloria, BOB & ALF PEARSON

Mencken, H L, PHYLLIS DIXEY
Mendel, WINIFRED ATWELL
Mendelssohn-Bartholdy, Felix, FELIX
  MENDELSSOHN
Menken, Alexander Isaacs, ADAH ISAACS
  MENKEN
Merlin, June, MAGICIANS
Merry Moments, HARRY LISTON
Mesmer, Franz Anton, Princess RUBIE
Meszharos, Mihaly, JIMMY CLITHEROE
Methane, Mr, JOSEPH PUJOL
Meyer, Orville, MAGICIANS
Mick & Montgomery, CHARLIE DRAKE
Micro, JIMMY CLITHEROE, THE
  ZANCIGS
Midsummer Night's Dream, A, BILLY
  SHAKESPEARE
Mill, Paul, SIFFLEURS & SIFFLEUSES
Miller, Joe, JAMES MADISON
Miller, Berenetta, Mlle ALMA
Miller, Judy, DELFONT & TOKO
Millie-Christine, CHANG & ENG,
  JENNY LIND
Mills, Florence, GRACIE FIELDS
Millward, Sid, DR CROCK
Minevitch, Borrah, LARRY ADLER
Minns, Clement, MAGICIANS,
  VENTRILOQUISTS
Mistinguette, SAARTJE BAARTMAN
Modley, Allen, ALBERT MODLEY
Moe, Ikey, JIMMY CLITHEROE, ISSY
  BONN
Moffat, Graham, WILL HAY
Momus, J W LISKARD, 'Jolly' JOHN NASH
Monarchs, The Three, LARRY ADLER
Montague, Pansy, LA MILO
Monty Python's Flying Circus, SPIKE
  MILLIGAN
Moody, Kathy, LEW GRADE
Moon, Ronnie, MISCELLANEOUS
Moore, Billy, YVONNE PRESTIGE
Moore, Dudley, PEG-LEG BATES
Moore, E J, MAGICIANS
Moorhouse, Syd, MISCELLANEOUS
More, Kenneth, TONY WRIGHT
Morisco, George, Mlle. ALMA
Morrell & Melville, EDDIE MORRELL
Morris, Barbara Ward, TED ANDREWS
Morris, Bob, SKETCH ARTISTES
Morris, Dave, CASEY'S COURT
Morris, Lily, HYLDA BAKER, QUEEN
  OF...
Morris, Ossie, STAN STENNETT
Morrison, Joe, DAISY SQUELCH
Morritt, Charles, MAGICIANS
Morton, Charles, FATHER OF...
Moses, Phoebe A. Oakley, ANNIE OAKLEY
Moss Empires, HERSCHEL HENLERE,
  LESLIE MacDONNELL, MAX

MILLER, BOB & ALF PEARSON
Moss, Tom F, HARRY FRAGSON
Motie, Rahnee, KORINGA, MAGICIANS
Mottley, John, JAMES MADISON
Mrs Dale's Diary, RONALD FRANKAU,
  JESSIE MATTHEWS
Mr Tower of London, GRACIE FIELDS
Much Ado About Nothing, DE HAVEN &
  PAGE, JAY LAURIER, BILLY
  SHAKESPEARE
Munro, Alex, MISCELLANEOUS
Murdoch, Richard, PETER SELLERS
Murgatroyd & Winterbottom, RONALD
  FRANKAU, TOMMY HANDLEY
Murray, MAGICIANS
Murray & King, MURRAY & MOONEY
Murray, Will, CASEY'S COURT
Murray, Tom, SIFFLEURS & SIFFLEUSES
Musical Elliott Savonas, The, BICYCLE
  ACTS (The Elliotts)
Mushie, p.11
My Fair Lady, JULIE ANDREWS

Nano, Hervio, Mlle ALMA
Napier, Joan Valantyne, HECTOR NAPIER
National Eisteddfod, ROVI
Nedlo, TED RAY
Neek, Hugh, TED RAY
Neiman, Fred, VENTRILOQUISTS
Nemo, Mr & Miss, p.13, JUGGLERS
Nesbitt, Max & Harry, MISCELLANEOUS
Nevada Ned, KING OF...
New York:
  Colonial, ALICE LLOYD
  Roof Garden, EVELYN NESBIT
  Hubert's Museum, QUEEN OF... (Gypsy
    Rose Lee)
  Palace, MAX BYGRAVES, MARIE
    DRESSLER, JIMMY DURANTE
New York Philharmonic Orchestra,
  TEDDY BROWN
Newell, Tom D, RICHARD HEARNE
Newley, Patrick, Mrs SHUFFLEWICK
Newton, Carol, ill.54
N'Gai, MAGICIANS
Nicholas, Grand Duke, LA BELLE OTERO
Nijinsky, Vaslav, LITTLE TICH
Nikita, Mlle, JIMMY CLITHEROE,
  QUEEN OF... (Adelina Patti)
Nirt, Red, TOMMY TRINDER
Nissen, Nick, TED RAY
Nixon, David, MAGICIANS, NORMAN
  WISDOM, WINDMILL THEATRE
Noble, Ray, AL BOWLLY
Nolan, Kevin, DEHL TRIO
Noonan, George, JACK HAIG
Norman, Karyl, BARBETTE
Normand, Mabel, CHARLES CHAPLIN
North & South, RONALD FRANKAU
North Wales Magic Circle, ROVI

Norworth, Jack, NORA BAYES
Nuffield Centre, MICHAEL BENTINE

Oakes, Harry, RONALD FRANKAU
O'Brian, Brian, Captain GEORGE AUGER
O'Brian, Frank & Violet, ill.55
O'Brian, Pat, ARTHUR TRACY
O'Brian, Patrick, Captain GEORGE AUGER
O'Connor, Billy, MAGICIANS
O'Connor, Cavan, ARTHUR TRACY
O'Connor, Tom, HUGHIE GREEN
O'Dea, Jimmy, MISCELLANEOUS
O'Dell, Professor, JIMMY LYNTON
Odell, E J, MISCELLANEOUS
Ogilvie, Sophie, MACKENZIE
   MURDOCK
O'Halloran, Tom, ill.55
Okito, THEO BAMBERG
Oldfield, Paul, JOSEPH PUJOL
Oliver & Twist, OWEN McGIVENEY
Olivier, Laurence, BERNARD MILES
Olma, KING OF... (Olmar)
Olmar, KING OF...
Olrac, Bobby (& Lillian), MISCELLANEOUS
Olympiers, The, LA MILO
On the Buses, REG VARNEY
On with the Modley, ALBERT MODLEY
Othello, IRA ALDRIDGE
Ovalden, Charles, CARL HERTZ,
   MAGICIANS
Owl and the Pussycat, The, ELTON HAYES
Oxford English Dictionary, ZAEO
Oxford: New, ill.48

Pablo, Ted, AHMED MADRALI
Paderewski, Ignacy Jan, WINIFRED
   ATWELL
Padley Brothers, VALENTINE
Paganini, Niccolo, MACKENZIE
   MURDOCK, CARL HERMANN
   UNTHAN
Palmer, Florence, ROBB WILTON
Palmer, George, GASTON PALMER
Palmer, Joe, AL JOLSON
Palmer, Kate, MISCELLANEOUS
Palmer's Ghost, Dr PEPPER
Pantzer Brothers, M. CANDLER
Paris:
   Casino de Paris, BARBETTE
   Moulin Rouge, JOSEPH PUJOL
   Musée de l'Homme, SAARTJE
   BAARTMAN
Parker, Henry, HENRY LLOYD-PARKER
Parker, Orville (Boss), MISCELLANEOUS
Parnell, Val, DON ARROL, LESLIE
   MacDONNELL, MURRAY &
   MOONEY, FRED RUSSELL
Parr, Catherine, MALCOLM SCOTT
Parrot, William, TALBOT O'FARRELL
Parsons, Nicholas, ARTHUR HAYNES

Pasta, Jean, JENNY HILL
Pasta, Letty, JENNY HILL
Pastor, Charles, BIG BILL CAMPBELL
Pastrana, Julia, JOE LAWRENCE
Patti, Adelina, QUEEN OF..., GRACIE
   FIELDS
Paula, Mlle, ANIMAL & BIRD ACTS,
   KORINGA
Paulette & Renée, JUMPIN' JAX
Payne, Graham, MISCELLANEOUS
Payne, Jack, PEGGY COCHRANE
Paynola, Tina, BERYL ORDE
Peabody, Eddie, MISCELLANEOUS
Pearse, Odin, STANELLI
Pedersen, Tilly, CARL BRISSON
Peek-a-Boo, WINIFRED ATWELL
Peel & Curtis, ISSY BONN, TOMMY
   MORGAN
Peel, Robert, BEATRICE LITTLE
Pennell, Joseph, TOM TINSLEY
Performer, The, GEORGE CLARKE
Perry, Vic, MAGICIANS
Peta & Paula, THE FIVE WHITELEYS
Peter, Edward, SCOTT & WHALEY
Peter Pan, THE LUPINOS, ARTHUR
   PRINCE, WEE GEORGIE WOOD
Peters & Lee, HUGHIE GREEN
Petersen Brothers, ill.54
Petrie, Willie & Alfy, G H ELLIOTT
Pettitt, Henry, HERBERT CAMPBELL
Pfau, JULES LÉOTARD
Phoites, The Three, MISCELLANEOUS
Phroso, AL CARTHY
Pierce, George, GEORGE & BERT
   BERNARD
Pieri, Antonio, AHMED MADRALI
Pierre, La, PEG-LEG BATES
Pierro, M., PEG-LEG BATES
Ping Pong, BILLY MERSON
Pink, Wal (& Co), SKETCH ARTISTES
Piper, Franco, BIRDIE BRIGHTLING,
   JUGGLERS
Planquette, Robert, FLORENCE ST JOHN
Pleasants, Jack, GEORGE FORMBY snr
Ponchery, H R, CAICEDO
Poluski, Miss, SKETCH ARTISTES,
Poluskis, The, SKETCH ARTISTES,
   DAISY WOOD
Pollock, Channing, MAGICIANS
Pollock, Jackson, MAGICIANS (Channing
   Pollock)
Poole, J J, GEORGE LEYBOURNE
Pop, White & Stagger, MISCELLANEOUS
Pope, Glen (& Ann), MAGICIANS
Pott, Victor, HARRY FRAGSON, ill.24
Powell, M Edward, Mme GENEIVE
Power, Amby, MACKENZIE MURDOCK
Prelle, Charles, ANIMAL & BIRD ACTS,
   VENTRILOQUISTS

Roscius, IRA ALDRIDGE, Master
   WILLIAM BETTY, SAM COWELL
Rose, Harry (Mr Robot), AL CARTHY
Rose, Julian, ISSY BONN
Ross, Annie, JACK SHORT
Ross, Don, GERTIE GITANA
Ross, Tiny, JIMMY CLITHEROE
Rossini, Mme, Mme GENEIVE
Rotol Airscrews, MUSHIE
Royal Academy of Music, HARRY CLAFF,
   PEGGY COCHRANE, STANELLI
Royal Astronomical Society, WILL HAY
Royal College of Music, CARLOS AMES,
   STANELLI
Royal Music Hall Performance 1912, ALBERT
   CHEVALIER, HARRY CLAFF,
   PIPIFAX & PANLO
Royal Variety Performance, MARIE LLOYD
   1928, NONI & HORACE, STANELLI
   (& Douglas)
   1935, HARRY CHAMPION
   1937, REVNELL & WEST
   1954, AL READ
   1992, LESLIE CROWTHER
   1996, VICTOR BORGE
Ryley, Mr & Barnum, Miss,
   MISCELLANEOUS
Rymer, George F, CHARLES CHAPLIN

St Dunstan's Ovingdean, MAX MILLER
St James, Freddie, FRED ALLEN
Sadler, Iris, QUEEN OF..., FLORENCE
   ST JOHN
Said, Ben, MAGICIANS
Sainsbury's, TINY TIM, KATYA VAN DYK
Salisbury & Kubelsky, JACK BENNY
Salvation Army, The, LILY BURNAND,
   SAM TORR
Samson (Alexander Zass), EUGENE
   SANDOW
Sand, George, ADAH ISAACS MENKEN
Saphrim, MAGICIANS
Santley, Joseph, Master WILLIAM BETTY
Sappho, NELLY LENNOX & KATE
   RALEIGH
Sarony, Leslie, THE TWO LESLIES
Sargent, Thomas Henry, MAX MILLER
Saunders, Dan, JENNY HILL
Saunders, Joe, GEORGE LEYBOURNE
Savo, Jimmy, JUGGLERS
Schaeffer, Severus, JUGGLERS
Schaeffer, Sylvester snr, JUGGLERS
Schaeffer, Sylvester jnr, JUGGLERS
Schnorbitz, MIKE & BERNIE WINTERS
Scott, Clement, FATHER OF... (Charles
   Morton)
Scott, Great, DU CALION
Scott, Maidie   [1], CHIC MURRAY
                     [2], CHIC MURRAY

Scott, Admiral Percy, MALCOLM SCOTT
Scott, Walter, JOHN HENRY ANDERSON,
   HENRY LLOYD-PARKER
Seeley, Blossom, QUEEN OF...
Selbini, Lalla, BICYCLE ACTS, RONNÉ
   CONN, THE GREAT LAFAYETTE
Selbo, KING OF...
Sells & Young, VALENTINE
Seppetoni, JAN VAN ALBERT
Seppetoni, Minna, JAN VAN ALBERT
Sewell, Gladdy, RONNÉ CONN
Seymour, Sid, DR CROCK, DELFONT &
   TOKO
Shakespeare, William, IRA ALDRIDGE,
   ISSY BONN, VICTOR BORGE,
   COLLINSON & DEAN, LEON
   CORTEZ, JAY LAURIER, BILLY
   SHAKESPEARE, WILLIAM F.
   WALLETT, BRANSBY WILLIAMS
Shaughraun, The, PAT FEENEY
Shaw, Bernard, LA BELLE OTERO
Shea, George, BARCLAY & PERKINS
Shepard, Burt, BIG BILL CAMPBELL
Shepley, Ida, RONNÉ CONN
Sheppard, Jack, HARRY HOUDINI
Sherrard, May, HYLDA BAKER,
   QUEEN OF...
Sherrell Brothers, CANNON & BALL
Shields, Cyril, MAGICIANS, SIRDANI
Shock, Joyce, GRACIE FIELDS, QUEEN
   OF...
Short, Ernest, LA MILO
Shrimpton, Bert, DR CROCK
Siege of Paris, NELLIE POWER
Silvester's Ghost, Dr PEPPER
Silverstein, Andrew Clay, ANDREW 'DICE'
   CLAY
Sinatra, Frank, RUBY MURRAY
Sinbad The Sailor, FRED EMNEY
Sinclair, Peter, KEN DODD
Sinden, Donald, TONY WRIGHT
Skegness: Indian Theatre, SHEK BEN ALI
Slater, Arthur, SIFFLEURS & SIFFLEUSES
Slater, Ralph, PETER CASSON
Smith, Canfield, VENTRILOQUISTS
Smith, Joseph, KING OHMY
Smith, Miss Ward, ANNIE MAY ABBOTT
Smith, Walter William, MAX BYGRAVES
Smith, William E, CHARLES D BERNARD
Smith, William P, Mlle ALMA
Smithson, Florence, JENNY LIND
Smoothey, Don, MISCELLANEOUS
Snakella & Travella, BILLY MERSON
Sober Sue, JIMMY LEARMOUTH
Sontag, Henriette, MISCELLANEOUS
   (Louise Pyne)
Sorcar, MAGICIANS
Sound of Music, The, RICHARD HAYDN
Sousa, John Philip, BI-BO-BI
Southgate, Elsie, STANELLI

316

Also published by Oberon Books:

The Private Lives of Noël of Gertie
A Talent to Amuse, A Bright Particular Star
Sheridan Morley
1 84002 091 1

Jack Tinker: A Life in Review
James Inverne
1 84002 018 0